THE ACADEMIC PRESIDENT
— EDUCATOR OR CARETAKER?

THE CARNEGIE SERIES IN AMERICAN EDUCATION

The books in this series have resulted from studies made under grants from Carnegie Corporation of New York and from time to time studies supported by The Carnegie Foundation for the Advancement of Teaching. These books are published by McGraw-Hill in recognition of their importance to the future of American education.

The Corporation, a philanthropic foundation established in 1911 by Andrew Carnegie for the advancement and diffusion of knowledge and understanding, has a continuing interest in the improvement of American education. It financed the studies in this series to provide facts and recommendations which would be useful to all those who make or influence the decisions that shape American educational policies and institutions.

The statements made and views expressed in these books are solely the responsibility of the authors.

Books Published

Berelson · Graduate Education in the United States
Clark · The Open Door College: A Case Study
Cleveland · The Overseas American
Conant · The American High School Today
Corson · Governance of Colleges and Universities
Dodds · The Academic President—Educator or Caretaker?
Glenny · Autonomy of Public Colleges
Henninger · The Technical Institute in America
Medsker · The Junior College: Progress and Prospect
McConnell · A General Pattern for American Public Higher Education
Perkins and Snell · The Education of Historians in the United States
Pierson · The Education of American Businessmen
Thomas · The Search for a Common Learning: General Education, 1800–1960
Weidner · The World Role of Universities

HAROLD W. DODDS

THE ACADEMIC PRESIDENT
⌐EDUCATOR OR CARETAKER?

WITH THE COLLABORATION OF
FELIX C. ROBB ⌐ R. ROBB TAYLOR

McGRAW-HILL BOOK COMPANY, INC.   1962
New York   San Francisco   Toronto   London

THE ACADEMIC PRESIDENT—EDUCATOR OR CARETAKER?

17295

PREFACE

Even a cursory observation of college presidents at work reveals that they differ as widely as the shapes of their heads. Generalizations regarding them are hazardous, and nothing is gained by efforts to "homogenize" the approximately two thousand personalities at the helms of our junior colleges, four-year colleges, and universities. Nevertheless, the truly successful have certain attributes in common. Chief among them are a quality that elicits the confidence of faculties and thoughtful laymen, and a gift for sustaining a climate of intellectual inquiry and a zeal for quality.

The presidential office will go the way of the buffalo if it loses its traditional character of educational leadership. Clearly no president can succeed by returning to the practices of his nineteenth-century predecessors, who were members of the teaching faculty as well as chief executives, with the duty of administering student discipline, conducting daily chapel, and preaching on certain Sundays. The presidential office can be preserved only by methods which take cognizance of present-day administrative duties inseparable from the conduct of large and increasingly complex institutions.

The office is in need of better definition; it has lost its uniform and consistent character. Today it finds itself suspended between two worlds. While it has moved away from the old world of relative simplicity, it has not yet come to terms with its new world of

v

complexity. It is hoped that this study will aid in rationalizing it in a manner that will preserve its historic, essential nature.

Our field work involved visits to approximately sixty colleges and universities. Because the problems are most apparent, and most acute, in the universities, we selected for the most intensive team study a number of representative universities, some tax-supported, others privately supported, and spread from coast to coast and from North to South. Our research group was composed of Felix C. Robb, then dean, now president of George Peabody College for Teachers; R. Robb Taylor, then instructor in sociology, now assistant professor at Wisconsin, engaged in studies of academic government; and myself. Not the least of my personal debts to my colleagues runs to their persistence in maintaining the point of view of a dean and a member of the faculty against one whose academic life had been spent largely in the president's office.

Our practice was to interview presidents, trustees, academic vice-presidents, deans, nonacademic officers of administration, members of the faculty of all ranks, and students. We were cordially received everywhere and were impressed by how frankly members of an academic community are willing to talk. Naturally each interview was held under a promise that names would not be disclosed, a circumstance that explains why we are often unable to cite sources or identify institutions.

This is not a "scientific" study of the type of a sociological investigation into the academic decision-making process and allied topics. While interviews were exhaustive and far-ranging, and opinions were weighed and cross bearings taken, no attempt was made to quantify in a statistical manner opinions and judgments we recorded.

We realize that our material reveals the influence of the practitioner in contrast to the academic scholar. We agree with David Riesman that the "common sense" of the practitioner is partly a falsified reality and with Robert W. Merry that there is some tendency toward a mutual exclusion between effectiveness in administration and effectiveness in the study of administration.

Nevertheless, we consider our approach to be valid, for experience contributes much that is not disclosed by the techniques of case studies or statistical analysis alone.

In deference to feminine readers, may we make clear that we refer to presidents as of the masculine gender solely for the purpose of convenience? We know that many excellent college presidents have been and are women—probably with a higher proportionate record of success than is enjoyed by their male counterparts.

We extend thanks to the hundreds of individuals who granted us interviews and directed us to other sources of information on their campuses, to those who attended our conferences, and to the scores who cheerfully responded by letter to requests for information.

Special acknowledgment is due to three who rendered substantial aid from the beginning to the end of our study: to Prof. W. H. Cowley for numerous suggestions and observations from his store of broad knowledge of the history of academic organization and governance, and particularly for making available a preliminary draft of his forthcoming book *Professors, Presidents and Trustees: An Assessment of the Conceptual Roots of American Academic Government;* to Prof. Robert W. Merry, a member of the faculty of the Harvard Graduate School of Business Administration and director of The Institute for College and University Administrators, who was our indefatigable counselor and friend throughout; and to Prof. Earl J. McGrath, executive officer of the Institute of Higher Education, Teachers College, Columbia University, for wise advice. We alone are, of course, responsible for views expressed or errors of fact or judgment.

Our thanks also go to Miss Lenore Sorsby for editorial assistance in the organization and treatment of our material which strengthened its presentation, and to the secretary of the study, Mrs. Ruth Eiler, for help in checking references and preparing the manuscript and the index for the publisher.

This study was made possible by funds granted by Carnegie Corporation of New York and the Carnegie Foundation for the

Advancement of Teaching; but, again, the statements made and views expressed are solely the responsibility of the authors. The seasoned interest of Vice-president James A. Perkins was helpful from the beginning, particularly because he rigorously refrained from any semblance of direction or interference.

We acknowledge with thanks permission from the following copyright owners to quote from their publications, as cited in the text: Eric Ashby; Association of American Colleges; The Beacon Press; A. A. Berle, Jr.; Columbia University Press; Fletcher School of Law and Diplomacy; President and Fellows of Harvard College; Houghton Mifflin Company; University of Kentucky Press; J. B. Lippincott Company; McGraw-Hill Book Company, Inc.; University of Minnesota; the estate of Abraham Flexner; Oxford University Press; Trustees of the University of Pennsylvania; Harold W. Stoke; and The Viking Press, Inc.

As a guide to the widely dispersed literature of our subject, Prof. Walter C. Eells prepared early in our study a comprehensive bibliography on academic administration with special reference to the presidency. This has been published by the U.S. Office of Education under the title *The College Presidency 1900– 1960: An Annotated Bibliography.*[1] For this reason no bibliography is appended to our text.

Finally, a personal note is in order. In discussing the office and the incumbent, this study sets forth what I think it should and can be. In no sense is it a record of how I performed in it. To the charge "If all you say is so important, why didn't you do it while you were in office?" I rejoin simply that I did not know enough to do it. As a result of our field work and some time for reflection, I came to reverse some old opinions and to a clearer distinction between a president's primary duties and the supporting functions that can prove so distracting.

Harold W. Dodds

---

[1] Walter Crosby Eells and Ernest V. Hollis, *The College Presidency 1900– 1960: An Annotated Bibliography,* Government Printing Office, 1961.

CONTENTS

CHAPTER I

THE SETTING OF THE ACADEMIC PRESIDENCY

Can a college or university president be an educational leader and still find time for the other things that he must attend to—or that his publics think he should? Cynics answer "no." We are more optimistic, but the answer will not be easy. That his "position has declined in academic status" and that "the faculty here no longer look to the president but to the provost" are views repeatedly expressed in academic circles. The postwar years have brought about extensive changes in methods and organization of university administrations, but the position of the president as a force in education continues to decline.

In attending to the life of the mind, a college or university cannot neglect the claims of the body and physical things. Even the most educationally minded president faces a constant struggle against becoming enmeshed in a network of supporting activities—business management, public relations, fund raising. They are essential and often possess a quality of urgency calling for prompt attention by someone, perhaps in the face of set deadlines. Unlike a revision of the curriculum, they cannot safely be put aside to await a more opportune moment.

1

EDUCATIONAL LEADERSHIP,
THE PRESIDENT'S PRIME FUNCTION

Some hold that the president of the future will not be able to function as an educator at all, indeed that it is futile for him to try. Let him find some good deans, they say, and delegate all educational problems to them. Then he may devote himself to his supporting functions, with—presumably—the bonus of a certain ritualistic grandeur on ceremonial occasions, such as commencements or convocations honoring distinguished personages. If this view be correct, the outlook for higher education is far more dismal than we are prepared to admit. We cannot conceive that the president, as the number one man in the organization, can delegate to academic vice-presidents, provosts, and deans an overriding responsibility toward the university's primary role.

Instead of devoting himself chiefly to secondary activities, we believe that the president must preserve his educational leadership, that it must indeed be enhanced. This is not to suggest that these activities are not a part of an institution's educational success or that the president can or should divest himself of final accountability for their efficient operation. But in no area can he do it all himself; he must entrust wide discretion to others. He reveals where his heart lies and sets the character of his administration by the choice he makes between those functions to which he gives his most personal, intimate, and continuing attention and those which he more generally leaves to others. We believe that implicit in the office he holds is the duty to participate actively in framing and carrying out the teaching and scholarly policies of his institution.

In so doing, a president will have to fight for time to contend with the public's conception of him as a sort of Jack-of-all-trades whose services should be available on call. Accordingly, certain answers to how he can be an educator do not rest with him alone but with trustees, alumni, the academic community, and the public generally. Substantial modification of their demands will take the combined efforts of all segments of his constituency. In many it will be a slow educational process of creating a better understanding of his true role; but it is essential nevertheless. Some presidents are more favored with understanding constituencies than others, but if the guild of presidents sets its mind to it, it could modulate extravagant expectations which usurp time that should be devoted to the teaching and scholarly growth of our colleges and universities.

In the last analysis, however, some of the most crucial solutions lie within the control of the incumbent himself. It is all too true that some presidents find in the supporting activities greater satisfaction than their primary educational function affords. When a president is more eager to sit down and discuss plans for revising the curriculum with a visitor than to show off new buildings, we can be pretty sure that he has strong educational aspirations.

WOULD TWO HEADS BE BETTER THAN ONE?

The job specifications of the American academic presidency call for a combination of managerial competence and talent for educational leadership, two capacities that some insist are mutually exclusive. Accordingly the suggestion has recurred periodically that the office be divided between two persons of different types, particularly when an institution has had an unhappy experience with a brilliant generator of ideas inept in securing concurrence and in exerting managerial oversight, or vice versa. Select an educational expert to have charge of the needs of the mind; select another, a man of affairs, and of weight in the community, to be responsible for other areas of management and fund raising.[1]

---

[1] This proposal to cut in two the traditional office of the president is not to be confused with the common chairman of the board–president relationship, under which the president remains the chief executive officer, nor with the chancellor-president relationship to be found in some universities. Under the latter the president may be assigned to administer an institution which is part of a larger complex (as at the University of California, where the titles "chancellor"

Such arrangements do not suggest a promising solution to the dilemma of educational leadership. Since every activity in which a college or university engages relates in some degree to instruction and the advancement of knowledge, bifurcation of ultimate responsibility, which is more than merely a division of labor, gives rise to inhibiting jurisdictional problems. This happens even between two congenial persons who are temperamentally disposed to cooperate. Someone, after all, must have the final executive word. As others have remarked, when two men lift a heavy stone, somebody must say "when." We cannot escape the belief that the president's constituency will continue in the future, as in the past, to hold him accountable for all that goes on and that he should have a reasonable degree of power commensurate with this responsibility.

It is a common complaint that managerial duties have displaced presidential opportunities for participation in education. The remedy lies in more effective delegation of broad areas of decision making to subordinate officers and the president's refusal to become involved in any but the major issues of management. "We presidents know the theory of administration," writes one, "but we find it difficult to delegate." Sternly surmounting this weakness will better reconcile managerial and educational functions than bifurcating the presidential office.[2]

VEBLEN'S CURE

Attacks fifty years ago upon the man and the office were not confined to the charge that the educator had been displaced by an operator and money raiser. Young men returning by the

---

and "president" are transposed), or he may be especially charged, under the chancellor, who is the head of the university, with educational responsibilities. In the latter case he may be known as "provost" rather than as "president," although his role may differ little if at all from that of the more usual academic vice-president. However, these broad arrangements do not introduce a bifurcation of ultimate authority or responsibility.

[2] Fuller treatment of the several aspects of delegation will be found in Chap. III as an element of the art of administration.

hundreds from German universities, with the coveted Ph.D. in their knapsacks, were eager to apply to America the Continental form of university governance, a form which, unencumbered by a president or a lay board of trustees, concentrated power in educational matters in a small faculty oligarchy composed of those who had achieved professorial rank.

The man who gathered into one bundle the criticisms of presidents as mere managerial creatures of lay trustees was Thorstein Veblen, whose scathing *The Higher Learning in America*[3] became the bible of professorial unrest. He berated presidents as "captains of erudition," thus likening them to "captains of industry" and, by inference, to the robber barons of the time. He advocated eliminating both president and trustees by the simple expedient of wiping them off the slate.

It would, of course, be idle to deny that Veblen and others had already at hand conspicuous examples of arbitrary and dictatorial presidential action detrimental to a university's proper freedom, or that many institutions were suffering from the ignorant meddling of trustees where academic discretion should have prevailed. The more informed trustee who, happily, is becoming more and more characteristic of our leading institutions, had not emerged as an influential element in most lay boards.

Yet the beleaguered presidents had something on their side, too. Since they were impaled on the twin charges on the one hand that they were mere politicians and money raisers and on the other that they were arbitrary academic slave drivers, subservient to reactionary tycoons, it is not strange that some complained that ". . . there are in our universities able professors and otherwise lovable souls to whom the very sight of a university president seems to be like . . . the waving of a red flag to an enraged beast."

When a scholar sits down to theorize about academic governance, he may question, with Veblen and other writers, whether,

---

[3] *The Higher Learning in America: A Memorandum on the Conduct of Universities by Business Men,* reprinted in American Century Series, Sagamore Press, Inc., New York, 1957.

after all, a president is really necessary.[4] Yet emotion blinded Veblen to some optimistic evidence. In particular, he failed to foresee the countervailing strength which academia would muster in support of its own freedom and ideals. A modern faculty knows that it must be ever alert "to keep the administration honest." Yet with the passage of years the "natural antagonism" between administration and faculty has softened. Professorial acceptance of presidents has grown with the increased weight and scope of faculty participation in decision making. Yet embers from the earlier fire remain and do flare up on occasion. Traces of what Woodrow Wilson described as ". . . the perennial misunderstanding between men who act and men who write" appear every day in face-to-face dealings between the administration and the faculty, and between the faculty and the trustees.

THE PRESIDENT HEADS A COMPLEX ORGANIZATION

In arguing for a single chief executive ultimately responsible for management as well as for education, we do not blink at the fact that the modern university—and, to a considerable degree, the college as well—is a complex system composed of a series of subsystems: a lay governing board, a professional faculty sub-

---

[4] I well recall a meeting of a group of conspirators at a professor's home in Princeton thirty years ago. It was the last year but one of President Hibben's administration, and the search for his successor had just begun. Yet it was the consensus of the meeting that it behooved the faculty to adopt some new restraining regulations early which would hold the new incumbent, whoever he might be, within the paths of righteousness. I do not remember that anyone mentioned the obvious danger that in restricting the potential of the new president for evil we might also be reducing his capacity to serve the faculty well. In any case, the meeting came to nothing, in part because the proposals for containing the president-to-be tended to hand control over to a faculty oligarchy, as is common abroad. It is natural that afterward I often looked back on this meeting with some amusement, remembering what they got two years later. I also recall an early office visit by an elder statesman of the faculty, before I had found a chair that did not spill me out on the floor, to remind me that the University had never had a better year than the one just past, in which my post had been vacant. H. W. D.

divided into departments according to specialties, students, administrators (both academic and nonacademic), librarians, athletic coaches, and service personnel ranging from secretaries, laboratory technicians, clerks, and skilled artisans to janitors and grounds keepers.

Whether it is true or not that college and university presidents often "make their responsibilities seem more tragically frustrating than they really are," they are undeniably busy men. And there is some truth in the self-portrait they so often paint, for each of them heads an enterprise involving a bewildering range of services. Can one think, for instance, of a business of comparable size that must employ Sanskrit scholars, accountants, glass blowers, philosophers, and curators of pregnant hamsters?

The American college and university system sends forth graduates into a broad diversity of occupations. It provides business with young salesmen, scientists, engineers, and executive trainees. It prepares teachers for our public school system. It supplies material for the skilled vocations and the learned professions, and it trains young scholars to carry on the great tradition. Increasingly it operates programs of continuing adult education, many of them planned for professional and business groups who have discovered that professors can be a source of useful as well as theoretical knowledge.

Along with a growing attention to specialization, the American college or university tries to impart to its students intellectual discipline and at least a modicum of cultural understanding, for it has committed itself to developing competent individuals in the broad ranges of the human personality. To this end it provides extracurricular cultural activities as well as the services of counselors, physicians, psychiatrists; it supplements these by social and athletic facilities, dormitories, and dining halls. It furnishes athletic extravaganzas for the entertainment of students, alumni, faculty, and townspeople. For good or ill it affords experience with sex, alcohol, tobacco, and good fellowship.

A college or university serves the world of thought through preserving society's fund of knowledge and transmitting it to others. At the same time, if it is true to its commitment, it is ceaselessly engaged in analyzing and criticizing this fund and searching, through the methodology of scholarship, for new knowledge to add to it.

The search for new knowledge has generated a host of esoteric specialties and subspecialties, which are reflected in modern curricula and elaborate research activities and facilities. Confronted by this complex, no president can hope to match the faculty in areas of its specialties or even to keep abreast with his former competence as an academic scholar. This tends to discourage him from participation in the educational process, in contrast to his predecessors of an earlier day, when it could be assumed that they knew something about everything.

Presidents all over the land are struggling with their problems with varying degrees of ardor. The process produces presidential headaches, occasional temper tantrums and ulcers, and some resignations. It is not strange that many, reviewing their careers at that melancholy moment when retirement is upon them, suffer from a sense of guilt that they have not been more effective forces in education.[5]

Obviously, to succeed, a president must be fired by a deep concern for education. It is equally observable that not all of them are. It follows that since presidents are chosen by trustees, trustees must be persuaded that supporting activities are only a part of the president's assignment, that his first responsibility is for the institution's educational growth and scholarly vigor. Parenthetically, we may remark that if more boards of trustees could master this principle, they would select fewer presidents for the wrong reasons and experience greater success in their choices.

[5] The rising interest of the Federal government in higher education is creating a new set of forces drawing presidents of private and state-supported institutions alike away from on-campus involvement in educational operations. While many presidents could delegate more of the representational duties of lobbyist, salesman, and educator, there remains a considerable area in which their presence as the institution's chief representational figure is demanded for protocol reasons if no other.

ENERGY IS NOT EVERYTHING

It is clear that the president is the target of competing demands which are often inconsistent and sometimes in outright conflict with each other. None escapes the burden of fund raising and public relations. "Representational pressures," created by calls to serve actively in educational, civic, and government bodies, are distracting and time-consuming.

Even if a president were dowered with inexhaustible energy, there is the time factor. No matter how well his administration is structured and how skillfully he delegates, no president can escape trouble-shooting interruptions and some personal attention to details. As one with a successful record as the head of a large and diversified university remarked, "It may happen that the most important task confronting a president when he reaches his office on Friday morning is to find two tickets on the 50-yard line for tomorrow's football game." It should not be so, but many can testify that under present-day conditions it is. So it is natural that a president, going over his day's work as he prepares for bed, finds little which was immediately concerned with the advancement of education.

We foresee no escape from the education–management–public relations dilemma. We do believe that its rigors can be lessened in favor of more effective educational leadership. The life of the educator-president will never be one of ease. He may envy those others who can take Saturdays off for golf or tennis, but he will go right on working on weekends and holidays. As he transfers his center of gravity from housekeeping to education, he will only be replacing one set of pressures with another more acceptable set.

THE PRESIDENT AS A PUBLIC FIGURE

Whether he likes it or not, the new president finds himself in the public eye and the subject of much personal publicity. It is heady wine, and he will watch himself for signs of inebriation. To former students, townspeople, government officials, donors, educators, contracting agencies, and the public, he personifies the institution. His office carries social status. He is sought after by all who prefer to deal with the top man, all who have something to gain by association with him. He is importuned by innumerable individuals and groups to attend meetings. Usually some kind of speech is involved. His support will be sought for all sorts of public causes, some good, some poor. He will be invited to serve as an officer of civic associations and a member of public bodies and agencies, especially when a figure who stands remote from political partisanship is desired.

The new chief executive will discover soon enough that nearly every invitation carries the bait that its acceptance will be good for his institution. Some will be pressed on him by influential people whose good will the institution needs. It is hard to devise and adhere to a formula for accepting some and declining others. Presidents of state and municipal institutions are particularly exposed to such external pressures. Some succeed in rationing their public appearances more severely than others, but alumni and taxpayers clamor for the personal touch. They are certain to criticize the unavailable as "remote" or lacking in civic feeling.

Although a too heavy indulgence by the president in public relations activities encroaches on time and energy for academic affairs, these duties should not be thought of merely as a barrier separating him from his educational responsibilities. Instead they are a means by which he realizes his primary function, for at the highest level they merge into statesmanship. Moreover, many a president finds refreshment in contacts with the nonacademic world, as well as a chance to extend his knowledge of what laymen are thinking.

He has an educational job to teach the public to respect his office and to make fewer demands for extracurricular service, in order that he may be a potent professional leader. Meanwhile it is eminently unjust to criticize him for not exercising educational leadership and the next day to bring pressure on him to take part in some activity unrelated, or only remotely related, to his chief responsibility.

CAMPUS CEREMONIALS

Anyone curious as to how a president spends his time before the public must examine campus ceremonials. Preparing for them takes quite a bit of his time, yet how well or how poorly he conducts them counts more than it should in the public's impression of the man and the institution. They range from impressive graduation exercises through ground breaking, dedications, receptions, Founders' Day exercises, and home coming to campus sings and Sadie Hawkins Day. This is a wide range indeed.

Still, some ceremonials have meaning in that they direct attention to the nature and aims of the institution. They afford the president an opportune moment for speaking on some phase of institutional policy. There is something about a colorful yet dignified commencement exercise which expresses both the personalities of our colleges and universities and their survival power through the centuries. A day set aside to recognize the university's interest in its honor students helps to restore a balance with athletics and extracurricular activities which automatically attract disproportionate attention.

Ceremonials that seem trivial to the faculty may be important to the students. They may also give the president a chance to improve the students' image of him as a human being interested in them. The president probably acted wisely who at the last moment canceled an important downtown appointment in response to undergraduate pleas that he, and not the vice-president, place a star atop the tree at the traditional Christmas-tree lighting.

Among the common ceremonials that might be abandoned we include the customary elaborate inauguration of a president. Occasionally it may be utilized for a profitable review of institutional goals, but usually it isn't worth the bother. Generally the new president has been at work for some months before the arrangements for the inaugural can be completed. This gives a faintly anticlimactic, ex post facto air to the affair. For the chief figure it is a treacherous occasion. If his inaugural address contains much more than platitudes, he risks exposing his plans prematurely. As a president who has succeeded remarkably in welding a set of diverse units into a more integrated university told us, "If I had announced in my inaugural address that we were going to do certain things, things we subsequently did, I would have scared hell out of the faculty." On the other hand, the new president may simply play safe and produce a thoroughly vapid speech. From our experience one might almost formulate a law of probability that his future success will be in inverse ratio to the degree of "old school" emotion generated on the occasion. Elaborate inaugurals have been discontinued in a number of institutions in favor of a simple local induction ceremony.

NO IVIED TOWER FOR THE PRESIDENT

Obviously, despite a college or university's dedication to thought, its administration, both academic and nonacademic, must be geared for action. For the president, no decision is "academic" or "armchair." Yet he and his administrative colleagues deal daily with men whose professional life is preoccupied with scholarly subtleties of meaning and refinements of expression. These hairline distinctions by nature tend to dilute both the desire and the capacity for action. To a practical businessman they are apt to seem not only unsubstantial but also puzzling and sometimes downright exasperating. It is the job of the academic president, who is part of both worlds, to bring the values and motivations of the highly individualistic man of thought and those of the more organizationally minded man of action into reasonable accord, so that each will serve the other well.

Of course, business and governmental executives face a similar responsibility for accommodating the demands of individuals for opportunities for self-expression with the requirements of the organization. But to equate the office of a corporation's chief officer with the university presidency is misleading without modifications appropriate to the position of the faculty in the university.

As Harold Seymour has remarked, the problems of a university president are more like those of the general manager of the Metropolitan Opera Company than of the president of the Metropolitan Life Insurance Company. Further, the office of the academic president differs from that of the chief executive of the usual business corporation in that the ultimate function of his institution—one might say its "end product"—is education rather than financial profit or production of material goods. In this it is unique.

SCHIZOID NATURE OF COLLEGES AND UNIVERSITIES

To succeed at his job a president requires a full comprehension, even more an acceptance, of the unique organizational and operational aspects of the society which comprises an institution of higher learning. Sociologists tell us that all societies develop appropriate systems of government. From this standpoint the university displays a sort of split personality. It stems from a constant internal tug of war between the demands of conformity and of nonconformity, between the need for order and the university's mission to cultivate individuality and self-expression.[6] Like any other organization, the university can exist only on the basis of methodical procedures supported by some hierarchy of authority. The success of each department or subdivision, as well as of the whole university, relates to group loyalty and response to the centripetal pull of conscious membership in an organization.

The processes of a university generate strong centrifugal forces by their inherent emphasis on personal creativity and intellectual independence in faculty and students. Great individuals, not great organization men, make a college or university

[6] Of course this tug of war goes on in varying degrees in all human organizations, even a most highly disciplined church hierarchy or military unit. But the difference in degree is so great as to constitute one of kind.

great. By stressing the values of self-expression and originality, by reason of its duty always to be challenging the *status quo* as well as defending it, the university inevitably nourishes conditions favorable to controversy but correspondingly unfavorable to organization. Since a university is a society of intellectuals, and by definition intellectuals resist being organized, the loyalty of a professor is, to a greater degree than among businessmen, an ambivalent mingling of loyalty to the organization with an opposing loyalty—indeed an obligation—to himself and his profession to transcend, although he cannot ignore, the demands of team play. In a way, he is in the situation of a man who cannot live apart from his wife but whose life with her is a continual strain.

Academia's most cherished awards are not given in recognition of effective committee work or efficiency as a dean. Indeed, the young man who seeks professional recognition and advancement in the academic world will hold his prior commitment to be his subject. His best hopes for advancement lie with the senior colleagues in his field of scholarship.

As in all organizations, the desirable condition of a university is one of *mobile equilibrium* between centripetal and centrifugal influences. The president's problem is to see that the state of mobile equilibrium is directed, in accord with defined institutional emphases, toward agreed goals.

THE DEMOCRATIC CLIMATE OF ACADEMIA

A generation ago, the president was frequently an individual of personal power on his campus, operating at times on authority almost as awesome as a medieval potentate's. Now, however, in spite of the survival of some extreme authoritarians here and there, academic leadership has shifted from the Napoleonic approach of earlier years to a more democratic, representative form of governance by conference. Although the modern president carries moral and legal responsibilities of leadership as broad as those of his predecessors, he discharges them in a more consultative manner. In these times, perhaps the most effective charge that a faculty can make against an action of the administration or, in certain circumstances, of the trustees is that "we were not consulted."

A president must be willing to accept a definition of educational leadership that brings about change less by the sheer power of his office and more by informal, friendly, and persuasive means —by the weight of his arguments, the marshaling of the facts. As a rule trustees nowadays respect the discretion of the faculty more fully and over a wider jurisdiction than did their predecessors. Indeed this respect can be so strong that governing boards sometimes become only rubber stamps of faculty actions within the area of operations. As one competent observer has remarked, faculties are now making decisions which in business are reserved to top management and boards of directors.

Logan Wilson has written:[7]

Without a more exhaustive inquiry than has yet been made it would be hazardous to state that there is a persistent correlation between the democratic organizations of the major institutions in this country and their educational eminence. On the other hand, it is equally fallacious to conclude that democracy is a "luxury" that the lesser colleges and universities cannot afford.

As to the survival of extreme authoritarianism, Wilson has this to say:[8]

Extreme authoritarianism can hardly be maintained in our larger and better colleges and universities, but it is fairly common in small, mediocre, and insecure institutions. In such settings the administration likes to surround itself with an air of infallibility, and the atmosphere may become so oppressive as to drive away from the campus all but the most subservient professors.

We may add that among the samples of colleges and universities which we studied those of accepted educational eminence were characterized by a large measure of faculty self-government, al-

---

[7] *The Academic Man: A Study in the Sociology of a Profession,* Oxford University Press, New York, 1942, p. 79.

[8] "Academic Administration: Its Abuses and Uses," *American Association of University Professors Bulletin,* vol. 41, no. 4, pp. 686–687, Winter, 1955.

though in varying degrees and forms, and that in each the trend in recent years has been to draw the faculty more and more into advance consultation on broad institutional policies formerly considered to lie within the exclusive domain of the trustees, advised by the administration. Our findings also support Wilson's opinion that if extreme authoritarianism exists, it is in less favored and secure institutions, although there are naturally striking exceptions among them.

During the past generation the general level of the democratic process and participation has moved upward throughout American life. William S. White,[9] in commenting on the changing nature of public administration in Washington, speaks of the growing use of the "consultative method of directing affairs" and how this is creating a new type of public official who knows how to "manage well by seeming to manage little," who possesses "the odd talent of getting things done collectively." Writers on business administration note a similar development of the consultative process. Corporate executives are discovering that they must evoke and compose the knowledge of self-conscious specialists and that subordinates carry out decisions more heartily if they have had their say while policies are being formulated.

Yet, from the standpoint of democratic sharing in decision making, the new spirit of consultation in government and business falls far short of the processes that characterize the academic world. This phenomenon colors its every action; it is quite familiar to directors of research laboratories, academic or industrial.

The officers of a business corporation labor under no illusion that they are a society of equals. In the last analysis, a directive is obeyed as such, and no subordinate feels that he has compromised his integrity as an individual by following it loyally. Not so in academia. Successful university presidents from non-academic life soon learn to curb their old compulsions to make rapid-fire decisions. They learn to cultivate patience and the habit of conferring. The academic president who cannot secure faculty consensus through methods of consultation exceeding those

[9] *Harper's Magazine,* February, 1959, p. 98.

obtaining in modern businesses, even where the consultative process is most highly developed, cannot expect to command faculty support. Under most circumstances the faculty can and will destroy him more quickly and decisively than will the trustees.

PRESIDENTIAL WORKING CONDITIONS

In most institutions recent decades have witnessed extensive improvements in conditions of work for the faculty. While salaries may leave much to be desired, as academics properly remind us, faculties have more money for research, more leaves of absence, more research assistance—all of which, to their European colleagues, seem like the wealth of Croesus. Although this improvement has been far from uniform, in pace-setting colleges and universities it has been marked, and others are struggling to the same ends.

In contrast to faculty progress, working conditions for too many presidents in expanding institutions (and which are not?) have worsened or at least have not improved *pari passu* with those of the faculty. Presidents have been given more administrative assistance than they used to have, but the expansion in the administrative force has too seldom kept pace with the expansion of institutional activities. The faculty is bound to criticize the added cost of any expansion of administrative staff, and too often the administration defers to them. The result is that many presidents have been too modest in looking after their own interests as chief executives.

LEADERSHIP IN VARIANT TYPES
OF COLLEGES AND UNIVERSITIES

There are many elements common to all colleges and universities, else this study would have been unthinkable. Each needs at its head an individual who is, or can become, its effective leader —guiding, unifying, representing, defending, and inspiring. Molded by such forces as geographical and cultural circumstances that define the region or regions to be served and the nature of the service, the wealth or poverty of alumni and friends, and the prevailing level of scholastic capacity in the students it attracts, each has its own special opportunities, requirements, and limitations which outlaw easy generalizations and defeat quick appraisals and panaceas. A president my succeed in one environment and fail in another.

No institution has all the resources it needs or has use for, but the relative wealth or poverty of the place makes a vast difference in the specifics of the president's job. It is one thing to be president of Yale, Wesleyan in Connecticut, or Rice of Texas; it is quite another to head an institution struggling to stay out of receivership. Lacking financial resources, the raw materials of success, a president is hard pressed to translate his efforts into notable academic progress. He knows he must involve himself personally in fund raising and public relations to a greater degree than his opposite number in a wealthier institution with better-organized support.

The college surrounded by institutions of greater prestige also presents peculiar problems, as do large universities in small towns, municipal colleges in which the spirit of localism is strong, state institutions which are a part of a cluster under the control of a single board, and institutions voluntarily related through affiliation agreements.

THE STATE UNIVERSITY PRESIDENT

Conditions obtaining in state colleges and universities taken as a group present variations from those in the privately sustained;[10] and the problems vary from state to state. They will be different, for example, in one whose legislature has a built-in agricultural base, distrustful of urban sophistication, from the problems of one more urban and industrialized. The task of the

---

[10] No one can predict how this may change in the future. In a sense private colleges and universities have always been in the public domain, but they are becoming more so as both state and Federal governments become increasingly involved in higher education.

president in a state where partisan political controls are strong will vary from that of his colleague in a nationally oriented state university over which they are relatively weak.

It is possible to exaggerate the difference between the "public" and the "private." For example, looking at the intramural aspects of both presidencies, we find them similar in many ways. Nevertheless, the heterogeneity of the "public" head's constituency is inevitably reflected in his day's work. Citizens, alumni, and non-alumni alike take a proprietary interest in their tax-supported colleges and universities and exert special pressures upon them either directly or through the legislature. With exceptions among private institutions in urban areas, tax-supported colleges and universities have developed into more comprehensive multiservice organizations than the privately supported, a circumstance particularly true of the land-grant colleges, which present problems of their own. When the drift of power to superboards and executive agencies of the government is coupled with rapid turnover and political susceptibility of regents, and complicated by a tendency of public officials to view the administration of public education as the same as any other function of government, the president confronts an all but baffling switchboard of pushes and pulls.

The press of the state is ever alert for news, preferably bad from the president's standpoint, and the frequent legal requirement that meetings of the regents be open to the public[11] contributes nothing to his ease of mind. The presence of the press is perforce a damper on freedom to think out loud, which naturally leads to evasion in the form of off-the-record meetings to argue out debatable questions.

The attitudes of legislative members are a constant concern to the head of a state institution, particularly when a legislature is sitting or is about to sit. Legislatures differ in the amount of time

[11] An officer of one eminent state university reported that pressure was emerging to open faculty meetings to the press and commented that if reporters were to be admitted, they should be required to remain throughout the entire session.

they require the president to spend at the capital during sessions. Some are content with one appearance before a committee per session, which permits him to delegate much to assistants. Others traditionally demand his almost constant presence and his answer to almost every question.

The presidency of a state college or university calls, too, for a certain political *savoir faire*. The term includes a knowledge of how government operates and what motivates public officials—in short, a comprehension of how things get done in government, as well as a capacity, if not a fondness, for living in a glass house. Because the president is a prominent state official and therefore fair game for anyone, his political *savoir faire* embraces a certain toughness of spirit to protect him from the abrasion of headline seekers who will attack the university on any issue at hand, inconsequential as well as great. It entails a personality capable of at least riding out a sort of periodic public clamor which the head of a private institution encounters much more rarely, if at all. His wife shares the headlines and his responses to clamor, which may impose a special problem of maintaining morale at home.

With every step toward progress, some have had to fight lonely rear-guard actions against hampering legislation or even a vendetta headed by a governor or other political figure. All honor to those who have surmounted their big and little crises, while promoting educational excellence. The growth and improvement in quality of state universities is one of the dramatic achievements of American higher education, with credit due to farsighted legislators, governors, and other state officials as well as presidents and regents.

EDUCATIONAL LEADERSHIP CAN COEXIST WITH BIGNESS

The president's role varies with the size of his college or university, whether it be "private" or "public." Obviously, the larger it is, the more systematic and adept the president has to be in selecting, organizing, and coordinating an able corps of associates in administration; in delegating to those associates; in sustaining the morale of the faculty, from many of whom he is remote; and in exercising overview. One of the troubles with an empire is that its leaders tend to lose touch with local realities. Yet some of the "obstacles" to the president's involvement in the academic affairs of a university may be invoked to cover a basic lack of interest, a personal fascination with public relations and management.

This is a harsh indictment. Too harsh, perhaps, if it were not that these same obstacles have not prevented some heads of great and growing universities from exerting a strong personal impact upon the intellectual life of their institutions. For example, some have stimulated at their huge state universities a campus interest in the arts so pervasive that it radiates throughout their states. These men—by frequent attendance at cultural activities, by showing an interest in faculty and students, by using occasions to talk to students and citizens about the place of the arts and sciences in society, and, not least, by finding the resources to provide adequate faculties, equipment, and quarters—have demonstrated that presidents of institutions with more than ten thousand students can still make a profound personal imprint upon the character of an institution and its students. The difficult trick is to operate the big organization so that it behaves as effectively with individuals as a smaller one.

Solutions to mounting problems associated with institutional bigness cannot await the emergence of presidential supermen— types in singularly short supply. If a result of enormous growth is an inevitable failure of the president to know what is going on in each of his colleges and professional schools, if the university becomes a mélange of unrelated parts, if communications break down throughout the system, if an "edifice complex" supplants essential concern for quality of teaching and research, if undergraduate students feel a cold impersonality about the institution, the time has come to consider some radical surgery. This would mean establishing new colleges and universities or imaginative reorganization of the behemoths.

President Douglas Knight of Lawrence College contends, as

have others with considerable reason, that in many ways the small-college president has a more complex and more taxing job than the head of a large university—at least he has more roles to play and a more intimate personal involvement. The informality of a small college obliges the president to be readily accessible on any and all phases of its operations. While there may be no significant difference in the number of persons gaining daily access to his office, odds are that, without the assistance and protective screening procedures employed by presidents of bigger institutions, he contends personally with more petty problems and grievances. On the other hand, the president of a small institution has in his favor the relatively homogeneous nature of a constituency whose preeminent concerns revolve around the teaching-learning function of the college. It is not surprising that many deliberately elect to remain in the college environment.

The institution which is halfway between the college and the university in size and program, in transition from a traditional college to a modern university, faces growing pains of its own. Eager to maintain the values and functions of a small college, it finds, for one thing, that decisions about staff expansion are difficult. The traditions of a small college endure in the face of new conditions calling for reorganization and change. The result may be a stultifying resistance on the part of senior faculty, trustees, and alumni.

Church-related colleges and universities, which originated in denominational zeal that piety be linked to learning, constitute another institutional variant. In these latter years, non-tax-supported institutions are steadily declining in the national proportion of students they enroll, and rarely today is a new independent college or university founded which is not church-related. Therefore, hope for maintaining in the United States a balance between public and private direction of higher education cannot ignore the strengthening of church-related colleges and universities, which "by cutting their own feed" are our most effective blocks to powerful political controls over all higher education. Churches are due more credit than they receive from secular sources for their support of institutions that serve the entire population. While church relationship assumes an organization from which funds may flow to the institution, church authorities are likely to exhibit more enthusiasm for founding a college than for giving it strong, continuous support and display a somewhat checkered record in financing them.

Our criticism would be that too often their concepts of quality should be more intellectual. If our thesis is correct, such institutions will not rise above the capabilities of the men chosen to lead them. Certain church groups follow a policy of restricting faculty recruitment to their own membership and thereby make the attainment of high academic quality difficult. We leave to their respective denominations all judgment as to the piety of their presidents. It is within our province, however, to state that the laity of the several religious groups should be gravely concerned about the limited academic qualifications of some of the presidents chosen to head their institutions of higher learning.

THE PRESIDENT AND HIS FAMILY

An important aspect of the presidency is the impact of the office on the man and his family. How the family react to their new life has more to do with his success than his public knows. From the moment of election, a president's wife and children are front figures in the academic showcase. Their activities will be mentioned in the newspapers and will be reviewed in conversations in the faculty club. He and they have entered the public domain together. His family must be prepared to see less of him. Days and even weeks will be consumed in out-of-town trips. Nights will be devoted to campus occasions, speaking, and dining out in official capacity.

Some presidents succeed better than others in carving out free evenings at home, and they are wise, but many tend to be monopolized by the demands of a briefcase heavy with urgent administrative materials. The home, once a relaxed heaven for the weary professor and a scene of informal fun with friends, becomes the locale for official receptions, teas, and other social events.

The buoyant, resilient family, however, will not take the presidency overseriously; their heads will not swell with its prestige; they will find ways to hold together as a family; and they will discover in high visibility the rewards and pleasures of measuring up to the demands of challenging circumstance and enjoyable associations which otherwise they might never have known.

In all this, the president can be immeasurably aided by his wife. Hers is a difficult role. If she plays it well, she adds to her husband's effectiveness, particularly in the social and representational realms. In selecting a new president, trustees rightly consider the wife. Indeed, we saw one table of specifications in which she was placed two lines above money-raising ability in order of importance.

The ideal president's wife possesses the capacity to enjoy public life, which to a less well-organized or less outgoing woman would lead to painful sacrifice, neglect, and frustration. Constituents may be as much impressed by the first lady's grace and good sense as by the chief executive himself. Nor is her influence restricted to the social sphere. There is the story, probably apocryphal but illustrative, of one who unconsciously worked a minor reform in the college. Solely because of her interest in the subject matter of two courses, she began dropping in on the lectures. In each instance, it is reported, the lecturer was moved to revise his notes, some of which had not been brought up to date for ten years.

Occasionally a president has been all but destroyed by an inept wife who broke confidences to indulge in high-level gossip or succumbed to pride of rank and the temptation to inject herself into the management of her husband's affairs. Thank heaven, most wives are gifted and willing partners who supplement their husbands and compensate for qualities in which they are deficient, besides providing sympathetic shoulders on which their men can weep.

OLD PERSONAL RELATIONSHIPS ARE ALTERED

If the president has previously held a high administrative post, the durability of his temperament under abrasive personal criticism and endless individual and group contacts has been tested. He has acquired some insight into how organizations work; but whether he is a novice out of the professoriate or a battle-scarred number two man in administration, probably never has he come under klieg lights such as play on the chief executive. He soon learns that he must exercise new controls over what he says and how he says it. He discovers that innocent observations are examined for hidden meanings. The humor in which he clothes a sharp remark may not survive in the second telling.

His old personal relationships will be altered, his privacy invaded. One new president reported, and others would agree, that what he missed most was participation in faculty gossip and the right to criticize the administration. As William Howard Taft found in connection with a more important Presidency, old friends will stop dropping in to spend the evening. To them he has become a friend in power. No longer will he be—nor can he afford to be— a part of his old departmental gang. He cannot play favorites, or even seem to. Old colleagues will be quick to sense whether he grows with the job or inflates.[12] They will be acutely sensitive to his degree of sincerity and candor.

SOME LIMITS AND LATITUDES OF THE PRESIDENT

Granted that the president cannot eliminate all external stresses that press on him, granted that he cannot ignore all minor internal problems or leave them on his desk in the hope that they

---

[12] One of my earliest recollections of an unwarranted swelling of the ego involved a young subordinate administrator known to all the faculty by his first name. On the day he was named president of the college, an older colleague met him with "Congratulations, Jim!" to which Jim icily replied, "Call me 'Mr. President.'" F. C. R.

will go away or solve themselves, he still has latitude—not often fully realized or exercised—in the *how, when,* and *who* of handling these matters, and he can even establish an order of priority as to *what* is to be given his personal attention.

Few presidents have succeeded in confining themselves to the irreducible minimum of routine business, social activities, and minutiae which press upon them. Any college transacts enough business to consume all the time of one who thinks that only he can adequately develop a contract, guard the petty cash, plan a building, oversee the janitors, curtail a panty raid, or represent the college. If he will allow it, a president can become a complete slave to his desk, telephone, and random interruptions, living in a whirlwind of disorder.

At one urban university we were told that local claims on his time would pull the best possible president away from the faculty and away from academic leadership. After a year or two in that institution the current president reports that he has all but given up trying to plan his day. The pace he follows and the sheer volume of business he attempts to handle leave him little time for an intellectual life of his own and truly make his work hard. He is busy with details, when what his university desperately needs in its president is guidance and a panoramic view.

Naturally, no president completely escapes grubby details. What he must watch is that he is not confusing sheer activity with a sense of accomplishment. For the extrovert there may be more fun, more satisfaction in rounds of social events or in personal attention to the details of constructing a new building than in closeting himself to prepare a forceful statement of views on an educational topic. It takes less energy to check on the quality of food in the dining halls, and it is more fun to attend a convention than to be an educational provocateur. Unfortunately, some presidents have needed a coronary attack for an alibi to relinquish details ; and not all succeed in doing so even then.

Any experienced chief executive knows that some of the daily crop of problems can grow into large, difficult ones. Someone must handle them, and handle them well. But woe betide the institution whose president cannot distinguish the essential from non-essential, who continually deals with trivia. He is the sort who believes that somehow things are all right so long as the dormitories are filled, the budget stays "in the black," and no major upheavals occur.

Given an intellect capable of raising and coming to grips with important educational issues, the president needs most of all a personality or ego that will allow him to share his management load. At the same time he must retain the final responsibility for things over which he has less intimate control because he has dared to delegate them.

Even after administrative minutiae have been cleared out and all delegatable matters have been assigned to a strong central administrative staff and to the deans, the president's freedom to act is circumscribed by rules and regulations, charter and bylaws, tenure of the faculty, respected custom, and beloved tradition, not to mention a galaxy of long-term commitments and stipulations of agencies, professional associations, governments, and a complex of public expectations.

Nevertheless, the president who makes a realistic analysis of his strengths and limitations in relation to his job and forms a determination not to spend his talents on minor issues will be rewarded by an immediate increment in educational influence.

THE CLIMATES OF PRESIDENTIAL SUCCESSION

New brooms sweep clean. Or at least they raise more dust than old ones. After the first wave of approval or dismay over his selection, the new president faces the first question: Where would I be wise to begin?

If he follows a "giant" in office, he must prove that his capabilities are adequate, if different from his predecessor's. If he is young and follows a respected and popular president, he may suffer some invidious comparisons, but he can take heart in the cruel fact that retired, resigned, or dead presidents are usually soon forgotten.[13]

Following a notable president usually means that the successor is heir to a valuable institutional momentum. He is fortunate if his predecessor's success was not solely personal but was achieved with the help of a workable administrative structure and an effective organization. He can then rely upon momentum to carry on normal functions during his first, tentative year.

In the folklore of the presidency there is a widely current notion that the worse the plight of the institution, the greater the opportunity of the president to achieve personal success. An institution which has been led into difficulty by its former president may afford an opportunity for his successor to look well by contrast at the start; but as soon as the new president attacks some serious matter, any relative advantage he enjoys is evanescent. While they can be valuable as guides to future conduct, the shortcomings and failures of a predecessor are hardly to be regarded as a godsend.

Perhaps the easiest president to follow in office is one who has not been personally popular but who has succeeded in keeping the college or university in good order, gaining in strength, and "on target." He has left a good legacy. Unfortunate personality quirks—such as impatience, aloofness, severity, impersonality, a grouchy disposition, or an irritating egoism—will not obscure his solid accomplishments. His successor may be a more gregarious type, but he had better not rely on charm for success.

Presidents who take office after an interregnum, or following a president who exhausted his physical and mental capital long before he retired, may have to contend with special problems. As a president approaches the end of a long term, he becomes properly sensitive regarding commitments which will bind his successor. At the same time, he does not want the institution to lose

---

[13] Except, perhaps, if the former president himself retires to an adjacent office where, as he becomes an adviser to the trustees and ambassador-at-large, he complicates his successor's life under the illusion that he is helping.

momentum. He tends to establish ad interim policies which, wise or unwise, often carry over to the next administration. At worst, under temporary leadership, a form of chaos may develop. This in turn will require the next president to devote a disproportionate amount of time to regularizing the university's operational procedures and coordinating the work of reluctant administrators who had been enjoying a season free of firm direction.

In our view, among the most difficult of all persons to follow is one who, long in service, has become the idol of his constituents. This is a phenomenon found more often in small colleges, where students are more apt to be sentimental about their presidents. Although successive heads of colleges and universities are not likely to engender a tradition of hero worship, where idolatry does exist, it may be that one successor must intervene before another can command enough respect from the hero's followers to be accepted as their leader. In any event, the man who follows a popular one, loved for his personal qualities, for colorful—perhaps carefully cultivated—idiosyncrasies, or for the fame he has brought the institution, must be prepared to endure a trying period. He will be the victim of searching comparisons, a lot of them unfair. A sense of humor will help him to keep his perspective. It may also save him from becoming an involuntary human sacrifice to the memory of his predecessor.

Perhaps this is as good a place as any to urge a new president to treat the memory of his predecessor kindly. He may find as he grows older that his first impressions require substantial correction, that his earlier opinions—worse, his earlier utterances—were naïvely unjust. "Let him not boast who puts his armor on as he who puts it off." Neglect of this admonition will bring adverse criticism even from the critics of his predecessor. Alexander Meiklejohn at Amherst and Tyler Dennett at Williams are examples of what obvious lack of respect for one's predecessor may cost a man, and Woodrow Wilson's failure to mention retiring President Patton in his inaugural address at Princeton was remembered later to his disadvantage.

THE NEW PRESIDENT AND FACULTY ACCEPTANCE

The president who is chosen by the trustees without faculty approval or in the face of strong faculty opposition will travel an uphill road at the start. It may even happen that a new president's legacy includes one or two disappointed faculty aspirants for his post and perhaps a faction in the faculty that actively resisted his selection against a preferred candidate. Under such circumstances he may have to earn the honeymoon period readily granted to those who come in under more favorable conditions.

Illustrative of such cases is one in which twenty faculty members signed a vigorous objection to the selection of the man who then became their president. When we visited the campus, they were still known as the "twitching twenty." The new president wisely undertook no reprisals. He persuaded a capable member of the twenty to accept an important administrative post and by tactful treatment persuaded the others of the group to grant him a fair trial period. His policy of frankly identifying the dissidents and forthrightly discussing with them their ambitions, doubts, and fears is an excellent precedent for others who find themselves in the same situation. It is vastly preferable to acting as if opposition had never existed.

THE PRESIDENT PREPARES TO LEAD
BY EXAMINING HIS LEGACY

The circumstances confronting a president new to the job, whether from the academic or nonacademic world, throw light on the setting in which academic leadership realizes itself. We therefore suggest some criteria by which he may both measure his legacy and enlighten himself on the nature and dimensions of his task ahead.[14]

[14] Criteria such as these may profitably be invoked by a president approaching retirement who is naturally beginning to think about what he will leave to his successor. Former President Henry M. Wriston suggests that if he is

1. *The governing board:* Is it strong, balanced, active? Is it an inert body, restricting itself to routine operations? Does its membership contain at least a nucleus of influential members appropriately sophisticated and concerned about education and the nature of a college or university?

2. *The faculty:* Gauged by other institutions in its class, has the faculty exceptional strength in several departments and schools which can serve as pace setters? Which are the weak ones that will require special attention? Is morale good, as attested by the institution's holding power of its faculty? Are departments headed by able persons? Does effective machinery exist to assure faculty participation in the formation of academic policy?

3. *Academic program:* Are the curricula a clear reflection of institutional purpose? Are they abreast of needs which they should serve? Do they show evidence of past planning and periodic revision?

4. *Finance:* Do sufficient funds flow into the college or university to permit a balanced budget without denying basic support to a strong academic program? Is the institution debt-ridden? Is the organization for fund raising and/or legislative support effective, and does it function without the constant involvement of the president?

5. *The administration:* Is the administrative structure sound and appropriate to the size and purposes of the institution? Are the deans leaders in their own right? Does the central administrative staff have its quota of creative minds who are able to share much of the president's load? Do disappointed presidential aspirants, if any on campus, evince loyalty to the new president and willingness to work together well in harness?

6. *Physical plant and equipment:* Are buildings well maintained, and is equipment modern and adequate? Has the physical

---

shrewd, the outgoing president will exact a promise from his successor not to look under the presidential rug for the first year. It is a sensible promise for a new man to make. So far as possible let his first examination be his own, so that he will not be influenced unduly by the strengths and weaknesses of his predecessor; let him postpone looking under the rug in order that he may interpret what he finds there in better perspective.

development of the campus proceeded in accord with long-range plans which have been kept current?

7. *Public relations:* Has the institution cultivated the active interest and support of alumni, townspeople, patrons, and citizens at large? Has the conduct of public relations relied on excessive participation by the president? Has the public relations program concentrated on the public image of the president at the expense of the institution?

A NEW PRESIDENT SHOULD TAKE TIME
TO GET ACQUAINTED

Especially when he comes from outside or has been selected from professorial ranks within, and therefore has not through personal experience gained a comprehensive knowledge of his own institution, the new president profits greatly by devoting a major portion of his time at the start to visiting departments, laboratories, and special agencies or bureaus before he starts to make major moves. Through early informal acquaintance with people and programs, he acquires invaluable information about the strength of departments and programs. During the time, he is not the only one who is learning. Faculty and administration come to know him under circumstances less exacting and more personal than faculty and committee meetings.

PRESIDENTIAL SATISFACTIONS:
THE PRESIDENT MAKES A DIFFERENCE

Let no president assume that his office does not make a difference. It is said that the cudgeling the presidency has received within and without the academic world deters able young men from undertaking it. Still, it enjoys unique influence and prestige simply because no matter how democratic a society of scholars may be or however consultative its processes, the role of chief executive remains indispensable. Further, practical experience has demonstrated that it is played best when it is unitary and not collegial.

Abraham Flexner, who was no blind admirer of academic presidents, wrote thirty years ago:[15]

> I do not believe that we should today possess at their present stage of development the best things in the American university, if we had had no university presidents; I further believe that we should probably not be afflicted with the worst, if great scholars and scientists had during the last twenty years possessed more influence in determining university policies. . . . To be sure, a permanent head insuring continuity of policy is necessary; an unwieldy faculty cannot, I believe, manage a university.

It is not accidental that notable steps forward in higher education have been identified with the names of individuals and still are. The fact that the correlation between the pace-setting colleges and universities and those with broad faculty autonomy is less than absolute is no argument for a weak president. In a democracy the one appointed to lead must lead. Never in living history has it been clearer that academic democracy, in company with our political democracy, will flourish or decline in proportion to its capacity to select and utilize its leaders.

Sooner or later a self-examining president has moments when he wonders why he ever took the job or what he is accomplishing that someone else could not do better. He will suffer attacks of loneliness; he will be irritated by days that slip completely away from his planned use of them. He will not win every tilt and tussle. His administrative grind and the pressures demanding response may make him feel like a captive squirrel in a revolving cage. He knows that one does not succeed merely by being busy. His accomplishment will be determined largely by how well he selects the strategic points at which to apply himself, how well he delegates less critical matters to others.

[15] *Universities: American, English, German,* Oxford University Press, New York, 1930, p. 184. The growing practice of trustee-faculty conferences is discussed in Chaps. IX and X.

THE OFFICE IS RICH IN SATISFACTIONS

Contrary to some well-publicized opinion, the office is rich in personal and intellectual satisfactions. To attack it as devoid of such joys or even as anti-intellectual, as some have, is unrealistic and naïve. Obviously its rewards are not those of the specialized scholar pursuing some fragment of new truth in library or laboratory, but they are real. The life of a scholar is not the only life of the intellect. As one president remarked, "I rarely think as hard or as fast as when I am out trying to get a million dollars. To assume that educational policy is made only in the classroom, or that the only rewards are there, is wrong."

Another, on resigning after sixteen years in office (which he deemed as long as one person should occupy it) to return to teaching and scholarship, denied that he was leaving because of the burden of fund raising. "I was engaged in it incessantly," he said, "and I enjoyed every minute of it." A third who resigned for the same reason wrote, "I regard my thirteen years as president here as having been not only a rewarding experience, but also a most enjoyable one. I wouldn't have missed it for anything." A fourth wrote, in language in which many would concur, "I stay at [the post] because I am so solidly convinced of the importance of higher education and of the transformation which can be worked by bringing out the latent talent of youth. Having this conviction, which makes the process perpetually exciting to me, I stay at the presidency because it maximizes my own personal impact on education."

Unless one values rewards such as these, he will become bored toward his main responsibilities and find his outlet in preoccupation with the more practical problems of housekeeping or succumb to an appetite for sitting on platforms. The president who spends most of his time doing things which come hard to him —whether it be work with people such as trustees, faculty, students, alumni, or the public at large, or necessary observance of administrative procedures—is making a too costly and probably unfruitful sacrifice for whatever satisfaction he derives from being called "Mr. President."

But if his basic devotion is to education, the successful president will be sustained by the satisfactions derived from his relationship with faculty, trustees, and alumni and its culmination in progress for the institution. He will have to forgo the joys of specialized research, but he can find intellectual satisfactions in being a generalist in a world in which specialists are a dime a dozen. He will identify in the graduates and their achievements the influence of the university he is privileged to lead as its chief executive. These things will bring him happiness.

CHAPTER II

THE PRESIDENT AND ACADEMIC LEADERSHIP

The memories of certain historic figures of acknowledged presidential greatness both inspire and haunt modern university presidents. Haunt them, for they often hear that no such greats exist today. Where are figures comparable to the giants of the past—the Eliots, the Gilmans, the Harpers, the Andrew D. Whites—men who by charismatic gifts wrought sweeping innovations that spread far beyond their institutions?

As a president reads their biographies, it is appropriate that he should search his soul, for if he does not lose himself in their tall shadows, the reading will illuminate the inmost center of his office. Here are brief vignettes of the careers of seven who by common consent are numbered among the giants. Their histories make pertinent reading today.

PRESIDENTIAL GIANTS OF THE PAST

Andrew D. White, president of Cornell from its founding in 1867 to 1885, was a historian, diplomat, and prodigious reader who preferred the scholarly life to administration.

A member of the New York State Senate when the application of the Land Grant College Act benefits was being decided upon, he came to know a fellow senator—Ezra Cornell.[1] He convinced this man of wealth and vision to support financially, ideologically, and with ardor the idea of a new university which would develop the mechanical and agricultural arts, as envisioned by the Land Grant College Act, but which would also include ample attention to the liberal arts. That the mechanical arts deserved university status, commonplace today, and that the two types of education should be brought together in a program and offer degrees of equal standing was a most heretical proposal which raised the level of blood pressures throughout college circles. It anticipated the struggle that stirred the British dons of Oxford two generations later, who heatedly opposed technology as a subject unworthy of an honorable place in the ancient university until the University Grants Committee ruled against them.

White surmounted similar opposition to the principle that the new university should be open to all the people without discrimination as to race, sex, or creed. He was also ahead of his time in his concept of the presidential office in that he turned over discipline and control of the curriculum to the faculty. Cornell's faculty continues to enjoy a comparatively large degree of decision-making power.

Over the years, White had repeatedly to defend his radical educational theories; his health was precarious, and his benefactor was unable to continue his financial support at the old level after the panic of 1873. So that the last years in the presidency of this inspired teacher and prolific writer were gloomy ones in contrast to his early success.

Charles W. Eliot, on retirement in 1909 after forty years as head of Harvard, was accounted by many to "tower above all

[1] Cornell is known principally for his financial backing of White. He has received less credit than he merits for the ideas he contributed, which became mingled with those of White, as well as for the support of his friendship and zeal in recurring moments of discouragement, when White wanted to withdraw from the whole enterprise.

other presidents." He was the first in office to give full time to administration, but he managed to study and reflect upon broad developments, which he so well understood. Bliss Perry, who knew him as a member of his faculty and through family relationships, describes him as ". . . primarily an organizer and administrator" and stresses his inquisitive mind and his fastidious mastery of speech, ". . . the fascination which was felt in Mr. Eliot's living, speaking presence; in his flawless courtesy of bearing, his habit of deferential listening, his swift, benignant smile, and above all, the tones of his incomparable voice." [2]

At Harvard, Eliot brought new dimensions to science which other institutions, still under the influence of the classical curriculum, were neglecting. He is most commonly remembered for the variety of elective studies that he introduced and for the strong group of scholarly professors whom he chose, almost single-handedly, to man his innovations.

James B. Angell was president of the University of Michigan from 1871 to 1909. Of all the "giants" we have selected for biographical sketches, he was perhaps the most modest. Tactful and rich in human kindness, he deemed no innovation worthy that did not elicit "substantial unanimity of the faculty." Rather than impose policies on the professoriate, he preferred the slower process of consultation, which ripens into conviction and consensus. Angell did not have the freedom of action enjoyed by his eminent contemporaries who were founding new institutions, and his career was less notable than theirs for revolutionary change, but his long administration covered a period of innovation-by-evolution that in sum constitutes a notable series of "firsts."

Daniel Coit Gilman, the founding president of Johns Hopkins, serving from 1875 to his resignation in 1901, achieved fame through his pioneering emphasis upon postgraduate study and scholarly research. He adapted the German concept of a university to American conditions and promptly propelled his institution to front rank in the country. Funds which seemed ample for

[2] *And Gladly Teach,* Houghton Mifflin Company, Boston, 1935, pp. 225–226.

the time were available from the bequest of Johns Hopkins, so that he could attract strong professors from other institutions to implement his dynamic program. The Johns Hopkins Medical School, with its high standards of teaching and research, which compelled Eliot to attend to the Harvard School of Medicine, exerted a pioneering influence on medical education throughout the country that is still recognized in university circles.

Gilman was not the first to insist upon conditions permitting freedom of thinking and teaching, the vital element that he had not found earlier in his brief presidency of the new University of California, but his memory is nonetheless distinguished by his early and effective championship of academic freedom.

Upon retiring at Hopkins at the age of seventy, he was persuaded to become the first president of the new Carnegie Institution in Washington. But there, frustrated by absence of the freedom that had become second nature, he resigned after three years. In short, Gilman at the Carnegie Institution did not represent the right man at the right moment in the right situation. He was inhibited from any notable accomplishment.

As Johns Hopkins is the unchallenged monument of Gilman, so the University of Chicago is that of William Rainey Harper, its founding president and chief executive from 1891 to 1906. A precocious scholar of Hebrew who had taught successfully at four institutions, he persuaded John D. Rockefeller that the new institution he was backing should become a world-famous center of graduate study and research. With Rockefeller's munificent support he assembled a brilliant faculty. If this was done somewhat at the expense of other universities, still it promptly placed Chicago at the top in terms of prestige. Further, it did much to set the pattern of university development that now prevails in the United States. Like Gilman, Harper insisted that the faculty have full freedom in teaching and scholarship, and this at a time when such freedom was still in contention in prominent quarters. Unfortunately, Harper's almost perfect record was somewhat marred by his agreement to the separation from the faculty of Edward

W. Bemis, whose attack on the management of public utilities was considered heresy in high quarters.

Benjamin Ide Wheeler, president of the University of California from 1899 to 1919, is credited with introducing the era of its greatness. A classical scholar who was serving on the Cornell faculty when called to California, he retained a liking for German ways acquired during his student days at Heidelberg. After only a year in office he presented to the regents a formidable list of fifteen urgent needs of the university; when he retired twenty years later, all had been achieved or were in process of accomplishment.

Wheeler was an administrative dictator with a large measure of the power of life and death over professors and their salaries. Even before his retirement the faculty took steps toward acquiring the wide influence in university affairs that continues to be one of its outstanding characteristics. Nevertheless, Wheeler set its present tone of respect for academic freedom.

Woodrow Wilson, president of Princeton from 1902 to 1910, when he resigned in favor of a political career, earned his place among the giants more as a reformer than an innovator. Awareness of his influence upon the future of the American liberal arts college has been overshadowed by his later public life. But he was a leader in awakening our colleges of liberal arts from intellectual lethargy and in reestablishing their national significance in the face of growing demands for vocationalism. He wrote and spoke convincingly, eloquently. Continually he stressed the importance of an "antecedent" liberal education as a preparation for the learned professions and succeeded in perpetuating his ideas in the "preceptorial system" that in the minds of Princetonians is one of the University's most valued aspects.

Wilson aroused dissatisfaction with the prevailing social system in our colleges and set in motion changes at Princeton which now are obviously at work in all. Although he resigned amid turmoil and dissension, which it took his mild-mannered successor a decade to heal, his ghost continued to walk the campus for years, and its influence was good. He did not suffer opposition gladly. By present-day standards his methods were autocratic, yet he generated a loyal enthusiasm in his adherents.[3]

THEIR CAREERS MERIT ANALYSIS

The careers of these eminent past presidents call for study by today's academic chief executives, less because of their administrative methods (although they were not inferior administrators) than because of their educational competence and contributions. They had scholarly tastes; each came to the office possessing an academic background. Each was a man of broad interests; several were leaders in the political and diplomatic, as well as the educational, life of the country. Although none was able to ignore the undergirding functions, including fund raising, without exception they gave educational philosophy, policy, and program top priority.

The three who founded new universities were not inventors out of whole cloth. In a sense they were borrowers, in that their ideas were already in suspension in academic circles, particularly among those who had come to respect the German universities as the ideal type of higher education. They were, however, innovators in that they adapted, less critically perhaps than they should have, Continental ideas to American conditions and embodied them in one form or another in their strong new institutions. They had the advantage of a fresh start, unhampered by institutional tradition, free to assemble faculties sympathetic to them personally, and favorable to their ideals.

Each of the three was backed by individuals of substantial wealth and influence, although two unhappily experienced financial difficulties later on. Gilman had to survive financial shock when the Baltimore and Ohio Railroad suspended dividends, com-

---

[3] For example, although he used it sparingly, he received authority from the trustees to dismiss members of the faculty at will. His selection of new members was made in limited consultation with members of the faculty, but his was always the deciding vote, and to him goes the credit for the group of remarkable young teachers he assembled.

pelling him to defer for several years both a new medical school
and the new hospital required by Mr. Hopkins's will. White, as
we have indicated, was severely handicapped when Ezra Cornell
suffered monetary losses.

The presidential giants whom we have been considering may
not have felt that they had great freedom of action, but theirs
was a malleable era, conducive to the expression of individualism,
often the rugged kind. Because their institutions were then
smaller, they could unify and direct the faculties' activities personally, in a way no longer feasible. The modern concept of
academic freedom had not yet broadened to embrace the range of
faculty policy-making prerogatives common today. External accrediting bodies were far from their present importance, and
state executive agencies had not made the inroads on institutional
autonomy with which many state universities increasingly have
to contend. In short, the presidency was a more natural habitat
for the brilliant scholar-educator and the academic autocrat
than in our time.

Even in the days of the giants, educator-presidents found it
difficult to continue their teaching and their former devotion to
scholarship. Yet who will say that they did not enjoy intellectual
satisfactions? None of them was above a few human frailties. But
they had the capacity for attracting a personal following; their
personalities made them welcome company among the intellectual
and social elite of the nation. They were sensitive to excellence in
men. They had energy to burn in a good cause.

All this does not mean, however, that there are no gigantean
men among today's academic presidents. Great leaders, like
great poets, are more easily recognized in history than among
men in the next room. How can we measure the success of contemporaries by the standards of another era? The settings have
changed. The prevailing mode of consultative leadership has reduced a president's visibility. He must now share with others
credit that quite naturally accrued to his presidential predecessors. As Adolf A. Berle, Jr., observes of present-day leaders in
business or government, ". . . any man who says 'he' did some-

thing is generally a liar by the clock. He and a great many other people combined did it. Nevertheless the responsible heads of a system are entitled to take credit for success, just as they are invariably tarred with responsibility for failure." [4]

In assessing today's presidents we need not be bemused by the glamorous qualities of past "greats" into assuming that none exists today. Despite housekeeping duties, more than a few, although not so many as one could wish, do find time for the life of the mind. As *primus inter pares* they manage to maintain the *primus* nature of the office. Many a modern president wrestles valiantly and effectively with problems that would daunt lesser men. If more were less involved in management, their contributions as educators, as well as administrators, would be greater. If, as a genre, presidents of the present are deficient, it is in their capacity to escape being overwhelmed by managerial operations, to excite, to inspire, and to lift leadership to the plane of statesmanship.

INNOVATION AS A MEASUREMENT OF SUCCESS

Without innovation no growth is possible; "to be upset is good for people." Accordingly a *sine qua non* of presidential leadership is a gift for sustaining a spirit of inquiry, self-examination, and readiness to entertain new ideas and embark on new educational ventures. A president should be an originator of ideas, but his success is not measured merely by the proposals which surge up within himself, to which his personal trademark can be attached. Many are put forward by members of the faculty; others he will absorb from the atmosphere of educational discussions in general. His leadership relates to his capacity for receptivity and his discriminating selection of the issues he raises and the programs he supports. The palm of excellence should not go only to the dramatically provocative, whose policy might be described as a sustained condition of academic revolt. Periods of purgation

[4] *Power without Property,* Harcourt, Brace & World, Inc., New York, 1959, p. 4.

in the life cycle of a college or university may be necessary, but no accomplishment survives long in a climate of superheated combat, which dissipates energies and warps judgments.

In other words, presidential achievement is hardly to be equated with simple zeal for battle; it cannot be divorced from what a president accomplishes in embodying his ideas in the frame of his institution; it must be measured with one eye on his ability to convert his college or university to those ideas. The president who wants his innovations to endure stops short of precipitating open rebellion with consequent repudiation of his point of view. Otherwise what he accomplishes is apt to be gadgetry, merely a compromise or temporary reorganization of processes, rather than any fundamental enduring change.

Without doubt, institutional changes achieved today without faculty acceptance will be evanescent. More than one president has lived to see a faculty repudiate a cherished reform, either by formal action or by equally effective conscious or subconscious sabotage—the same faculty that may have given it reluctant consent under real or fancied duress. No matter how good a majority vote in favor of his proposal may seem to the president when it is spread on the faculty minutes, if those who voted "aye" aren't soundly convinced of its merits, or at least ready to experiment, it will not march.[5]

Whether or not Robert Maynard Hutchins succeeded at the University of Chicago will be debated by educators for many a long winter evening. His defenders regard his years there as the University's most exciting, innovating period. And in many respects they were, even if marred by tension and controversy beyond the optimum for a university. There is no doubt as to his stimulating, provocative influence not only over his own institution but

[5] One damper on faculty hospitality to innovations is that their pros and cons take on the emotional coloration of absolutes, corresponding to tenets of religious faith, rather than present themselves as worthy experiments to be tried, modified, even discontinued, as experience dictates, without attributing censurable failure to anyone. It requires a bit of courage for a president to promote an innovation of the nature of an experiment, knowing that his prestige may be damaged if it fails.

in American higher education generally. He did good by making people angry. However, if measured by the number of innovations that have survived him at Chicago, his right to enduring fame as a university chief executive diminishes. In assessing the causes for the faculty's later repudiation of much of his program Chicago veterans cite two things: his impatience in pressing for the adoption of new ideas without sufficient faculty support and his difficulty in judging excellence or the lack of it in his associates. Presidents will find in his essay "The Administrator: Leader or Officeholder?" [6] a revealing self-appraisal of his career as a university administrator.

In our view it is not correct to attribute failure, or even second-class citizenship, to those who may lack the talents that make them well publicized personally but who operate quietly to improve the quality of their institutions. To lift a college from relative mediocrity to relative excellence is a notable achievement. If all our institutions of higher education were good by standards copied from the best, who can measure the resultant revolution that would occur in the life of the nation? Progress throughout all levels is inspired by emulation as well as by innovation. We agree with the Ecclesiasticus whose praise of famous men did not overlook those who had no memorial but ". . . whose seed shall continually remain a good inheritance."

THE HUMAN SACRIFICE

Notwithstanding one's regard for the patient man who succeeds slowly, without the drama of radical innovation, one cannot exclude from the honors list some successful failures, the "human sacrifices." Such a one was probably selected because the institution was recognized to be in need of radical renovation. In these circumstances, trustees expect the new president to clean out decay in the curriculum, remove deadwood from faculty and

[6] *Freedom, Education and the Fund: Essays and Addresses, 1946–1956,* Meridian Books, New York, 1956, pp. 167–196.

staff, and set the college or university on a new, more excellent course.

Accordingly, they choose a strong personality with well-defined views. But when he begins to do what he was called to do, self-interest and deeply ingrained habits and traditions, shared by influential seniors on the faculty, by certain members of the board, and by some prominent alumni, prove to be powerful enemies of change. Personality difficulties, tolerated at the start, become magnified into serious presidential handicaps. Thus, exhibitions of impatience with the prevailing tempo of academic progress, sharp expressions of criticism which escape his lips, or a sort of drive that is interpreted as general hostility to what has gone before alienate earlier friends who may turn out under pressure not to be so anxious for reform after all. In short, progress toward the very goals for which he was appointed make the reformer *persona non grata* to enough trustees, faculty, and other constituents to wreck his continued usefulness.

The end is resignation or dismissal following the rancorous churning and wrenching that in academia are a prelude to forced separation. Many will mark him down as a failure. His methods may have been rough and his patience insufficient for the occasion, but he will probably be gratefully remembered by his successor. Meiklejohn of Amherst and Dennett of Williams, referred to in the previous chapter, are prominent figures on this list to whom it is proper to point after three decades. Both were judged by many contemporary observers to be failures; each was temperamentally unsuited to the milieu in which he worked.[7] By word and attitude each aroused gratuitous hostility but each brought ultimate good to his college.

A predestined human sacrifice may be aware of the rough road immediately ahead when he accepts the call. But if he does so intending to become a martyr, he will succeed with but limited

---

[7] John Erskine describes Meiklejohn as a gifted teacher, a magnetic leader of youth who sharpened the wits of his students. But ". . . he was handicapped by his inability or his unwillingness to see that an idea, to function at all, must function through human beings as they are at the moment." *My Life as a Teacher*, J. B. Lippincott Company, Philadelphia, 1948, p. 50.

benefit to the college or university. For as he lays about him with his scourge, he does not do so in the perspective of responsibility for the next stage—to rebuild on the foundations of the old.

CAPACITY FOR STIMULATING IDEAS

As a group, presidents are criticized for lack of any clearly formulated and enunciated philosophy of education by which they can appraise how they are doing. More lenient judges credit them with possessing at least a subconscious philosophy that colors their actions whether they or their public are aware of it or not. Obviously a president should not only possess a mature and consistent philosophy of education but be able to interpret it to faculty, trustees, and the lay public generally. That his philosophy will exert a deep influence in his decision making is equally clear. The effect will be felt without constant self-examination to make sure that each decision minutely conforms to some element of it, say, Section III, subsection (*a*).

The clear formulation and enunciation of the purpose of a college or university, on which every president worth his salt must reflect, is not a simple matter, as it was in the Middle Ages. As Sir Eric Ashby points out, when he does so reflect, he gets a mixed answer, for the purposes of a modern university conflict with each other, and each has its representatives at the faculty senate table. Some hold that the essence of a university is ". . . a leisurely and urbane attitude to scholarship, exemption from the obligation to use knowledge for practical ends . . . an opportunity to give undivided loyalty to the kingdom of the mind." At the same table, however, sit those for whom the university has ". . . urgent and essential obligations to modern society. . . ." He concludes, ". . . if the university repudiates the call to train technologists, it will not survive; if it repudiates the cultivation of non-practical values, it will cease to merit the title of university." [8] Since these views have not been reconciled and prob-

[8] *Technology and the Academics,* St. Martin's Press, Inc., New York, 1958, pp. 69, 78.

ably never will or should be, universities—and their presidents—find themselves searching for a *modus vivendi* by which the two can be accommodated.

While humanists and technologists differ temperamentally regarding their centers of values, the mutual accommodation of the two is handicapped by the failure of each side to develop meaningful ways for expressing and demonstrating the significance of its subject matter to the other. Each continues to talk to the already converted. One benefit accruing from periodic institutional self-studies and forward planning is the compulsion on each half of the "two cultures" to make itself comprehensible to the other. The aim is not a shallow permissiveness of one for the other, inasmuch as the truth in each point of view will always depend to some degree on tension with the other.

A president of mental vigor and cultural interests sets intellectual fires on his campus. Without a certain springiness of temperament that leads him to entertain—and enjoy—challenging, even grandiose, ideas and enables him to meet faculty peers and pundits with a sense of intellectual security, he will quench the flames lighted by the more creative and penetrating minds in the faculty. America's presidents gain the respect of their faculties when their administrative realism is wedded to intellectual receptivity. They know enough to recognize a fresh, promising idea. By the time it has become common knowledge and won common consent, it is probably beginning to move out of date. Former President Wilbur of Stanford is credited with saying, "If the faculty accepts my idea without objection or hesitation—I know I am at least ten years too late!"

A president whose heart is centered in education will not content himself with reconciling diverse opinions, important as this function is; he will go further. He will be a parent as well as a midwife of ideas, not omitting those he knows will be contested. We have observed that if the faculty accepts him as an educator, if he is skillful and considerate in planting the seeds of ideas, and if he refrains from applying arbitrary pressures, his proposals are received with respect if not with universal approval. Indeed, members of the faculty pay him the highest compliment within their power when they say of him, "He is one of us" or "Everything he does takes educational values into consideration." Such presidents may tell you that their influence is restricted to "insinuating" new ideas without being detected at it. But if they really believe this, they do themselves a grave injustice.

On the other hand, a president who is not accepted as an educator may well discover that to be identified as a proponent of a new idea is the kiss of death for it.

Professors commonly believe that their presidents are not their intellectual peers. They may be restricting intellectuality to research scholarship and so are being unfair. Still, the judgment may be correct. We have observed an occasional misguided president who, at least until he learned better, pitched his message on a low, even jocular, level in an effort to be known as a "regular fellow." His notion of fulfilling the demands of educational leadership and earning the good will of the faculty may be to have them in for dinner.

The president who wants to make memorable improvements on his campus will emulate his eminent nineteenth-century predecessors by judging his success in educational terms. He will take advantage of the multiplicity of small occasions and minor matters that somehow escape delegation to convey an educational accent or to increase his fund of knowledge. Informal campus contacts may consist of nothing more than chitchat, but they may also supplement the information that he gets through usual administrative channels. The moments of a walk with a young teacher from one building to another can be vaporized in observations about starlings and pigeons, or they may be exploited by a kindly inquiry about his courses and his plans for the future, capped by a word of encouragement. A slightly unwelcome visitor may become not a nettling interruption but a chance to probe for an idea. The possibilities of such informal methods are endless. The way in which they are utilized is one of the imponderables of leadership.

One acid test of his leadership is ability to follow through, for a good idea that has survived examination and debate must still be translated into decision and decision into action. As a president succeeds in this area, he grows in respect and influence even beyond what he can attain through needed plant expansion or faculty salary raises.

It is a master stroke for the president to become so deeply involved intellectually and emotionally in the educational side of his work that he will shunt ancillary pressures to others instinctively. He will not evade his ultimate responsibility for management and finance, but he will find men and ways to relieve himself of constant involvement in their details. He will exchange them for others that promise a higher order of durable satisfactions. His preference for these explains why he is not in a business post, where his troubles might be fewer, his weekends freer, and his pay better.

If, as we tell it, the services which one man can perform sound more like wishful thinking than practicable possibilities, we repeat that we know presidents who are succeeding as influential educators and who are improving their institutions in the process. We are suggesting nothing that we have not observed presidents practicing.

Uninterrupted service as a college or university chief executive pitched at the level we have been discussing is wearing. The individual must make conscious efforts to "recharge his batteries" regularly. Although few presidents take sabbatical leaves, they have as much need for them as the faculty. It would be better if they became an accepted pattern. Too many presidents suffer from varying degrees of chronic fatigue, from mild to serious, sufficient in any event to keep them habitually below the top of their form. When he utilizes his travels, his attendance at national meetings, and his visits to other campuses to pick the brains of others for new ideas, he is combating parochialism, for he is tapping external sources of strength beneficial to even the most restless and original minds. But such activities are not to be considered as meeting his need for periods of recreation. Although state laws may prevent him from traveling abroad at university expense, whenever possible a president will profit from an occasional visit to universities in other countries. He will gain both recreation and new ideas from contacts with educational systems different from his own.

TENSION AND CONFLICT

The president needs a nervous constitution which will enable him to live habitually at a focal point of conflicting pressures. His office, described as one of the most conflict-centered in the land, is replete with tensions to be reduced to manageable levels by qualities inadequately summarized as getting along with people, a talent which may signify merely a facility in avoiding issues that generate contention. A president who shuns conflict neglects an essential obligation. The result is that he contributes to his institution's mediocrity rather than to its excellence.

The president must bear in mind the welfare of the college or university in the large. He can be sure that his overview will conflict with the individual interests and personal ambitions of various members of the faculty, clustered, as they are, about special fields, departments, or component schools and colleges. Many presidential decisions are bound to bring disappointment— perhaps grievous—to someone. When President Eliot observed that the most important single quality in the academic administrator was "the capacity to inflict pain," he did not mean that presidents should find a sadistic pleasure in causing others to suffer. He was recognizing that most presidential decisions concern conflicts of personal interests or principles sincerely held and that members of academia are sensitive people, apt to be disheartened professionally as well as hurt personally by an adverse verdict.

A president will do what he can to prevent normal and desirable tension from degenerating into strained personal relations which wind up in rancorous and damaging strife; but he will also do everything he can to avoid "peace at any price" and the sterility of one big, dull, happy family. He tries not to smother conflicting views but to make use of them. A lively president, we were told by one who has earned his reputation for liveliness, will keep his faculty in a kind of "healthy turmoil" which generates fresh ideas, supplies a climate favorable for their consideration, and releases ambitions while stimulating self-criticism.

Nevertheless, at times the restless president will discover that he is doing what golfers call "pressing his drive." That is the moment for him to suspend his role of instigator-protagonist and allow the institution time to consolidate its gains. He will avoid bombarding the faculty or trustees with a constant barrage of ideas. After all, faculties have continuing responsibilities for teaching and scholarship and trustees for wise guardianship, as well as for innovating. A president will therefore be alert for symptoms of intellectual indigestion.

COURAGE

At the risk of resorting to platitudes, it needs to be said that the academic leadership calls for courage.[9] Any incumbent whose tenure spans more than a brief honeymoon period will have to defend the institution against outside attack from influential quarters and the freedoms of faculty members and students who espouse unpopular causes. He may, for example, have periodically to protect the library against assaults by self-appointed censors or protect the right of the students to invite controversial speakers to the campus. Superficially these issues may seem unsubstantial, perhaps unworthy of a president's attention, but, as many can testify, they may on a moment's notice burst into a conflagration. In such instances he cannot afford to appear timid or vacillating before his constituents, trustees, faculty, alumni, or the public.

A president often needs a different sort of courage to combat procrastination in doing what he knows should be done for edu-

---

[9] We recall an interview with a faculty member which revealed an inadequate concept of the presidential office. After describing his own spirit of intellectual independence, he observed, "I should make a poor college president, because there are times when I have to stand alone."

cational improvement because he hesitates to undertake the protracted, often heated, discussion that is characteristic of faculty action. Some have impaired their influence by unwillingness to risk being defeated by the faculty on educational issues in which they believe, forgetting that leadership does not consist in advocating only popular causes. Defeat on a single issue or an honest mistake frankly admitted need not spell doom for a president or justify invoking faculty intransigence as a reason for transferring the center of his energies to ancillary activities.

As a matter of fact, it is more apt to help, by keeping him human. Also by making the faculty, trustees, or alumni aware that their views are considered. Paradoxically, an occasional faculty victory over the president may clear an atmosphere becoming too tense for comfort. It may indeed make acceptance of his position on subsequent issues more likely. Still, we cannot endorse the suggestion that a president should put forth an occasional project simply for the low motive of having it beaten down by a restive faculty as a harmless outlet for their energies.

Perhaps the most common test of courage and devotion to one's educational philosophy is offered by external attacks on academic freedom; they are difficult because they usually emanate from anti-intellectual prejudices and fixations. They pit the essential idea of the college or university, that it is a center of rational inquiry, against the pattern of other organizations designed to serve special interests or promote party lines. The difficulty is doubled by lack of common assumptions from which to begin, or a common vocabulary to use in discussion between the two worlds, so that seldom does one fully grasp the meaning of the other or why the other feels as deeply as he does.

Few trials have been more severe than those of the presidents of Wisconsin colleges in the McCarthy era, the California presidents during the loyalty-oath crisis, the Southern heads in the current period of racial tension, or the state university presidents who have had to stand almost alone against the attempts of public officials or politicians to commandeer their institutions. Weak executives seek to conceal or sublimate their convictions, but stormy times are an opportunity for strong men to emerge to become figures of influence far beyond the boundaries of their campuses.

ATTENTION TO ASPECTS OF THE STUDENT CULTURE

One of the great forces in education, too often neglected by university heads, is the tone of student life on the campus. Whatever may hold at postgraduate levels, although teachers may not always admit it, it is probably true that half of an undergraduate's education comes from fellow students and sources other than formal instruction. Thus the prevailing campus culture is both an effect and a cause relating to both the lower and higher limits of what one student receives from others, including the faculty, and what he contributes to his education by his own native efforts.

Our interviews confirmed the belief that in even the largest and most complex universities the students' image of their president, whether fair or distorted as to his interest in them, has a direct bearing on their attitudes. If his conversation at a fraternity dinner, for example, stimulates intellectual exercise, tempered by a bit of wit, the students' own intellectual sights are lifted as their respect for him rises. If he gives a dinner in honor of the football team but never invites students in other activities, including the intellectual, to similar occasions, he depreciates his office. More, he misses an opportunity. Undergraduate conversations overheard as he walks across the campus are yardsticks of the level of campus tone. Incidentally, the impression that male students discuss only athletics and sex and female students only clothes, men, and social activities is quite inaccurate.

Robert M. Hutchins set an exhilarating mental pace for students by taking outspoken positions himself. Able presidents prefer to confront students with challenging issues rather than to argue constantly, defensively, the merits of the *status quo*. One who is afraid, who feels he must protect his institution or himself from student criticism, who shivers in fear of student indiscretions and their public criticism will have little influence over his student body.

The president has to take the initiative in making contact with representative students. Still they want to feel him their friend, that he is available to them even if they don't understand his problems and habitually criticize him for not paying enough attention to them.[10] Of course, no president of even a good-sized modern college can be a Mr. Chips to the students, but a certain aura of Mr. Chips, lending a considerable element of strength to the office, survives in the typical college and many universities.

As the late James L. McConaughy, sometime president of Wesleyan University, Connecticut, remarked, " 'Prexy' is particularly the title of a college administrator; it suggests emotion, often affection, . . ." but Prexy Sloan of General Motors ". . . does not quite click." [11] True, the image of a kindly scholar-philosopher, lovingly intimate with his boys and girls, is a luxury that only a small college can approach. Yet something significant will be lost on the day when the conventions of the presidential office divorce it from all association with students, when the incumbent receives his information about them wholly from others.

A president can get considerable information from students about what is going on, or at least what they think is going on. Only a few may come to know him personally, but many, including campus journalists, will note how he comports himself and will appraise him accordingly. Since his opportunities for contacts with students are few, he will naturally utilize strategic moments and strategic groups for making himself known. An annual dinner in honor of their governing body, at the president's

[10] Gilman's biographer describes him as "head of the family." When he headed the University of California, "There was never any hesitation or slip in addressing a student by his name. Every student knew him personally." Obviously no president of the University of California or of Johns Hopkins can approach this today.

[11] I am told that "Prexy" has generally been dropped from campus usage, although I can testify that the term survives to some extent. In any case, the idea behind it lingers on. H. W. D.

home if possible, at which topics of common interest are frankly treated is an illustration of a tactical occasion.[12]

Although student publications are potential trouble spots, the president will hold his press conferences with their reporters with few holds barred if he wants to get his message across. Some set aside scheduled office hours when students may see them without an appointment, although those who come at such times are apt to speak for a fringe of constant complainers.

Despite the pressures of management, fund raising, and public relations, a good many presidents do find time to involve themselves in the student culture. They are fortunate if they enjoy dealing with burgeoning minds, for there is no such thing as a five-minute conference with an undergraduate on any serious concern. Many manage occasionally to get out of the office and observe student life in its extracurricular setting—the dining halls, dormitories, assemblies, fraternities, and the student center. Students, even though they may not talk with the president, interpret these appearances as signs of interest in them, and this is good. Presidential contacts with students too frequently have to do with serious discipline cases, town-gown disturbances, or similar unhappy emergencies.

Of course, certain problems and issues repeat themselves with each class as successive students pass through similar stages of interest, doubt, and agitation about the same sorts of things. This repetition may become boring to the president, as it may to those members of faculty who are not born teachers, but if the president becomes fed up after two or three years, he may well be laboring in the wrong vineyard.

---

[12] In my experience one fruitful topic of conversation on such occasions is the organization of the university, the several responsibilities of the trustees, faculty, administration, and alumni organizations, topics ordinarily outside the range of students' concern but knowledge of which improves their understanding of the institution's operations and goals. H. W. D.

PRESIDENTIAL EMPHASES

The fulfillment of a president's purpose for his college or university is less a matter of esoteric philosophy than the embodiment of generalized aims in a series of specific, achievable goals. No one can match the president as potentially the most effective person to guide the thinking of both faculty and trustees toward higher degrees of specificity and clarity.

Once clear goals have been established, it is important for the president to say loudly and often what they are. His publics—even the faculty—do not hear him the first time he speaks, so he finds he must say the same thing over and over. But he will strive to find different ways of saying it appropriate to each audience. When asked how often a college president could make the same speech, Woodrow Wilson is said to have replied, "I don't know; I am still making the same one." And so he was, so far as his central message was concerned. But his mastery of the English language and the variety of ways in which he conveyed his message saved him from "vain repetitions, as the heathen do" in their prayers.

No one will dispute his duty to keep himself and his institution abreast of the times. This entails conscious selection of emphases: those matters which are to receive top attention must be within established goals, and there must not be too many of them to be sustained at one time. It is a never-ending problem of choices, and few chief executives can afford the luxury of choosing only salients of their personal preference.

Although it is usually in the best interests of the university for the president to be free to do what he likes to do, because he probably does it best, it is only human for him to be tempted to rationalize personal preferences into crying needs, to the neglect of the broad front. This he must watch, or the less well-attended salients will suffer in resources, quality, and morale. Presidential attention that brings new strength to one program is promptly noted and frequently makes others feel neglected. Even a windfall gift to one department or purpose may affect the morale of others, for such is the nature of the deadly sin of envy.

Since the president has only the usual twenty-four hours in which to live and to perform his multifaceted job, another kind of emphasis which he has to decide upon is whether to spend more time with schools, departments, and agencies that are ambitious to improve and ready to work with him aggressively or with those that are content with mediocrity, unable or unwilling to contribute cooperative effort in their own behalf. It is clearly more fun to work with the first than to try to fire the second with zeal for self-improvement. Yet he cannot neglect the latter, else his institution will follow a haphazard and unbalanced line of progress.

But no earthly president has any magic metrical gauge by which he can decide where to apply the major part of his time and attention at any given period. There is only common sense and his own sensitive antennae, supported by information about what is going on throughout the college or university. Indeed, a chief function of a president's information service is to help him to wisdom in settling this question. Inevitably the decision will be influenced in considerable measure by the play of external pressures, availability of new financial resources, and internal emergencies. The point is this: these factors should not be decisive of themselves.

Our studies establish the proposition that the president whose armory of weapons includes a reasonable command of administrative skill will most readily achieve progress on a broad front without scanting personal attention to salients. The man possessed of this skill is less apt to progress by fits and starts, at the mercy of circumstances; he is able to keep representatives working for him who thus release him to attend to things that require more of his personal attention or will profit most from it.

A president may find adventure and genuine satisfaction in setting himself one or more semiprivate goals that are particularly close to his heart and working toward them patiently and quietly as individual projects, rather as a scholar sets himself to writing a book. So long as such pets are in harmony with the institution's purpose and are not whimsical, they yield well-earned gratification and perhaps immeasurable profit to the college or university as well. They can quicken him to a sort of do-it-yourself, rifle-shot campaign for funds, which may be surprisingly rewarding.

Clearly, those who have been noted for personal fund raising without benefit of organized campaigns have done their best when the objective was closest to their hearts. These semiprivate goals may take the form, for example, of quiet cultivation of an over-looked source of financial support for some neglected facet of university life about which the president feels deeply; the development of some special feature, such as a center for the creative arts; the introduction of a new school or department; the improvement of dormitory conditions; or a solution of the "fraternity problem." A president is free to alternate among his private and personal goals from time to time, whereas, in dealing with major program commitments, he must resist the temptation to move blithely from one to another or forever to be "greasing the wheel that squeaks the loudest."

A RADICAL PROPOSAL

Walter Jessup once ironically told President Virgil Hancher, "If you can figure out a way to devote at least ten per cent of your time to the really important things you will be ahead of the game."

John J. Corson, who has surveyed many colleges and universities, has compiled a composite analysis of how two university presidents spend their days which indicates that they have been able to assign more than 10 per cent of their time to educational matters. He concluded that they devoted 40 per cent of their time to financial matters, 20 per cent to public relations, 12 per cent to physical facilities, 10 per cent to general administration,

18 per cent to "meeting with faculty representatives" and other educational activities. He concludes that[13]

> The foregoing summary analyses of how two university presidents spend their time do not reveal a statesman, educator, and modern-day Mr. Chips or Mark Hopkins. Rather they depict the university president as an executive concerned predominantly with financial matters, public relations, physical facilities, and other administrative affairs. They picture the university president as spending less than one-fifth of his time working on educational matters and keeping in touch with his faculty or with his students.

Although Mr. Corson observes that his ". . . quantitative approximations offer no precise depiction of what the presidents do . . ."—one brief telephone conversation may be more significant and call for a greater expenditure of energy than an hour devoted to routine matters—it seems that many presidents devote even less attention to educational operations. Had he included a larger representation of presidents, it is probable that the average percentage of time assigned to education would have been lower.

Today the need for educational statesmanship is so compelling that we make bold to recommend a bootstrap operation, the objective of which is not 10 or 20 but 50 per cent of presidential time for education. If this ratio of 50 per cent of attention to main function compared to the aggregate of all other functions could be introduced across the board in institutions of all types—and within the next decade—it would contribute to an educational and intellectual awakening by which our society might face its future with a sense of greater security than it knows today.

Clearly this is an approximation, quantitatively and qualitatively, of a desirable proportion and is not to be interpreted narrowly. No president can rigidly adhere day in and day out to a "50 per cent rule." It is proposed as a guide, not as a basis for statistical accounting for each hour spent throughout the day. The emphasis it represents, however, is closely related to the probability of academic success. A fund-raising campaign, a legis-

---

[13] *Governance of Colleges and Universities,* McGraw-Hill Book Company, Inc., New York, 1960, pp. 60, 61.

lative session, or the like will intervene, although they are not devoid of educational aspects. But if the administrative organization is adequate and staff work has been well developed, interruptions will be fewer and less diverting.

In adopting the 50 per cent rule, the president will recognize that more time is to be credited to education than is consumed in specific attention to curricula, research programs, and faculty appointments and promotions. Energy devoted to reading, study of educational issues, writing for publication brings definite educational rewards to him and his institution. When he consults with trustees on educational programs and personnel, he engages in a form of teaching, and the same is true when he centers his addresses to alumni and public on educational issues and does not content himself with pleasant commonplaces. Attention to financial and budget matters, planning a new library or laboratory entail decisions on educational emphases. But his definition of educational activity should not be so comprehensive as to encompass virtually all his dealings with nonacademic administrators, trustees, alumni, and the public generally. The major portion of the time he spends in these areas belongs to the category of supporting activities. That they bear some relationship to the functioning of the university does not justify their inclusion in the "50 per cent" as we conceive it.

One of the many facets of his primary function is that the president's job summons him to be an aggressive partisan for a point of view on academic questions and issues. How else can he fulfill his acknowledged responsibility for continually challenging the *status quo* in his own college or university, as well as in higher education generally? Not all his constituents will approve his position on a given issue, but they will respect the man who reveals integrity, informed intelligence, and courage.

Before presidents can exercise leadership, they must know something of the basic problems faced by all colleges and universities in common with their own institutions. Such insight demands an awareness of the forces shaping our society—economic, social, political—not for the purpose of simply following currents of opinion but for assessing them and, if need be, resisting them. None can be a professional authority on all educational issues, but most can inform themselves generally if they make time for reading and contemplation. The vital questions are intriguing enough to challenge the talents of any president, even a latter-day giant, and to merit fully 50 per cent of his time.

Our nation gropes, without notable success at this moment in history, for adequate policies concerning many educational topics. There is no dearth of problems from which a president can choose; some are organizational, others pertain to the region, the nation, and the world; none is easily answered. Guidance to their solution rests with those who are capable of enlisting a following; it cannot be supplied by mere group dynamics. What person is more strategically placed for this purpose than a college or university president, who, having carved out time for study and discussion of these momentous questions, has attained the stature of educational statesman? From his home base of achievement on his own campus, such a one can move with confidence and public respect to a position of national leadership.

We are fully aware that the dilemma of the modern president is real, that to urge him to make 50 per cent of his time free for educational matters will be considered by many a radical proposal. Many a seasoned, conscientious veteran will think it impracticable, even visionary. Nor do we underestimate the obstacles to its effectuation. It is, we repeat, truly a bootstrap operation. It can be realized only as the modern president is able to buy time from involvement in those supporting activities which he cannot ignore. He will be helped by a reasonable mastery of the art of administration, to which we now turn our attention.

CHAPTER III

THE PRESIDENT
AND THE ART OF
ADMINISTRATION

THE ADMINISTRATIVE ENVIRONMENT

Much that the president does, much of what we consider to be his prime responsibility, is accomplished by and through others, who discharge allotted duties as individuals but who also function as elements of an organized entity moving toward a common purpose. The president's job as chief executive requires that he cultivate, organize, release, and channel the potential of the group toward organizational goals. To do all these things well he must utilize the art of administration, whose purpose is simply to enable people performing a variety of activities to work together to a common end. The head of a modern, complex university or college will study to be a good administrator to escape being drowned in administration. But he will not deceive himself by thinking that merely by following textbook principles he will qualify as a leader, least of all a leader in education.

Nonetheless, if he has not inherited a sound administrative structure, well staffed, among the first things he must do is build one. While the correlation between a good administrative organi-

zation—from provosts or deans to superintendents of grounds—
and a president's educational potential is not a statistical absolute, the number of presidents who have found it necessary to attend to the former before they could get to the latter and whose
effectiveness as educators was thereby noticeably enhanced is too
large not to suggest a causal relationship.

Expert craftsmen know the value of good tools, and efficient
administrative techniques are good tools. Of course, no amount
of technique will compensate for one's inability to project a personality that quickens a spiritual and intellectual thirst for
excellence in one's colleagues. No amount of obedience to the
formal canons of good administration will imbue others with a
spirit of self-examination, a zeal to profit from past mistakes, if
the president does not himself set the example. But good tools
enable the president better to ". . . share in the thinking and
creative work of the faculty." [1] One of the most successful presidents we know was praised by faculty and colleagues for the
manner in which he employs orderly processes of administration
without becoming their slave or permitting them to become a
barrier between himself and the faculty and students.

The dean of another university praised his president for "leadership expressed through being the kind of man he is; it is not
accomplished through administrative machinery. Scholarship
stands out in his speeches." We would agree, remarking that this
president also possesses in large measure the gifts and human
understanding of an efficient administrator, although more careful observance of operational channels and clearer signals to his
administrative colleagues would increase his effectiveness.

Presidential skill in administration is no Johnny-come-lately
aspect of the academic scene. True, the fairly informal arrangements that served to inspire, coordinate, and direct the activities
of an institution when it was small and compact falter and break
down when it starts to grow into a multifaceted university. Yet

---

[1] Algo D. Henderson, "Finding and Training Academic Administrators,"
Public Administration Review, vol. 20, no. 1, p. 20, Winter, 1960.

the earlier college or university had its problems of administration. While the presidential greats described above did not lack administrative capacity commensurate to the requirements of the time, some successful ones of that day appear to have disregarded the most elementary principles of administration. An occasional one may do so today. By virtue of boundless energy, extraordinary talent for generating sparkling ideas, or brilliance in outmaneuvering the faculty while still retaining its tolerance—if not its undivided loyalty—or because of particularly advantageous institutional circumstances, a rare one seems to succeed by liberal use of autocratic methods, almost in defiance of the basic canons of good administration.

But today such presidents are biological sports who produce no progeny. The blunt fact is that the environmental circumstances under which the inept or unconcerned administrator could conceal his incapacity are disappearing.

If the consequences of indifference to some simple elements of the art of administration are not glaringly apparent during the tenure of a sitting president, they become manifest in his legacy to his successor. A case in point concerns a man who came to retirement age after serving his university first as a teacher and later as president. He had raised it in both public and professional esteem; he had erected buildings and, although not to the extent which had been programmed, he had increased the endowment. He had preached the need to raise standards until trustees and alumni caught something of his enthusiasm; he had supported academic freedom against adverse pressures. If a faculty member came in to ask support and he thought the project a good one, he might answer, without looking at the budget, "We must do it and find the money somewhere." This pleased the faculty, naturally. But the lack of regular procedure was hard on the finance committee of the board of trustees and the treasurer of the university. The president was regarded favorably by the faculty, but he was also criticized for being a poor administrator.

For one thing, powers of decision which he should have retained drifted away to others. As a result, unfortunate feuds sprang up among key officials. The president neglected to keep trustees and colleagues informed—he ignored channels. The situation degenerated into administrative disorder. These difficulties fell to the lot of his successor. Although academic progress had been made, it was the consensus of the faculty and staff that it would have been greater, and the financial position better, had the administration been more efficient.

The accomplishments of his administration were of no mean order, far beyond those possible had he been only an administrator in a narrow sense. Our point is that there is no inherent incompatibility between the gifts he possessed and an attention to administration.

CRITICAL VIEWS OF EXPERTS IN MANAGEMENT

Management experts who survey colleges and universities report that many educational institutions suffer from grave operating inefficiencies, that presidents as a class churn around in administrative turmoil, handicapped by insufficient and incapable staffs and unable to make use of what they have. They tolerate weak assistants who cannot or will not accept responsibility, or they distrust strong ones. Their administrative organizations, these experts say, are not well structured; areas of responsibility are poorly defined; the chain of command is hazy. The faculty complains because it gets the runaround. Business costs soar, because housekeeping methods are wasteful, even obsolete. One cannot deny that these charges are often embarrassingly true.

Students of management go even further. They charge that presidents often not only are incompetent administrators but actually reject the relevance to university conditions of the canons of administration formulated by experts on business and governmental organization. "The assumption," writes Corson, "that the university is different and not subject to assistance from the considered experience of other institutions seems to be the crucial barrier to imaginative development of new and improved means of governance." [2]

College presidents share this attitude with academia in general and accordingly have shown little desire to promote analytical studies of their office (apart from confidential management surveys frequently instigated by the trustees), such as business and governmental executives undergo. The signs indicate, however, that now that all other forms of human association are coming under the miscroscope, we are at the beginning of at least a small boom in academic research into the workings of the organization of academic people themselves. This enterprise will take on greater dignity and acceptance by colleagues if the presidents encourage it.

It would be quite unjust, however, to attribute the inclination of seasoned veterans in the academic presidency to view the apostles of administration with a lackluster eye only to professional inertia or to bigotry. These anatomical and physiological analysts of the body academic leave the presidents cold, because they consider that their exhortations neglect the lifegiving element, the *élan vital*, which above all else must emanate from presidents—the quality that makes others follow them. Presidents know that their success depends upon the personal values and influence they exude in a society in which, if a choice had to be made between an environment conducive to free-ranging imagination of teachers and scholars and one of nice orderly organizational processes, the ballot should unhesitatingly be cast for the former. The educator-president and the faculty both resist making a fetish of administration and fear that preoccupation with administrative methods will impair—even destroy—intellectual sensitivity. Moreover, whatever help the development of a generalized science of administration may offer harassed presidents lies largely in the future. Their basic needs, immediate and more specific, can essentially be met by some elementary, well-recognized principles of administration.

[2] John J. Corson, *Governance of Colleges and Universities*, McGraw-Hill Book Company, Inc., New York, 1960, p. 200.

Like all arts, the art of administration is to a degree an acquired skill, one that can be cultivated by study and practice. In improving his practice a president can, if he will, learn a great deal from nonacademic organizational experience. In perfecting his skill he will be under no illusions that his life thereby will be made one of ease, but he will gain sea room for that attention to educational leadership which the nature of his office implies.

PROFESSORIAL SKEPTICISM ABOUT THE ADMINISTRATOR

In arguing for the importance of administration, and certainly in dignifying it as an art, we take issue with cherished professorial tradition that "a dean is too stupid to be a professor but too bright to be a president." The tradition holds that administrative talent and imaginative educational leadership are not found combined in one person. Therefore, since they are mutually exclusive, one must choose. It is charged that, unfortunately for the cause of higher education, the administrator usually wins.

In order to establish this dichotomy, administration is interpreted as the management of routine operations in which little or no imagination is needed.[3] Nothing could be more misleading as to the qualities a chief executive requires, whether in government, business, or education. (Indeed—and no credit to academia— one can name from personal acquaintance a good number of business executives who are doing more creative thinking than many college presidents.) Peter F. Drucker says that administration is ". . . a creative rather than an adaptive task."[4] Its detractors do not perceive that there is a skill to it as valid in a university context as the art of conducting a scientific experiment is in a laboratory. One of them called administration

[3] Abraham Flexner, who was intensely critical of what he termed America's "rage for organization," fell into this trap when he wrote, "Efficiency in administration and fertility in the realm of ideas have in fact nothing to do with each other—except, perhaps, to hamper and destroy each other." *Universities: American, English, German,* Oxford University Press, New York, 1930, p. 186.

[4] *The Practice of Management,* Harper & Brothers, New York, 1954, p. 47.

". . . perhaps the most overrated commodity on the market to-day . . ." [5] and thereby undoubtedly expressed the honest opinion of many faculty members. To many professors, the concept *administration* suggests regimentation; regimentation spells restrictions on freedom; and the less there is of it, the better.

Moreover, why should money be dissipated on administrative paper-shufflers when the library needs strengthening, my department sadly lacks a new professor to round out its curriculum, my laboratory equipment is inadequate for my research, and faculty salaries leave so much to be desired? The very terms "economy" and "efficiency" are apt to arouse faculty fear that its participation in decision making will be diminished. This attitude should not be lightly dismissed. For it bears repeating that a certain incompatibility exists between organizational law and order and the play of individualism that produces an inspiring teacher or original scholar.

The design for an experimental "New College" projected by a group of professors from four New England colleges, acting under a grant by The Fund for the Advancement of Education, is an interesting reflection of this psychology. According to their report, "It is recommended unequivocally that the faculty have a dominant role." To assure ". . . some independence from his faculty," the president is to be chosen for a fixed term of five years. Although nothing is said about eligibility to serve again, if he is to succeed himself, he must endure the rigors of reëlection. "Presumably he would be elected (although not initially) by the Senate [in which the faculty would have a majority vote], instead of holding office under a board of trustees. . . . Whenever feasible, he will be chosen from the faculty and return to it. If not a member of the faculty on his appointment, he will become one at the conclusion of his term." [6]

[5] Lloyd P. Williams, "Some Heretical Reflections on Educational Administration," *Journal of Higher Education,* vol. 27, no. 4, p. 182, April, 1956.

[6] *The New College Plan: A Proposal for a Major Departure in Higher Education,* Amherst, Mass., 1958. One main emphasis of this new plan, so far as college governance is concerned, is centered on the composition and functions of the governing board. Two alternative plans are considered: One is a

It is difficult for a president-administrant to be a hero to his faculty. Heroes are the creatures of one's culture, and, as we have noted, academic culture has little place for heroes of administration.

Feeling a certain guilt evoked by the widespread campus opinion that too much money is already being spent on administration, conscientious presidents are reluctant to add needed aides to their organization. Many universities have outgrown their "administrative breeches." Too often pressures are met by the simple expedient of giving deans and supporting officers more work to do without the help they need to free them for attention to high-level policies. Like presidents, other officers of administration need time to read and think. Faculties profit from the administration's being adequately and competently staffed. On the whole those colleges and universities which have been courageous enough to spend money on administration have progressed the most.

THE METHODOLOGY OF THE ADMINISTRATOR CONTRASTED WITH THAT OF THE PROFESSOR

When one moves from a professorship to a presidency, he soon discovers that the professional demands under which he worked as teacher and scholar prepared him inadequately for directing a complex organization, for galvanizing and coordinating the work of hundreds or thousands of individuals representing various vocations and divergent, and often irreconcilable, views on institutional policies. Immediately he must subject himself to a new set of disciplines. For the personal freedom of his old life of teacher

---

board of trustees of the traditional type, in which event the president would ". . . act with the advice of a powerful standing committee representing the faculty." The other would substitute a ". . . Senate in which members of the faculty would have a major vote." The latter is preferred with the way open after ten years to institute a board of trustees "if necessary." "Hopefully, the fund-raising needs would be taken care of ultimately by the alumni and persons friendly to the college."

and scholar he must exchange a more regulated life of long office hours and orderly procedures.

As Prof. Robert W. Merry has observed, "The need for an administrator to take action on a great many matters in a relatively short space of time prevents thorough scholarly exploration of each matter that arises." Every executive must arrive at judgments by methods that are the antithesis of the methodology of scholarship and from evidence which is heavily empirical—this for the sake of reaching decisions that are at once prompt and capable of standing up in practice. He must be willing to accept the risks and responsibilities which such decisions entail. A fluent flow of logic and excellence in formal presentation of a case will not compensate for an action that turns out to have been a mistake.

A second psychological adjustment required of the professor-become-president is to accept as a fact of life that for him self-realization is attained in, and through, an organization. For previous reliance on himself as his chief source of ideas and center of action he substitutes faith in the principle of organization as a "conscious planned order of relations between men." He views the requirements of organizational processes not as limitations on his freedom, as he may have done before, but as a means of enlarging his freedom.

For him to adjust to a life filled with new sorts of externally and internally imposed disciplines, without succumbing to the concept of the administrator as one who merely shoves papers around, is not as easy as it sounds. Unhappy tensions between president and faculty frequently stem from his disregard of elementary organizational processes, which, in turn and perhaps quite innocently, derive from his eagerness to get things done and an insensitivity to the human-nature side of organizational life.

Quite possibly we have made the elements of administration by which a professor-president can buy time to be an educator sound more awesome than they are. If anyone should be deterred by his lack of that practical experience acquired by a businessman who has worked up to become head of an enterprise, we remind him that the art of academic administration is not so difficult and esoteric as all that.

On the basis of personal experience and from observation of others we conclude that the most critical areas for the president-administrant can be reduced to three. Each is familiar, easy to express in words, but difficult for many to apply in practice. They relate to (1) the practice of consultation, (2) the principles of delegation, and (3) the structure and staffing of the administrative organization.

ADMINISTRATIVE SKILLS: THE CONSULTATIVE PROCESS

Since the governance of a college or university is characterized by an extraordinary emphasis upon consultation, an understanding head rarely says, "I direct." Rather, he says, "I suggest" or "I raise the question whether . . ." and thereby gains a more sympathetic hearing and a stronger chance of securing consensus. While the business side of an institution is administered more bureaucratically than the academic under a recognized, accepted chain of command, the spirit of consultation spills over there also, to a degree not yet general in business. Many a president has undoubtedly wished that he could give a military kind of order to someone just once, or at least circulate through his staff and faculty a memorandum in the stern language, for example, of a directive by a bank president. But he resists the temptation, knowing that his success relates to his belief in the principle of consultation as well as to his skill in practicing it. Consultation aimed at integration of diverse viewpoints usually gives better results than the participants could have contributed as individuals.[7]

Bitter issues tend to be resolved by consensus as more facts emerge and thoughts expand. This is particularly true of universities, since their strength rests ultimately in the synthesis of the diverse contributions of professional nonconformists.

[7] See, for example, the discussion of integrative unity in Henry C. Metcalf and L. Urwick (eds.), *Dynamic Administration: The Collected Papers of Mary Parker Follett,* Harper & Brothers, New York, 1940, pp. 32ff.

A president, as a man of action, will patiently continue to talk and consult on major issues while consensus is building up. Skill in consultation stands on a par with mastery of the art of delegation in conserving a president's time and making his influence felt. A basic element of such skill, as in the whole decision-making process, is the capacity for eliminating minor and tangential variables, for holding one's own sights, and for tactfully keeping those of his conferees firmly fixed on the fundamentals.

The goals of the consultative process are a wiser decision than the president alone is equipped to make, a wider sense of ownership in the decision, and a more direct responsibility for carrying it out. To treat it as a manipulative tool for securing one's way is treason to the principle. It is also foolish, because the fraud is soon found out.

The consultative process must be open and free. The knowledgeable president will see that all views are fully explored, particularly those that run counter to his own. This he does, not only as a matter of intellectual integrity and to save time in reaching a decision, but for the vital reason that, as discussion proceeds, his own views may be altered. Our field studies showed that a faculty will forgive much in a president who keeps to this rule. The most pervasive praise we heard for the head of one institution we visited ran to his practice of developing the negative arguments of a proposal better than the opponents had done themselves. He was equally praised for knowing when to lower the boom on more talk. For once the president feels that all elements have been adequately explored, his duty is to decide and make his decision known. Faculty and administration will respect the one who decides in lucid terms and gives clear signals. One who postpones decisions hoping for unanimity may be considered a warm-hearted person, but his leadership will suffer from the resultant frustrations. In one university we visited the president seldom announced a conclusion until he had sampled with meticulous care a large number of opinions and cleared with those even tangentially involved. The standing quip of his administrative associates was, "Now let's check with Tony [the janitor] and then let it go!"

The president who practices consultation seriously will get into the discussion early, before rigid lines have been drawn or conclusions can be presented for his approval or disapproval. One president whom we interviewed makes it a rule, whenever a committee begins consideration of a major matter, to review with the members in a preliminary way the issues as he anticipates they will arise, so they will not be ignored, glossed over, or concealed in the final report. Of course, before a president begins "anticipating" issues, it is important that he know what they are.

DELEGATION

By common agreement among presidents, their most prevalent administrative weakness is inability to delegate work to others. In no area is faith in the principle of organization put to a more severe testing. As one observes, "Delegation is a prime quality under which a lot of other aspects of university administration can be classed as subordinate headings." Transferring authority to others runs counter to the conditioned reflexes of the scholar-president to do it himself. Yet he must learn delegation or be inundated in a tidal wave of trivialities. The effort may take some will power. As one admiring vice-president remarked of his chief, from the depth of experience with others, "Our president is an expert at delegation." And he added, "It's tough if you come from the academic world."

To make it even tougher, neither the academic world nor the president's various publics accept presidential delegation as readily in practice as they do in theory. Administrative officers and the faculty want the president to be available. But they also want prompt action on things in which they are interested. The combination is impossible if he does not delegate. In responding to the many pressures to be accessible and his native predisposition to be helpful, many a president finds himself attending to problems which could be as well or better treated by others.

As a president watches his institution grow from a relatively simple organization to a complex one, he may be surprised at how deeply habits of being easy to see, appropriate to the early days, have become essential to his happiness. He once carried the institution in his hip pocket. Now he misses the friendly associations with a larger number of colleagues. The lament by a president to a dean whom he met in the lunchroom suggests a sense of loneliness. "Why haven't you been in to see me and tell me what's going on in your college?" he asked. Nor was he much comforted by the reply: "But you told us that you had delegated wide powers to the vice-president and that hereafter we were to take up most things with him." Another president reports that people became accustomed to dealing with him rather than with subordinates when the institution was smaller. Now they resist using the new channels, which do not run so directly to him. He is aware that his office has become a bottleneck of procrastination and indecision.

We know a president who early in his career had a dream, in the form of a series of propositions on a printed page, which helped to change the course of his life: "There is a great deal to be done. If I could do it myself, it would, of course, be done better than by anyone else. But, since I can't do it all, for there are only twenty-four hours in a day, I must delegate. Even if the work is not done as well as I should do it, it will be done relatively well. In any event, it is more apt to be done than if I tried to do it." And then, as a footnote in fine print at the bottom of the page, this helpful admonition: "Probably it will be done better."

The operative words are in the footnote to the dream. As a matter of fact, he presides over a large number of people who are better fitted for their particular jobs than he is: "It is only a convenient fiction to speak of the president as a person who delegates authority because he cannot do the whole job by himself." [8] Thus a proper humility becomes a prime qualification.

[8] Edmund P. Learned, David N. Ulrich, and Donald R. Booz, *Executive Action*, Harvard University, Graduate School of Business Administration, Division of Research, Boston, 1951, p. 88.

HOW DOES ONE DELEGATE?

Perhaps the first principle to be remembered is to delegate authority as close as possible to the seat of the actual operation itself. The downward thrust will help to counteract the tendency present in all organizations for everything to rise to the top. There are cases of presidents surrounded by a whole corps of lieutenants who are supposed to take business off their shoulders but in fact make more work. This is in part because presidents have failed to make the dispersed decision-making authority stick and because the higher echelons have not delegated enough through the lieutenant level to the lower ones.[9]

The value of the downward thrust may, however, be destroyed by failure to establish sufficiently rigid cutoff points on appeals. We have observed that when a dean is always willing to hear an appeal by a student from a decision by an assistant dean, when the vice-president for business affairs cheerfully does the same in respect to actions by the superintendent of grounds, and the president reviews the steps taken by both (and any organization includes its share of people who will exhaust all avenues of appeal), everyone's work burden is increased. Of course, the right of appeal from a lower echelon to a higher must be preserved. In insisting that it not be employed frivolously, the president will undoubtedly be criticized for indifference toward unjust decisions of his own subordinates. He can be comforted by the fact that this policy, once accepted, will bring greater contentment to all in the end.

In his enthusiasm it is a temptation for an outgiving academic president to make curbstone decisions on things within the domain of a subordinate administrative officer without clearing the matter in advance. He may even forget to inform him afterward. Naturally this sort of thing makes for misunderstandings. And because

---

[9] This situation is not to be confused with the truth that able assistants make work for their chief because they generate ideas and press them upon him. One might almost say that the easiest way for a president to achieve a serene life is to surround himself with mediocre help.

it was based on incomplete data, the snap judgment is apt to be wrong.

Our field studies support the principle that in delegating, the president will guard against bypassing the administrative superiors of subordinates; he will drill himself to respect organizational channels, although if he is careful to keep the superiors informed, he need not be ironbound to them. Those who reported to us that their chief adhered to these elementary rules spoke with pardonable pride. Others, whose chief did not, revealed by their manner an unspoken irritation and frustration.

A president will have it understood that he holds himself free to talk to anyone as an aspect of communication, of getting away from his desk, and not because of distrust or disregard of anyone's superior. Normally, he will arrange that a major decision be communicated by the junior's superior, or at least as one in which the superior has shared. In any event, he will never, except in exigent situations, transmit to a subordinate a major decision which falls within the jurisdiction of his senior officer without clearing it first.

In delegating discretionary authority a president will realize that if he instructs the delegatee on every detail, he virtually dictates a conclusion. It is enough to outline alternatives and possibilities and so reinforce the self-respect and self-confidence of his agent. We recall one president who checked every reference to see that a subordinate's conclusion was letter-perfect. This habit was tolerated because of affection for a lovable personality, but his successor is warmly regarded by faculty and administration for following a different course. As a result the administrative staff work shorter hours but get more work done; they are able to take more Saturday afternoons and Sundays off, and everybody, including the president, is enjoying a richer home life.

This new incumbent is being praised for another reason: he allows a matter, once delegated, to stay delegated. When a president engages in hasty or haphazard retractions of assignments to others or intervenes at random in the use of another's proper discretion, he creates confusion. But, worse, he injures the subordinate's self-respect and renders him reluctant to accept responsibility. It requires more than the ordinary degree of Christian charity to continue loyal support of a superior who bounces in and out of delegated matters. The abler the subordinate, the less tolerance he may exhibit.

Delegation of discretion does not imply that the principal should cease to pay further attention to a matter of importance. " 'Hand out the jobs but don't forget about them' is a kind of adage with me," writes one eminent president-administrant. When he delegates a problem, he arranges a schedule of progress and sets a deadline for accomplishment. One result of "keeping in touch" is improved morale among the administration through the knowledge that the president not only holds them responsible but also has a continuing interest in their performance. The dean who told us that he would be happy if he could have just one hour every two months with his president had a legitimate grievance.

By keeping in touch with the juniors, the senior can make available his own reserve of experience and his familiarity with the broader aspects of the problem without encroaching upon their discretion. Furthermore, in this habitual "reciprocal relation" he discovers a useful means for evaluating the points of strength and weakness of the junior. Keeping in touch gives him a chance for a relaxed review of mistakes in the exercise of delegated discretion, for analyzing in what particular the judgment of the agent erred and how missteps can be avoided in the future. This is one aspect of in-service development of young administrators.

Moreover, keeping in touch increases the probability that a policy will be carried out as framed. Arriving at an agreed policy of major importance through the consultative process of colleges and universities is bound to be a slow business. The delays may measurably be reproduced at the executive stage. All heads of complex organizations are familiar with the possible resistance to the execution of a policy at the delegate level, owing perhaps to absence of enthusiasm for it, perhaps to sublimated opposition to it, or because of honest lack of a sufficient grasp of its implications.

Presidents of the United States and secretaries of the Department of Defense, for example, have been frank about the difficulty of getting a decision executed, however thorough the prior consultative process may have been or however complete the consensus may have seemed. While this circumstance is immeasurably more serious in the area of public administration, academic and business institutions are not immune from it. The mere allocation of responsibility for an action will not assure its execution.

OF COURSE DELEGATES WILL MAKE MISTAKES

From the president's point of view, delegation of discretion is a risk-taking process commensurate with the issue at stake, for he is still accountable for performance. Of course junior officers will make mistakes, but, as Harold W. Stoke shrewdly observes,[10] they will be fewer than those the president will make if he tries to do the work over again. He must reconcile himself to actions which he does not thoroughly approve.

Accordingly, an essential article of the president's creed will be to stand behind the actions of his agents. As our interviews repeatedly confirmed, no policy endears him more to his administrative colleagues. Whatever differences he may have with them he will express privately. If a mistake requires correction, he will seek to make it through the person of the agent; he will not reverse him publicly except under the most exigent circumstances. He will avoid as the plague browbeating subordinates in staff meetings, rebuking them for moving too fast without clearance or for failure to move fast enough. A wise chief will try to increase and not diminish the prestige of his associates; he will remember that to merit their loyalty he must be loyal. Unfortunately, some presidents ignore this sage counsel.

Probably the most difficult of all, the president will discipline

[10] *The American College President,* Harper & Brothers, New York, 1959, p. 40.

himself to seeing others receive the credit for policies which he originated. Not all are capable of such acts of self-denial. It may help to remember that credit for originating an idea that is carried out by another is one of the most evanescent rewards of the president's post.

THE ADMINISTRATIVE ORGANIZATION: STRUCTURE

As colleges and universities increase in size and diversity, the structure of their organization becomes of more critical import. Structure influences behavior for good or ill; therefore, attention to it will save both time and worry for the person at the head of it. Extrapolating our personal experience and our observations of others, the temptation is ever present to let organization lapse into obsolescence, to suffer the waste and annoyances of poor organization, to neglect the need for frequent review and possible modification in line with the personal capacities of individuals and their varying development.

A new president often finds it necessary to make sweeping changes in organization. Because of personal inclinations or other reasons his predecessor may have preferred not to undergo the strains in personal relations, the disruption to familiar routines involved in keeping the administrative structure abreast of the times. Wisdom, of course, suggests that a new incumbent suspend judgment as to both structure and personnel until he has come to know the strengths and weaknesses of each. Often enough he will discover that by reassigning duties he can maximize the strength of individuals whose services are worth retaining and minimize their weaknesses without the need to mount a radical overhaul.

The new head will have to feel his way with some care, since situations vary too drastically to admit of any ideal table of organization.[11] At best, the organization chart of any college or

[11] A short but comprehensive account of the evolution of separate positions in the past eighty-five years is provided by John Dale Russell in "Changing Patterns of Administrative Organization in Higher Education," *The Annals of the American Academy of Political and Social Science,* vol. 301, pp. 22–31,

university is a photograph representing but a static instant of time, rather than a living, changing panorama. So there is profit in periodic reexamination of the chart, for it may well turn out that either the chart or the assignment of functions to individuals appearing thereon, or both, require revision. A regular scheduling of such revisions provides occasions for revising assignments, for continuing those services in which an individual excels and transferring to others those for which he has proved unfit, or even for separation from his office with minimum danger to his self-respect.

A basic canon of organization is to keep the structure as simple as possible. An elaborate structure is no more a proof of a university's greatness than is a champion football team. What constitutes simplicity for one spells unwieldy complexity for the other. The organization recommended in the Willits study of the University of Pennsylvania, comprising seventeen deans, thirteen directors, seventy departments, an elaborate set of assistants to the provost and deans as well as to financial and business officers, plus numerous committees would be excessive in a smaller and more tightly knit institution. Yet for all, big or little, the utmost possible simplicity should be the goal. Dean Acheson writes, ". . . where people are organized for thought, the simpler arrangements are kept, the better." [12]

Nevertheless, certain familiar principles of structure are pertinent to all. Organizational units will be built around related functions; each will operate within a defined area of responsibility and authority under a specified chain of command, of which the administrative officers and faculty are fully informed. No subordinate will be accountable to more than one superior, although he may serve several agencies. Vagueness and overlapping in administrative relationships lead to power vacuums which invite

---

September, 1955. Russell points out that four major areas, each often under a vice-president, can be discerned in recent attempts to rearrange this structure toward greater efficiency, viz., academic program, student personnel services, business and financial management, and public relations.

[12] *The New York Times Magazine,* Oct. 11, 1959, p. 89.

—even demand—occupation by someone, with the consequence, for example, that the business-management side may gain ascendancy over the academic side to the detriment of orderly progress toward the institution's educational goals.

A sound, flexible structure according to functions is important, but it is only a beginning. The way in which it is employed and its pervading atmosphere are fundamental. Because, as we have noted, the spirit of consultation colors intra-administration relations as well as administration-faculty relations, many organizational decisions are best made under informal procedures, rather than by reliance on formal memoranda passed from one to another or down from above. An over-all atmosphere of mutual trust and respect makes for consensus, with paper work confined to the minimum necessary to preserve the essential data woven into decisions and to maintain appropriate records of them. Elaborate documentation may do nothing more than contribute a sense of security to an executive who distrusts his capacity for firm decision. Faculties and administrators rightly chafe when a procedurally oriented president demands a lot of "busy" paper work from them, details of documentation which may relate but remotely, if at all, to the bases of final decisions.

Though a backbone of formal patterns of communications is essential, a pervasive atmosphere of good will which moves administrative officers to keep in touch with one another generates communications of its own. One of the happiest groups of top-echelon officers we encountered humorously reported that the reason they kept their office doors open up and down the corridor was that each might hear what the others were saying to callers; in this way they diminished the need for formal media of communication between them. University administrations vary in respect to this happy circumstance; but our evidence supports the well-known fact that there is a positive correlation between good will among their members and the university's success. On the other hand, we observed instances of what happens when administrative officers distrust their colleagues or jealousy intrudes—the president, as well as the university, suffers debilitating and inhibiting strains.

It would be wrong to assume that the optimum state of harmony is one so complete, so pervasive that it eliminates the tensions that give life and energy, or that it can be attained only by submerging individuals in the depersonalizing requirements of team play. For one thing, the spirit of controversy and individualism endemic to academia will save it from enslavement to the "organization man." We have known men, newly come to academic administration from "outside," to be startled by the frankness, even the heat, with which opposing opinions were expressed in meetings of the president's administrative council, with nobody paying much attention to who was superior and who was inferior in rank, and then to see those same persons go out to a friendly lunch together afterward. This seems to us wholly desirable.

WHO REPORTS DIRECTLY TO THE PRESIDENT?

Since the time has passed when a university president can see all colleagues who have problems, in building his administrative structure he must necessarily distinguish between those officers who as a matter of course report to him directly and in turn transmit his instructions to their subordinates and those who habitually report to, or through, others. One president whom we interviewed had on his arrival at his new post counted at least forty people who considered him to be their immediate superior. His solution was to establish an inner cabinet composed of six men—two vice-presidents, two executive deans, and two directors—and to assign all other officers of administration to one of this half dozen.

The situation is not unique to the large universities. Two presidents of eminent liberal arts colleges confided to us that they were considering the establishment of a new top echelon of officers immediately under them to whom others would report. Each was contemplating the creation of three vice-presidents with quite similar job specifications in accordance with an increasingly common pattern. The new positions can be described as "academic policy and internal affairs," "fund raising," and "a general administrator for over-all policy."

There is no escape from a hierarchy of authority from a broad base at the bottom to a narrow top. The obvious danger in this pyramiding of authority is that the president will either consciously or unconsciously establish himself behind a wall of a small inner cabinet, believing himself to be saving time for educational policies when he is in fact diminishing his influence over them. When he does so, the faculty and deans and others who are not members of the charmed circle will be quick to note and resent it. This is especially true because the creation of new positions at the top of the administrative pyramid has been most conspicuous in recent years in the areas of business, finance, fund raising, and external relations and because the officers in these branches are apt to have easiest access to the president's ear.

At one university we found measurable faculty apprehension over the bare physical layout of offices in a new central administration building. Several officers designated to report directly to the president occupied the top floor with him, but only one, the academic vice-president, was an academic man. The inference drawn by members of the faculty was that the president would naturally be more subject to influence by his nonacademic aides. Deans were troubled by the new order, by which their ideas and requests reached the president through an intermediary and his decisions were filtered back to them through the same agent. In this instance time may prove their fears groundless, that their disquiet arose merely from growing pains, from the inescapable need to discard some of the informal methods of the past.

Unless the chief executive succeeds in maintaining contact below the high altitude of the inner circle, he will make others both less eager and less able to discharge the "representational" function he expects of them. He has a duty to get beyond the inner circle to others in the organization, to satisfy their sense of worth, to make sure he understands what is going on, that his policies are understood, and to increase the impact of his personality. More than one successful corporation chief executive makes it a practice to ask vice-presidents to bring subordinates with them to conferences in his office before anyone has committed himself to a decision, and to press them to join frankly in the discussion in the presence of their immediate superiors. The president, himself, will not be above changing his mind in the presence of new light that may be generated.[13]

The practice is worthy of emulation by academic heads. It can throw new light on a problem which might not appear in a recommendation of a vice-president alone or in an "agreed paper" without, at the same time, undercutting the superior.

STAFFING THE STRUCTURE

While the organizational chart is a useful guide, it is, of course, the quality of the individuals who staff it that really matters. Here the principle is clear; the difficulty is again one of execution.

Faculties complain, and rightly, when the personalities or practices of administrative officers do not reflect the goals or spirit of a president whom otherwise they respect. Accordingly, a president will choose strong administrative assistants with an appetite for responsibility. A president suffers when deans, for example, lack it. Removing a dean who is timid about making decisions may call for some courage. The incumbent may be popular on the campus, and in many colleges and universities his post has become an all-but-tenured position after the manner of a professorship. As with presidents who turn out to be unsatisfactory, "honorable exits" for deans are not always easy to arrange. But until the president makes a change he will continue to be held captive to ancillary tasks.

---

[13] The theory that the head of a business increases his efficiency by limiting his span of control to contacts with a few top officers may be seriously questioned. Professor Merry reminds us that an alert corporation president keeps in touch with more than the "inner circle" who report directly to him. As he follows through on various activities in process, he maintains contact with many of those of lower management level who are doing the spadework on particular problems.

Vice-presidents and deans must be hatchet men on occasion. They should be able to explain their no's in a persuasive manner and say "yes" with warmth. Otherwise they will obstruct the progress of a president known to be striving for the greatest possible release of faculty potential. A grudging "yes" can be a stronger morale depressive than an explanatory, sympathetic "no." Although a president needs others to help say "no," he cannot delegate all the no's to others and reserve for himself the "yes" decisions and the popularity that goes with them.

Moreover, as a president needs officers who can say "no" to others, so he needs men who can say "no" to *him*. An administrative staff of yes-men can only propel a president into ill-advised decisions, whereas a staff encouraged to challenge him when issues are under consideration are his best protection. As Logan Wilson puts it, they must be free "to talk you down." When the board of a college or university, or a business corporation, finds that only the most lionhearted have the courage to tell their chief executive that he is making a mistake, they may well begin to prepare for trouble ahead.

On the other hand, a president can reasonably insist that when opposing points of view have been freely and vigorously presented and he has made his decision, his administrative group unite to carry it out. The president discourages anything that smacks of sycophancy, but he has every right to expect this sort of loyalty.

Some university heads are temperamentally unqualified to work with strong colleagues, are overly fearful of potential empire builders. Such disrupting figures do exist, of course, and on occasion possess a profound capacity for troublemaking. But the president who sees in every strong personality a potential threat to his leadership will enfeeble his administration throughout.[14]

[14] Germane here is a story about Casey Stengel, for many years the picturesque manager of the New York Yankees. As recorded by James Reston, when asked if he would play Mickey Mantle in a certain all-star game between the American and National Leagues, Stengel replied, "I always figure that with Mantle in center field I'm a better manager."

THE ADMINISTRATIVE COUNCIL

Virtually all presidents have something which they call an administrative council, composed of both academic and non-academic officers. Usually it meets regularly, perhaps once a week, sometimes on call of the president, in which case its meetings are apt to be sporadic. The use made of administrative councils differs widely. We have been present at staff meetings which were consumed in protracted debate over questions that could have been disposed of by a simple decision of an administrative officer. When this sort of thing occurs, the psychological benefits of consultation are undone by irritation over time wasted.

We have attended other meetings that were exclusively occupied by significant questions and that materially helped to supply not only a solution but a coherent sense of unity in policy and its execution. One method of assuring this happy result is to circulate agenda in advance, which of itself tends to exclude trivia and gossip. Although consensus is one of the goals, rarely are questions decided by formal vote; usually the president follows Abraham Lincoln's policy that only his vote counts.

It is incumbent upon him to see that an informal atmosphere dominates but that business gets done. The colleagues of one recently inaugurated president were enthusiastic about his conduct of cabinet sessions as well as of other meetings. He has substantially reduced the number of meetings he attends, but he packs so much into those that there has been a great gain in new work accomplished. A notable feature is his technique of summarizing discussions, ticking off the major points of agreement and disagreement, and then driving toward a conclusion; he makes sure that a question does not drag on needlessly from one meeting to another with the participants not sure whether it has been settled or postponed. When he announces a decision, he makes clear who is to execute it. A reminder-memo of this decision is sent to the individual the next day. To many in academia this brisk procedure will seem too militaristic for their palates, but those who were a part of it approved.[15]

Another president keeps the eyes of his cabinet focused on education by circulating materials concerning developments in academic theory and administration and asking for comments thereon. One unique device he employs to alert his colleagues to issues being raised outside their own institution is to pass around a list of the topics coming up at the next meeting of a foundation of which he is a trustee. A by-product of the ensuing discussion is an addition to the stock of ideas which he brings to his fellow trustees.

Others stimulate thinking by sending around clipsheets made up of excerpts from important speeches, abstracts of pertinent research findings, and various items that otherwise the cabinet members might miss. Then they set aside time to discuss the more significant ones. Another device, common in business, that is being increasingly employed by colleges and universities is the "staff retreat," by which the president and his chief subordinates get away for a weekend or longer to probe together the bigger issues with more sustained attention than is possible amid the interruptions on the campus. This consultation-in-depth establishes a background for the actions to be taken in the months or even years to follow. Sometimes members of the faculty are added to the group; occasionally some trustees attend. More rarely the retreat becomes essentially a joint meeting of trustees, administration, and representatives of the faculty. Stevens Institute's Atlantic City Seminar, Chicago's Lakeside Conference, and Pittsburgh's Planning Session held at a resort in western Penn-

[15] Candor compels me to admit that many of the weekly cabinet meetings over which I presided were occupied with relative trivia. Subject to the demands of important questions on the agenda, each member was encouraged to raise anything on his mind. Undoubtedly the understanding of each other's operation was improved. This was my original purpose, for my predecessor had assembled his administrative colleagues but once in twenty years and communications had suffered accordingly. But the practice would not have been tolerable in a larger and more complex university. As I look back, I am convinced that our meetings would have been more meaningful had they been based on more formal agenda. H. W. D.

sylvania are random samples of institutions that have found retreats profitable.

PERSONAL ASSISTANCE FOR THE PRESIDENT

However successfully a president delegates to administrative subordinates, many matters will continue to rise to the top, and by no means are all that settle in the president's office trivia. They include questions which, because of their delicate nature or because of the importance of the people who raise them, must be treated at the top. Issues of policy arise that are not covered by existing rules or practice under which subordinates normally exercise discretion. Others involve the coordinating of activities and policies of high-level subordinates, and no president can divest himself of this ultimate, synthesizing responsibility. If he does not do it, it will not be done.

To reduce the turmoil in his life to a point at which he can concentrate on significant problems, he requires adequate *personal* assistance. We know from both experience and observation that presidents shrink from building a purely personal staff, because it would seem to be spending money on themselves. This is an honorable self-denying attitude, but it does nobody any good. As a group presidents suffer from grave deficiencies in assistance personal to them.

An indispensable assistant is a fully competent private secretary. Business has discovered that these rare people merit a salary quite above the going scale throughout the organization. A university president is well advised to imitate business practice. The way many presidents permit themselves to be bowed down under a heavy correspondence is almost an occupational disease. A private secretary who comes to learn the president's mind, who knows what he will say before he says it, who can refer letters to the appropriate offices for attention can lighten his burden of correspondence more effectively than a dictating machine, which, after all, only enables him to work more after hours. If she does not develop a power complex or an autocratic manner, she can also save him time on the telephone. If she meets people easily and graciously, she will shunt to other offices many callers who originally thought they must see the president himself. She should be a discreet person, for she will be a focal point for many questions, pressures, and pleas for help as well as information. Hers is not a quiet, closeted life.

Another indispensable post is that designated as "assistant to the president." Many presidents make use of this officer in a multitude of ways involving various levels of responsibility. Occasionally the assistant to the president performs virtually the function of a vice-president without portfolio. Generally, however, his duties are of a lower order of magnitude and are determined more by the personal traits of the president than by systematized duty assignments. He, too, can protect his superior from becoming snarled in relatively minor details which are, at the same time, not unimportant. He also handles a great deal of the president's mail, either over his own signature or by drafting letters for presidential signature. He does trouble shooting for his chief whenever feasible.

The assistant to the president receives callers on behalf of his chief, entertains visitors, and arranges interviews with faculty and administrators for those who merit or demand attention by the head office. He is the president's liaison man in respect to many details with administrative officers and faculty. He may represent the president at occasions which the latter cannot attend; he may make speeches to alumni and civic groups. He must exercise great tact in dealing with sensitive people and in diverting self-important bores. Besides ability to sustain an intimate personal relationship with his chief, he needs the capacity for hard work without regard to office hours.

A NEW TYPE OF PERSONAL ASSISTANT IS INDICATED

Nevertheless, however efficient may be the "assistant to the president," on his level, the academic president is still confronted with "too much to do" and "too little time to do it." We therefore propose that the president of the larger college or university especially give thought to the possibility of a different sort of personal staff officer, one who is fitted by temperament and experience to share his thinking at the highest levels at which he operates, one who will serve him by extending his range of knowledge in the whole broad area of his overseeing and coordinating functions. The role of such an aide will not be to make decisions on behalf of the president but to serve as his counselor and friend in the region of his top responsibilities.

Traces of such an officer are to be found in varying degrees in a number of universities, although rarely clearly identified as such. Line officers naturally give service similar to that which the personal staff officer we propose would perform; they are, as a part of their normal operating functions, already helping the president to know what is going on and to maintain an institutional overview. We do not suggest any change here. We do argue the advantage of designating, full time, to the role of high-level personal aide, one person who will not be troubled, dominated, or compromised by operating responsibilities.[16]

He must resist the temptation to substitute for his chief. In no case should he come between the president and the line officers or infringe on the authority or blur the responsibility of those to whom discretionary authority has been delegated. If he comes between the president and the line officers to whom the head must continue to look for advice and to learn how matters look from their sight lines, he will defeat his purpose. A personal assistant is not a deputy in respect to executive power; he is not an administrative coordinator of other men's activities.

In proposing that a president frankly and publicly add a new high-level man to the organization to be his personal assistant, we walk on delicate ground. The concept of the corporation presi-

---

[16] In smaller institutions the function of the personal assistance officer we advocate will probably be naturally combined with that of the "assistant to the president." However, even in such combined form it constitutes really a new and higher office demanding qualifications exceeding those of the usual "assistant."

dent's personal staff has not proved simple in business practice, and much argument has developed over it. We propose no organizational blueprint, nor even a title for the office. For want of a better title we call him the president's personal assistant to suggest the personal nature of the post and to avoid the ambiguities in the term "staff." Presidents introducing the idea must do it experimentally and adapt it gently to their particular institutional circumstances.

In the first place, the sort of help we have in mind is one which line officers cannot, by the nature of their duties, give adequately. They have their assigned responsibilities for decisions and the consequences thereof, as well as for informing and advising the president. They come to him with their problems and their recommendations. The competent ones are, of course, able pleaders for their areas and their own points of view. Their vision of the over-all institutional picture tends to be obscured by the immediacy of their own particular functions. Although there are some who, in Stoke's phrase, are masters of the art of "incomplete disclosure," it is only natural that, in all honesty, line officers will subconsciously stress the aspects favorable to the action they want the president to take. Loyalty to colleagues may also lead them to withhold significant factors regarding others. In short, the "feedback" that the president receives from his operating administrative subordinates cannot be expected to tell him all he needs to know.

By common confession, presidents know too little about what is going on. Conventional bureaus of institutional research cannot alone fill the gaps in the normal flow of information to them. Neither is formal statistical and financial reporting the complete answer by any means. Needful as such are—the more complex the institution, the more needful—much of the knowledge from which wisdom is distilled for the most critical and difficult decisions lies in the realm of imponderables. Much of what a president should know can be gained only from persons.

As one respected by the faculty a personal assistant can convey faculty views, useful criticisms, and suggestions which might otherwise escape his chief, since they often do not appear in formal conferences or formal reports and recommendations. He may discover trouble brewing of which the president otherwise might not be aware until it explodes. He can render an invaluable service by telling the president when he is wrong.

As the personal assistant supplements the president by countering and diverting the pressures of minor matters, he can serve as a watchdog to see that his chief is not neglecting major matters because of other pressures. He will subtly hold the president's feet to the fire on matters which he may prefer to ignore. He will see that an important presidential decision, once made, is correctly reported to the proper quarters. There is ample evidence that a president's neglect to acknowledge a memorandum which he has requested of, say, the department of economics or delay in communicating with a committee which has requested advice as to next steps is demoralizing to the faculty. A personal staff assistant will help him to follow through.

Another not inconsequential service is to see that his principal is adequately briefed in advance on matters that are about to require his attention. Too often, for example, presidents preside over meetings in ignorance as to the questions coming up. It is not inspiring when they have to fish around to learn what it is all about.

A president cannot possibly read all the mass of publications, reports, and surveys that come to his desk. If he is to keep abreast of what is going on in the field of higher education, he needs help of one who is competent to screen material and bring significant items to his attention.

Finally, a president needs someone with whom he can speculate out loud on any and all subjects and about all sorts of people without embarrassment or fear that his confidence will be violated, one who will bear with him patiently when he blows off steam.

As we have sketched the service that such a personal assistant can render, it is clear that the post calls for an exceptional individual with a gift of thinking objectively. He must certainly be acceptable to the faculty and worthy of their respect, or he will be considered just a secret service agent from the president's office.[17] He will recognize that he will fail in his duty to inform the president on "how things are going" unless he respects the professional dignity and discretion of the faculty. Accordingly, some academic background is advantageous.

The personal assistant is not an inspector general who investigates, approves, and condemns. On the contrary, he should be the sort whom the faculty will seek out because they derive help from talking with him. In President Franklin D. Roosevelt's phrase, he should have "a passion for anonymity" and be able to find satisfaction in highly significant work devoid of the glamor of authority to pronounce decisions. He and the president must be able to convince others that he is not a crown prince waiting beside the throne.

We are fully aware that we have portrayed an extraordinarily difficult position, one in large measure outside the customary line and staff organization. If the job specifications seem to describe an improbable collection of self-denying virtues, we rejoin that persons possessing them can be found. The magnitude and urgency of the president's need for such a roving assistant justify a fair trial.

We suggest that the post be combined with that of the secretary of the board of trustees, with staff assistance appropriate to expanded duties.[18] The two can be formed into a natural unit.

[17] We are aware that the chief obstacle to the implementation of our concept of this new office is the real danger that he will be received as nothing more than the president's spy in the camp of the faculty. Obviously he must be one who, by virtue of the respect in which he is held and his qualities of mind and personality, is able to cleanse himself of this taint. We believe, however, that the concept can be made to succeed. The magnitude and urgency of the president's need for this sort of roving assistance justifies its trial.

[18] Institutions which have not already done so will profit by abandoning the tradition that the secretary of the board should be a trustee, acting on a voluntary, part-time basis, and by recognizing that a more professional type can facilitate the work of both presidents and trustees. This topic is treated further in Chap. VIII.

Moreover, the secretaryship of the board is a familiar office. By joining the two, the introduction of the new role of personal aide will therefore be more in conformity to normal practice and less alarming to administrative and faculty colleagues than might otherwise be the case. As secretary of the board he can work himself into his broader responsibilities from the base of the already customary and accepted.

CHAPTER IV

THE PRESIDENT
AND THE REALM OF
THE FACULTY

The president's relations with the faculty are discussed repeatedly throughout this book, for all aspects of his work touch them to some degree. No president is so foolish as to follow a studied policy of neglect or even of planned isolation from members of the faculty. A president's respect for their place in the governance of the institution is a measure of his trust in them. And if he does not trust them, how can he expect them to trust him?

HOW FACULTY PARTICIPATION
IN COLLEGE AND UNIVERSITY GOVERNMENT HELPS

It is unnecessary to expatiate on the desirability of wide faculty participation. Since faculty see themselves as self-employed professionals rather than as employees, enthusiasm in a common enterprise is proportionate to the sense of ownership they have in it by virtue of sharing in the decisions that govern its course. Quite rightly they believe that broad faculty autonomy is necessary to preserve freedom in teaching and scholarship, both directly and as setting the collateral conditions which enable them to exert their full professional potential.

Individual faculty members of the same college or university will express quite contradictory opinions as to the amount of self-government they enjoy. Some will insist it exceeds that in all other places where they have been; others, that it is no more than a skillful device by which the administration secures backing for what it wants to do.[1] At the same time all agree that the institution with a tradition of good administration-faculty relations is most able to attract good men. Faculty participation at levels of high policy makes the members more willing to entrust administrative matters to the administration—where they belong. If excluded from this level, they will concentrate attention on minor things as the only way to preserve their self-esteem. But the fundamental argument why presidents should respect faculty discretion is the cardinal truth that if an institution is to prosper, it must utilize the intellectual application and imaginative thinking of more than the president, vice-presidents, and deans.

IS FACULTY CONTROL IRRESPONSIBLE?

Nevertheless, there are two considerations regarding the exercise of faculty discretion with which presidents are familiar and which faculties should bear in mind. One is that the latter do not share a collective responsibility for the income side of the budget commensurate with their part in deciding how the money shall be spent, although some are active as individuals in raising money for their programs or may on occasion aid the president in bringing the university's needs to the attention of the legislature. True, faculties do not adopt budgets, but their voiced ambitions

[1] For example, at one institution we visited in which the president's method of operation was to press for prompt decisions with a minimum of "buck passing," we were told by one person that faculty participation had become mere window dressing, while another expressed satisfaction that discussions were less protracted and that decisions were made more promptly and were generally sound.

and demands are a major force in deciding how funds shall be allocated and the purposes for which new funds are to be sought. Nevertheless, faculty government is an exception to a basic principle of popular government that those who hold the power of the purse must likewise be responsible for providing the funds.

The other consideration peculiar to faculty government, in degree if not in kind, is the absence of an individual, personal accountability for one's actions such as pertains to other professions, with only remote collective accountability for the decisions taken. Professors are not as personally responsible to the laymen they serve as are lawyers, doctors, and clergymen, nor do they suffer directly in standing and pocketbook if they fail to satisfy clients, patients, or parishioners. True, in publicly sustained institutions, both the collective and individual actions of the faculty may be examined by the regents or the legislature, and in private institutions by the trustees or influential elements of the public. When this occurs, an individual can rely on the organized defense of his colleagues. It is the president who meets the brunt of the attack; in line of duty he must repeatedly defend actions by the faculty in areas over which he has little or no control. For this he deserves more credit than the faculty are often willing to pay. As the harassed president of a state university, in which faculty participation had recently been expanded, wrote us:

> The faculty committees desire a great amount of autonomy and power but are not fully cognizant of the repercussions which their actions may bring about. . . . Critics of the University do not come to the committees to vent their displeasure at some of these actions, but rather to the president. As a result, I found myself cast more and more in the role of an arbiter between the faculty committees and the students, parents, and the general public.

Yet we should not have it otherwise as to either responsibility for budget balancing or personal accountability to the public. A change would impair beyond recognition the function which colleges and universities exist to perform. But the foregoing considerations attest the duty of a relatively sheltered profession to maintain within itself high standards of sensitivity to social needs and professional honor and responsibility.

ARE FACULTIES GOVERNING THEMSELVES WELL?

Nevertheless, the serious question has been put by some thoughtful trustees and by occasional faculty members themselves: Are faculties exercising their governing powers as well as they should? We discovered little evidence that they are giving any systematic thought to a general theory of the optimum scope and nature of their part in government and what in their own interest can better be left to the administration in this day of growth in size and diversity. The truth is that they have paid more attention to their rights than to their own internal problems of government. Faculties find the same difficulty in drawing the line between policy framing and administrative execution that trustees do. Too many individuals nourish the erroneous idea that the only way to keep control is to have a finger in every issue, to control the details and perhaps administer them as well.

A self-examining faculty starting out to appraise the soundness of its ideas about self-government and the adequacy of its machinery for the purpose encounters problems not dissimilar to those of other complex organizations with a controlling desire to govern themselves democratically. Love of direct democracy, town-meeting style, still haunts the campus despite enormous college and university expansion. Faculties have been slow to accept the principles of representative government and to abide by them. They complain about the administration without due consideration of the countless details it takes off their hands, thereby freeing them to concentrate attention on their professional function, scholarship and teaching. Instead of greater faculty participation in fringe matters, the need today is for a more reasoned attitude toward delegation to administration. Given proper controls, delegation will not reduce but will enhance the power of the faculty. Where, for example, would popular control of our civil government be today had not the scope of the administration's discretion been broadened? As with our legislatures, committees and individual members must be free to express criticism of any aspect of the institution's activities, and consultative machinery must be routinely available to challenge administrative actions as well as decisions by their own faculty agencies.

If faculties have stressed a pattern of democracy more suitable to a Greek city-state or an early New England town than to a modern American university, if the machinery of faculty participation has rusted, if the effort to modernize structure and procedures seems more burdensome than to endure the wasted effort of the familiar, if proposals for new arrangements have been thwarted by a few with vested interests in the old, the president must accept a fair share of the blame. He is not only the presiding officer of the faculty but also its chief executive. Accordingly, the faculty naturally looks to the administration to initiate modifications; making faculty government work is part of its job.

THE GENERAL FACULTY MEETING

Something of the altered nature of academic government is reflected in the common fate of the old-time faculty meeting. In many universities the traditional monthly sessions of the whole faculty have been replaced by one or two a year, at which the chief business is a talk by the president on the present state of the university and the outlook for the coming year. What he communicates makes a difference; but what he can say to make such meetings stimulating is a problem. If he seizes the opportunity to discuss finances, assuming this to be a topic of general concern, he will be criticized for not discussing education; if he discusses education, few beyond those immediately involved in the aspects he talks about will be interested. He cannot possibly produce a new pension system or a liberalized plan for leaves of absence or a new building program on each occasion. He might want to raise some controversial educational issues to challenge faculty attention and stimulate thought, but if he should, he might generate hostility toward policies he hopes to work out through a period of more relaxed discussion.

Although in the larger institutions where the traditional monthly all-faculty meeting has been preserved, only a few attend unless a controversial proposal has stirred interest in a wider group and has brought out those who come only to vote against it; yet these meetings are worth preserving until the university has become too big and complex and faculty interests too diverse to make them meaningful beyond recovery. They can be used to foster an atmosphere of institutional unity and as a forum for a wider consideration of actions and recommendations of faculty agencies than a senate affords; they can be an instrumentality by which the faculty holds its agents to account. Only an inadequate president will denigrate faculty meetings as merely occasions for blowing off steam and expressing grievances; if they are nothing else, it is his fault.[2]

[2] Unlike others of its size, the University of Wisconsin has declined to give up monthly meetings of the whole faculty and special meetings on call, in part because of a feeling that the professional schools should not become too autonomous. At these meetings broad educational policies are considered as well as other phases which concern the whole body. A proposal to change degree requirements, for example, requires approval by the general faculty. Other subjects of general interest are illustrated by a proposal to put the ROTC on a voluntary instead of a compulsory basis and representations to the regents reminding them that the location of new buildings was an educational matter and insistence that every effort should be made to preserve the native beauty of the campus against proposed encroachments. Discussion at many meetings is described as "something less than lively, but there is always the possibility that a tussle will develop." Attendance is usually small, ranging from 150, in an eligible faculty of more than 1,200, to 400 if a subject of wide concern is to come up. The general faculty meeting is prized as an opportunity for anyone to hear its legislative deliberations and engage in them if he will. A documented agenda is circulated in advance. The meetings frequently go into a Committee of the Whole for the consideration of matters in process preparatory to formal action at a subsequent meeting.

INFORMAL POWER CENTERS

The loci of faculty power are not visible to the naked eye. One must look to the constituent schools and departments, to a small number of important committees, and perhaps to the senate. Nor can one overlook the informal, extralegal centers of power which are not revealed in the membership of senates and committees empowered under the bylaws to act for the faculty. Of course, influential individuals are inclined to gravitate toward each other and to exercise a strong collective influence, and a knowledgeable president will know who they are. There have been times and places in which a professorial oligarchy, perhaps a gerontocracy, exercised more power than formal faculty agencies, able to obstruct the fondest aims of the president, or even a majority of the less active and aggressive faculty members. They may stay in the background while carefully plotting their moves, or they may be a prominently articulate group. At one place we were told of the existence of a parallel decision-making group, composed of older professors with some infusion of young men, which met more or less regularly to consider courses of action which the university should take. When the president learned of the meetings, he asked to be invited; but rarely are such power centers so organized and so easily identifiable. An evil form of an extralegal power center exists when a few faculty members, with plenty of time to sit around the club, arrange collective action to block changes desired by their more hard-working colleagues.[3]

[3] The testimony we received from one professor will be concurred in by others. "We have powerful people who hold no official position but exert a kind of veto power nevertheless. Here," he said, "they are the people who attract research grants which give them three or four staff associates and a dozen graduate students. It's good publicity, so they have power."

INFLUENCES WEAKENING
UNIVERSITY-WIDE PARTICIPATION

All universities are big in comparison with those of the earlier days from which many traditions of faculty government derive— and the big multiservice university is rather a congeries of disparate schools and institutes than a university in the original sense. There is a bit of fiction abroad today in the concept of academia as a society of scholars. Academia has undergone a considerable fragmentation corresponding to the fragmentation of knowledge. A common interest in teaching that used to bind this society together has been diluted by emphasis on research—a more specialized, individual activity.

Presidents report repeatedly that faculties accept little responsibility for thinking of education as a whole; they pass on specific educational matters without taking the trouble to inform themselves about education in the large, or they refrain. As in business, the effect of specialism has been "to direct a man's vision away from the goals of the organization." For the specialist, his "functional work becomes an end in itself." One need not endorse Ruml's proposals for more effective use of faculty time to be shaken by his indictment of the incompetency of a liberal arts faculty to fashion a curriculum. It should be taken more seriously in academic quarters than it has been.

In many places in the last two decades or so, willingness and thoughtful preparation for participation in faculty government have had increasingly to compete with the diversionary pull of the "second job." This pull can become so strong as to turn a university connection into little more than an accommodation address for receiving and answering mail. Consultantships and research grants by foundations, business, and government may enhance one's concern for productive scholarship but may easily drift into a responsibility to external agencies, particularly so for one who has achieved tenure, to the neglect of one's responsibility to his own institution. "Where your treasure lies there will your heart be also."

Within reason, consultantships to government and business, as well as generous grants for project research, render individuals more proficient as scholars and teachers and broaden their equipment for a part in faculty government. Moreover, an energetic man who is the busiest outside may be most effective inside. The rule of reason should control one's outside activities, but it is hard to define and even harder to apply to individuals except by bureaucratic rules resented by all academic people. The difficulties are insoluble outside the faculties themselves.

A president may counter the glamor of outside temptations by providing interesting work inside, but his opportunities here are limited. The caustic observations on faculty government of a president who could not arrange a committee meeting because one member would be in Washington all week, another would be away consulting with an industrial firm, and a third was scheduled for a quick trip abroad are not without significance. One may also question whether a professor who telephoned a colleague that he could not meet him this week in New York but would see him next week in Buenos Aires was habitually giving much thoughtful attention to his role in faculty government.

PRESTIGE OF PARTICIPATION

But perhaps the most serious handicap under which faculty self-government labors is the questionable standing attached to participation in the organizational process. Our interviews returned mixed testimony, as between institutions and individuals in the same institution, regarding the prestige, or lack of it, of service on faculty senates and committees. That institution is fortunate which has a substantial number of distinguished teachers and scholars who regard participation in the general affairs of the university as an obligation and are willing to devote time to it. But often they have to be sought out; they are not apt to be looking for the job; nor, unfortunately, are they always those best fitted for it.[4]

We heard opinions from presidents and faculty alike that faculty government is not representative; it is in the hands of politicians, sometimes described as oligarchs or bureaucrats, who are looking for an escape from the frustration of teaching and scholarship. Young men are advised to "keep off committees" if they wish to get ahead. "Our best men shun committee work but we could not get along without those who do not." We were told more than once that no man who views committee work as an important duty can be a true scholar. "The ideal faculty man . . . ought properly to find administration (including service on committees) distasteful, and will resist being drawn into it." By another: "Professor Blank is probably the most powerful man in the faculty organization, but he hasn't published a thing since he was given tenure."[5]

Surely it is illogical to call for a wide play of faculty discretion but fail to honor those who carry it on. The truth is that all organizations depend for the conduct of their organizational operations upon a relatively small group of activists who shape opinion, man the important assignments, and carry the bulk of the load. They come to know the problems, they accumulate experience in how to get things done, and they are willing to work. Although campus mores may compel them to deny it, they even enjoy the work.

Without diminishing the duty of the administration to involve the best of the faculty in the governmental process and to infuse

[4] In holding that the analogy of faculty government at Oxford and in German universities is faulty for America, Abraham Flexner gave it as his opinion that were we to follow their example, ". . . the best minds would stick to the laboratory or the study; inferior persons, executively minded, would probably get control." *Universities: American, English, German,* Oxford University Press, New York, 1930, p. 184.

[5] Whatever may be Professor Blank's proficiency as a scholar, on the testimony of others and on the basis of a long interview, he seemed to us to be extremely gifted in interpreting and promoting faculty views.

new blood in the persons of younger men, we question whether the attack on the "old pros" is just. The charge that faculty control is in the hands of the mediocre may indicate only that the concept of excellence needs to be more broadly defined. In any case, a majority of the faculty can turn the "mediocrities" out if they want to, if they are willing to do the work themselves. Until then why abuse those who are willing?

SENATES

Many large institutions have taken recourse to faculty senates, sometimes called "councils." They are usually elected in a manner to assure representation of the component schools and are charged with speaking for the faculty as a whole. Frequently they include certain ex officio officers of administration. Occasionally, however, they are large bodies composed of all the faculty of a certain rank, in which case an executive committee and their subcommittees do the work.

The legal powers of the senate differ from institution to institution. In a small university the senate's essential function may be to investigate and prepare recommendations for action by the general faculty. In others its power of decision may be almost as broad as the faculty's, subject to prescribed reports to the faculty and perhaps approval by it. Approval is granted more or less *pro forma* unless the issue is contentious. The most important faculty committees may be committees of the senate, to which outsiders are sometimes coöpted. A senate or its committee on educational policy may be an effective agency for passing on proposals emanating from the various schools and for raising standards where they are low. The president may or may not meet with the senate, but a subcommittee on conference with him is bound to have prestige.

A faculty's esteem for its senate may be lowered by a proclivity for busywork. It may circulate its minutes, but they are too detailed for anyone to read. Accordingly at some places after a good start senates have declined in prestige. Yet even if early expectations have not been realized, the senate is valued as an agency always in being to support faculty interests before administration and trustees when the occasion arises.

If the senate is inert or bogged down in busywork, the president must share the blame. To make it meaningful, he will recognize that it exists outside the framework of departments and schools and that, while not intruding on their domain, the senate can help to combat excessive autonomy in the component schools. He will see that important issues of university-wide scope are presented to it. Senates are least useful when headed by a president who controls their agenda and clogs them with inconsequential presentations and insignificant topics. Under such circumstances, the faculty may justifiably regard the senate as having been reduced to the status of a "company union."

COMMITTEES

Now that direct democracy no longer suffices, the efficiency of faculty self-government is closely related to its committee system. If faculty government should indeed be in the hands of the mediocre, its faults will appear most glaringly in the make-up and functioning of committees; perhaps the system is obsolete, or its component units are preoccupied with trivia. Taken seriously, committee work is more demanding upon the president (who, although he cannot begin to attend all their meetings, may be an ex officio member of all committees) than on faculty members. As one wrote us, no president can well maintain that ". . . contrapuntal harmony among the various groups that go into the intricate structure of an institution" unless he gives attention to the form, membership, and functioning of the committee system.

However members are chosen (by election of the faculty, by selection of the senate, by presidential appointment, or by a mixture of all three methods), the president who seeks to maintain quality must pay attention to the personnel of the committees. He will work to maintain their representative character by tapping the reservoir of quiet, thoughtful people who are apt to be overlooked. He will use his influence or appointing power to introduce young men into the process, but he will want important committees to include their quota of experienced people who already know how to get things done.

At the same time he can work to prevent capable faculty committeemen from being caught up in too many assignments by seeing that they are well distributed. One institution limits each of its faculty to one committee membership, which may be overly restrictive. Others curb excessive committee activity by declining to reduce the teaching load of committee members, on the ground that every institution has the right to expect some "citizen service" from each faculty member. At one university we were told that if a man complains about his load, the administration first looks at his committee assignments. Nevertheless, the administration will recognize that high quality of service on vital committees takes time; it will not drive the "citizen service" obligation too far.

A president will be at pains to maintain good liaison between the faculty committees and the officers of administration, academic and nonacademic; he will see that the natural urgency of the administration men to accomplish results does not truncate their cooperation. He must deal honestly with all committees and be prepared to see them disagree with him. In short, he must respect their findings.

It has been charged that presidents tolerate committees chiefly because they can be manipulated to support what the administration wants to do anyway. This is unfair. Despite their well-known proneness to discursiveness, compromise, and delay,[6] committees serve the administrator by bringing faculty ideas and points of view to bear. He knows that committee members who have studied a problem can give him wise counsel and informed support for the actions he takes. This is not exploitation but cooperation.

---

[6] A friend has coined a law for committees as a supplement to "Parkinson's Law" for administrators: "If one consults a sufficiently large number of people for a long enough time, one can develop insurmountable opposition to the most innocuous idea."

Where faculty government is extensive, a proliferation of committees—some active, some dormant, and some which were never of any consequence—is common. The total number of hours spent by members of the faculty in all-university, school, and departmental committee work may be little short of appalling. It is easier to create a new committee than to bury a dead one. A president should resist the temptation to appoint a committee as a way of resolving each controversy or for evading an administrative decision he should make himself.

THE COMMITTEE SYSTEM MAY NEED RATIONALIZATION

No rationalization of an obsolete committee system is possible without a thorough study leading to a sophisticated philosophy regarding the optimum relationship between the framing of faculty policy and administrative execution. The second step toward reforming an obsolete committee system is to analyze its weaknesses. A complex committee system creates a confusing power structure in which decision making is so dispersed and so fuzzy that it can be mastered only by a faculty bureaucrat who knows the ropes. "You need to know the appropriate committees to clear through; then you find that the system doesn't work in the same way for the next case which may look similar." Even the president may be at a loss as to which committee to consult, although he will be criticized if he consults the wrong one. Such a system abounds in embarrassments, which would chafe faculty members more than they do if it were not for their abiding faith in committees as defenders of their freedoms.[7]

The prestige of committee service naturally runs with the importance of the particular committee in the scheme of government. It is a safe generalization applying to many colleges and universities that if all existing faculty committees were abolished and replaced only by a few exercising truly consequential func-

[7] I used sometimes to counter complaints of too much time consumed in committee meetings by offering to have the administration take over the work. I can recall no case in which my offer was accepted. H. W. D.

tions, eminent faculty members would be less reluctant to serve. Faculty controls are not jeopardized if the right to raise questions is clear and grievance procedures are kept open.[8] Standing committees naturally deal with particular segments of institutional operations. Accordingly when a subject arises of general importance transcending normal operations or calling for intensive study and investigation, the common practice is to organize an *ad hoc* committee. This device gives a chance to coöpt faculty leaders who may evade routine committee duty and to choose those with special contributions to make to the subject at hand.

Those who fear that faculty power is declining, owing to the "intrusion" of the administration in day-by-day operations, might consider the growing participation of faculty committees in areas of policy administration which traditionally were not included in the faculty domain. The expanding practice of faculty committees to consult with the trustees on the choice of a new president is discussed at some length in Chapter X. Another example of faculty influence is the growing practice of consultation on campus development exemplified by faculty committees on new buildings and space utilization. Their membership commonly includes several appropriate administrative officers; if not, the practice of close consultation with the latter prevails. The standing Campus Planning Committee at Wisconsin reports to the general faculty; it is viewed as a faculty agency despite the ex officio membership of certain officers of the administration. A faculty com-

---

[8] The comprehensive survey and report of the Stanford Committee on Committees adopted in 1959 was intended to make the system more efficient. The so-called "academic" committees are elected by the Executive Committee of the faculty. The "presidential" committees, designed to facilitate the work of the administration in cooperation with the faculty, are appointed by the president, usually in consultation with the Executive Committee. A most important innovation was an advisory committee to the president. It is composed of certain officers of administration and the Executive Committee of the Faculty. The functions of certain committees were combined or transferred. The changes are considered an improvement, but how well they have cured what was formerly termed a committee-ridden system is debatable. Where formerly there were twenty-five committees, there are still twenty-one. In spite of the customary complaining, the prestige of committee service at Stanford has been relatively high.

mittee at Chicago makes representations to the business officers. The Stanford faculty committee on land development consults on occasion with the trustees. While concerning itself primarily with the location and design of academic buildings, it has had a part in planning the area of Stanford's spacious campus set apart for industrial exploitation as a source of revenue to the University. It has not tried to substitute its business discretion for that of the trustees, but it has influenced the architectural character and dignity of the new development to harmonize with the academic atmosphere of the campus proper. As with all committees, a faculty committee on campus development operates in inverse effectiveness to the time it spends on minor matters. Deliberations in the name of democracy on the details of a pathway from the gymnasium to the cafeteria, as in one example reported to us, are a travesty of its function.

FACULTY-PRESIDENT CONFERENCE COMMITTEES

Another instance of increasing faculty influence in government is the standing committee for consultation with the president. Such a committee may be elected specially by the faculty for this purpose, supplemented perhaps by some presidential appointees. Or if the senate is a small body, it may itself be the advisory committee; more often it is a subcommittee, perhaps the executive committee, of the senate. Presidents who consistently use a standing advisory committee by discussing frankly any sort of problem that is not too delicate to talk about report that it is extremely helpful. When a too optimistic budget has to be cut, as, for example, when legislative appropriations have not come up to expectations, the existence of a well-seasoned system of consultation is invaluable.

We observed one practical instance in which such a committee meeting regularly with the president, free to discuss anything on the mind of either, would have substantially eased a habitual state of tension; and there are probably a good many others. If an advisory committee is introduced following a period of active faculty dissatisfaction, a president may find it overeager to make decisions which properly pertain to administration; but if he is patient and willing to confer freely, respect for the administrative function and trust in his administration builds up as experience accumulates.

PLACE OF DEANS IN ACADEMIC GOVERNMENT

Deans are usually appointed by the trustees on nomination by the president, often for fixed terms subject to renewal. Corson observes that in the major institutions the dean's office has become the critical position in educational leadership. This is true in the sense that deans are more in touch with daily operations and that the president must look to them as essential agents in attaining organizational goals. But, unless the president has abdicated his office of educational leadership, his position is the most critical of all from the standpoint of the impact of his major decisions, the spirit of excellence he exudes, and his responsibility to see that the deans reflect and implement his policies for the organization.

Most crucial of all the offices of dean is that of the "dean of deans," coming to be known as the academic vice-president, a top-ranking coordinator of academic affairs. He should be the man to whom the administrative reins are handed in the absence or disability of the president, second only to him in the administrative hierarchy. He is the president's alter ego in many matters, not as a means of escape but to widen and deepen the force of the latter's participation in education. While a president cannot see all who solicit an interview or crave his intervention, a sagacious one can, by his known interest in the faculty and in educational policy making and by reasonable accessibility, work to prevent the existence of an academic vice-president, or "dean of deans," from obstructing the channels between him and the other deans and faculty members. The vice-president who resents a dean, departmental chairman, or member of the faculty talking directly to the president or appealing a decision to him, as an occasional one seems to do, misconceives his function. Such a one constricts communication with the president and is not protecting him so much as his own vanity.

Despite the emergence of the academic vice-president, the deans remain effective agents by which a president multiplies or diminishes his influence in the educative process. However, as appears repeatedly throughout this book, educator-deans do not absolve a president from personal involvement in education. In the language of one acute president, "When he relies on transmitting his ideas through an academic hierarchy, when he depends on deans to interpret and carry them out, he rarely gets beyond making a speech about what ought to be done."

The processes by which a president decides whom to nominate to the board for a deanship vary, but in any case the faculty generally has much more influence here than in the selection of the president. Although outright election by the whole faculty or the faculty of a single school is practically unknown in the United States, it is not uncommon for a committee, or faculty of a particular school, to present a single nomination or a slate of names. The regulations may not stipulate advance consultation between the committee which makes the nomination and the president, but the best results obtain when there is.

At Chicago, for example, a committee of the division over which the dean presides makes nominations to the chancellor. At Washington University, St. Louis, an exceptional procedure requires that the chancellor must refer annually his appointment of a dean to the council of the appropriate school or, if the school has none, to the council of the general faculty. Although reappointments are customary, the faculty cherishes this prerogative as "a protection against possible presidential abuse."

The president is usually free to reject all the recommendations of a nominating committee or school and to send them back for reconsideration and presentation of new names; and many presidents can cite instances where they have done so. Presidents of institutions in which the custom of faculty nominations prevails admit that the process may entail some grief before agreement is achieved. They also report that the greater confidence inspired by faculty participation eases the path of the dean.

It is true that in many institutions the president is still free to nominate deans to the trustees without any legal requirement for consultation. Some presidents view any faculty participation in the selection of administrative officers as hazardous. However, it is wise to take careful soundings among the faculty to assure acceptability, even if consultation is not prescribed.

This in no way negates a president's right to final say as to whom he will name, for certain considerations are involved which a faculty may overlook. Clearly, a dean should be sympathetic to the aims of the president and able to represent him effectively. He should enjoy the confidence of the faculty; he should also be one with whom the president likes to work, without his being compliant. As was said in the previous chapter about officers of administration generally, an experienced president prefers strong deans: a dean who must constantly be led by the hand is an encumbrance. As one president expressed it, an effective dean is a "noxious dean" because he will raise problems, not shove them out of sight. But—and this is a requirement a faculty might overlook—deans should be more than spokesmen and promoters for their areas. They are, or should be, a top-level element in the decision-making process in the large; they should possess the aptitudes of a generalist with an all-college or university point of view.

They need a talent and a respect for administration. Some deans of an earlier day, most effective in personal dealings with individual faculty and students, would explode under today's burden of supervising subordinates, chairing committees, and similar duties. One who tries to curry favor with the faculty by "talking down" administration is shouting to the wind, for the faculty will judge him by his actions, not by any "sweet talk."

We like the once universal custom of teaching deans, but it is increasingly difficult to sustain, especially in fields of rapidly changing subject matter. Although naturally there are exceptions in both camps, deans of the smaller professional schools seem better able to carry a reduced though respectable teaching load than do deans of the large undergraduate colleges. A dean who finds himself so pressed that teaching has to be sandwiched in among administrative duties, who merely meets classes and does not teach well, should withdraw from it. We encountered some persuasive opinions that some of the poorest teaching today is done by otherwise proficient deans who cannot find time for adequate preparation. They are frequently absent and, more or less perforce, resort to subterfuges and substitute teachers to keep a class going.

DEPARTMENTAL CHAIRMAN AND FACULTY GOVERNMENT

In those schools which are subdivided into departments, the chairmen are critical figures. They are closer than the deans to the faculty. They rank just below the deans in the success of a president's administration. The all-but-universal sentiment favoring democratic conduct of a department's business reveals that faculties appreciate their potential and why they so often insist that they are "chairmen" and not "heads." [9] Good men must often be persuaded to accept appointment.

Departmental chairmen are chosen as a rule by one of three methods: appointment by the president or dean of the school, nomination by the department or a committee thereof and ratification by the president or dean, or election by the department. In any case it is important that the selection be agreeable, or as agreeable as possible, to the department, and a president or dean will not appoint without at least consulting key members. If he does, the new chairman may find himself in the deplorable position of the one who announced at the opening departmental meeting of the year, "Gentlemen, I have the unfortunate duty to inform you that I am now your chairman."

Because the chairmanship is an onerous post and because faculties are alert against dictators, short rotating terms may be pre-

[9] The faculty of Harvard College take pride that their chairmen, who customarily serve for brief rotating terms, are simply administrative agents of the departments and are in no sense "heads." On the other hand, the chairmen at Chicago have a great influence with the administration.

ferred, at least in theory. Rotation, however, has its drawbacks. The chairman is, or should be, a leader, much more than a "paper pusher" or mere housekeeper. He is the one chiefly responsible for forward planning of the curriculum, of fields of scholarship and of personnel, and it takes time to develop and execute plans.[10] When short terms and rotation are the rule, responsibility for these functions is dissipated.

A weak or lazy chairman may not destroy a good department, but he is not one to pull a poor one out of the doldrums. One capable of leadership among intimate colleagues in a democratic setting is best. Dictators are not good risks. The Chicago committee appointed to investigate the factors affecting faculty appointments and promotions concluded that ". . . historically, many of the truly great departments were built by one man, acting dictatorially. The worst departments were built in the same way. On the other hand a strictly egalitarian system tends toward a middle result."[11]

A too hard-driving or autocratic chairman serving over a period of years may bequeath an unfortunate legacy. The greater his academic reputation, the more easily he can, if he chooses, hold the department wedded to old curricula and old fields of scholarship in which he gained his fame. Colleagues may grumble, but they have learned that it is easier to be yes-men than no-men; or they resign and go elsewhere. When he retires, the department loses the guidance of an overpowering personality and, unschooled in the practice of self-government, may find itself on dead center.

Although some chairmen complain that their position is not sufficiently defined in the bylaws and regulations, their influence is great or little according to their persuasiveness and the innate respect they command from their colleagues. Although the faculty prefer a chairman rather than a "head," they nevertheless expect

[10] The position of the chairman in faculty-personnel administration is treated in the following chapter.

[11] *Report of the Subcommittee on Appointments and Promotions (to Tenure)*, 1959. The report was published as a privileged communication, not to be divulged to unauthorized persons. The University authorities have kindly granted permission to quote from it as above.

him to lead and to promote with the administration their case for higher salaries, early promotions, larger staff, lighter teaching loads, and better working conditions. At the same time, the dean and president look to him to stimulate faculty activity and productivity, to build strength economically, and to win over all those who resist plans for improvement, particularly proposals which they feel reflect upon themselves. To meet both conditions, he needs strength in his own right.

THE PRESIDENT AND THE CURRICULUM

In one of his reports on the state of the university, former Chancellor Kimpton of Chicago, after remarking that his previous energies had been largely directed to urgent business and budgetary matters (including the university's extensive urban redevelopment program), gave warning that he now planned to give attention to education. "Faculties in general," he remarked, "become concerned when the head of their institution rattles his Phi Beta Kappa key instead of his tin cup. And with some justification."

Faculties desire that their president be a Ph.D., chosen from academia; they expect him to make significant speeches on educational topics. But as jealous professional guardians of the curriculum and fields of scholarship they entertain mixed feelings regarding his place in the educational process. Undoubtedly a goodly number prefer that he does not mix in curricular policy making, and we heard criticism of some who were browsing in pastures reserved for the faculty. On the other hand, we also heard criticism of presidents who by remaining aloof denied the faculty the opportunity to "battle ideas" with them. A professor of political science expressed what is probably the prevailing faculty position when he wrote that the legislative function in curricular development belongs to the faculty; the president can propose and attempt to persuade. Unlike the President of the United States, he cannot use patronage as a weapon or make his will prevail by "going to the people." On the contrary, he must make it plain that he is not going to the people and that the personal fortunes of faculty members are not affected by agreement or disagreement with him.

A president may have little influence in day-by-day curricular changes, but as one remarked, if he looks ahead two, three, or five years, if he anticipates issues by throwing out challenging ideas, not only can he cultivate divine discontent which prepares the way for innovation, but he can have a great deal to say as to what path it will take. Success requires tact, sensitivity to faculty prerogatives, patience, and persistence. "You have to wait for things to come to a boil," remarked one president, "but often you have to turn up the gas."

Some deans whom we interviewed underrated the capacity of the faculty to produce fresh educational ideas, holding that significant innovations toward progress habitually originate with the administration. They were confusing origination with the process of seeing a new proposal through the machinery of discussion, criticism, and finally to adoption. "My best suggestions as to how I may lead educationally," writes one president, "come from the faculty." An experienced educator-president knows that, given encouragement and opportunity, members of the faculty do produce new ideas.

Faculties may or may not represent the most conservative profession of all.[12] But if they respect the president and deans, they do not protect their private interests so zealously and cling so stubbornly to old personal opinions that nothing but logrolling or a watery sort of compromise is possible.

Moreover, good ideas often come to the administration in the form of complaints and unsatisfied needs personal to the individual. A good president or dean will welcome their expression, for unsatisfied needs are opportunities and may open up broad areas to innovation. They may also prove to be formative sources of colleague appraisals of a department or school.

Prof. Paul H. Buck, former provost of Harvard University,

[12] David Riesman asserts that they are suffering from a stalemate of success which smothers enthusiasm for progress.

has remarked that no radical proposal survives its customary period of faculty discussion unless the president makes a pet of it. Its implementation rests with the administration, although, in the words of former President Goodrich White, it must run ". . . the gauntlet of prolonged faculty discussion and debate." The adoption by Harvard College of its program of general education, which stimulated the faculties of other colleges to take the idea seriously, is a case in point. There is danger, however, that an eager president will indulge himself in academic minutiae in an effort to influence education. Since he will only dissipate both his energy and influence, even in respect to the liberal arts college where he may feel at home, he may have to discipline himself against meddling. The faculty of one university can produce impressive evidence that the departments to which a former president had devoted himself too enthusiastically declined while those which he left more to themselves fared better.

ADMINISTRATION-FACULTY COMMUNICATIONS

Despite the prominence of the consultative process in academic government, with its scores of committees, its faculty senates and councils, complaints of insufficient administration-faculty communication are common, particularly in large and rapidly growing universities. As Prof. John Dale Russell reminds us, any profession tends to develop its own esoteric vocabulary and thereby to clog the channels of exchange of information with others. For example, to many teachers the institution's financial report is a closed—or, worse, a misleading—book. Administrators who wrestled with the faculty over the allocation of "overhead" received from the government in respect to research projects will testify how the substitution of the term "indirect costs" helped to clarify the concept. Copies of the institution's annual financial report may be distributed to the faculty with the best intentions; but if it was prepared more to meet the concepts of the accounting profession rather than the needs of nonexperts, it will convey misinformation rather than enlightenment. Financial officers charged with preparing it may well consider the oft-imitated innovation introduced years ago by Governor Alfred E. Smith, by which the finances of the state of New York were summarized in everyday language a taxpayer could comprehend. Surely university administrators can do likewise.

Some institutions circulate periodic newsletters. Of course their value relates to what they talk about. The weekly letter at Iowa State University includes news of subjects before the board and strives to inform the faculty of actions taken before they read them in the newspapers. Wisconsin issues a semimonthly publication called *Memo* which the administration considers an excellent method of keeping the faculty informed. In addition to news of current events the editor does not hesitate to "throw out fliers" which stimulate reactions favorable and unfavorable. Obviously the success of a faculty newsletter relates to how successfully it departs from the typical business house organ, with its wealth of personalia and its stress on keeping everyone happy and proud of the corporation by which he is employed.

Student publications, particularly the campus newspaper, are read by the faculty and staff, and from them they learn—correctly or incorrectly—much of what is going on. The accuracy of student reporting frequently leaves something to be desired, but it is improved when members of the administration make sure they know what they are talking about and are prepared to conduct a press interview with all possible frankness. The danger of misrepresentation remains, but a rule of defensive silence is more damaging.

Faculty senates have a duty to inform their colleagues which they may or may not fulfill. As indicated earlier, if their minutes are monopolized by records of busywork, many will not take the trouble to read them. A faculty council or committee advisory to the president affords two-way communications if it is diligent in reporting to the faculty, if each side talks freely, if controversial subjects are not eschewed, and if the president is not afraid to share confidential information as background material. In so doing, a president knows that he is running some danger in behalf of the cause of good communications. The testimony of one faculty chairman that "we have had some trouble in preserving secrecy within the council when secrecy was important" described a common human frailty and the risk his president ran, "who spoke off the record with great candor." We agree with Stoke that presidents are too inclined to withhold information when keeping a matter confidential is of no great importance and when disclosure would increase understanding and inspire confidence.

The effectiveness of regular faculty meetings as opportunities for communication relates to how a president conducts them as well as to what he discloses. If he suppresses controversy, if he conveys the impression that proposals emanating from the administration are to be adopted without debate (as some still do), he destroys the occasion as an opportunity for communication and weakens the honest support his proposals might otherwise enjoy. The contrast in faculty attitude toward a president who required that questions must be submitted in writing in advance with that toward his successor who cheerfully "fielded" questions from the floor need not be elaborated.

When communications are deficient, the cause roots as often in neglect as in hesitancy to disclose. The busy administrator, conversant with a problem and its ramifications and beset by pressures to meet deadlines, tends naturally to assume that others must be as aware as he is, that the bother of explaining is unnecessary.

Faculty members are similarly inclined. Communications is an intrafaculty problem as well as an administration-faculty problem. Even between cognate scholarly disciplines intrafaculty exchanges are often piecemeal and haphazard. To a scholar intent upon his project the cost of maintaining communication, in terms of more meetings, more memoranda to be drafted (and read), more attention to distributing copies of correspondence is not worth the time which would be subtracted from his research. Furthermore, how many faculty members are really interested in what is going on in areas other than their own, and apart from what might be called "common terms of employment," is debatable.

The advertising world has made us familiar with mass media of communications, and some of their mechanistic nature has rubbed off on our colleges and universities. True, the machinery for the exchange of information and opinion has not generally kept pace with the need to combat a sense of being out of touch, and we do not underestimate the desirability of improvement. Yet, however helpful formal media of communications may be, they are but a bit of human engineering. In no sense can they substitute for that interchange and understanding which is a natural by-product of well-conducted processes of consultation. When a president becomes absorbed in the main business of his institution, the back of the communications problem is broken.

A PRESIDENT'S PERSONAL RELATIONS WITH INDIVIDUALS

We agree that that president succeeds best who gets away from his desk as often as is humanly possible, shows an interest in the members of his faculty, and tries to know them. Fortunate is one who receives voluntary invitations to meet with departments or schools for a give-and-take talk about their ambitions and requirements. In spite of its relative remoteness in large institutions, vestiges of an earlier pastoral relationship to the staff still attach to the presidency. When its occupant expresses a personal concern in cases of family illness or bereavement, he is acting like the human being he is. One was warmly praised for his habit of writing a note to a man who had published a book or received some professional honor or recognition or had made a noteworthy contribution as chairman of a committee or something of the sort.

Presidents differ over the propriety of close personal relations with individuals. As we remark later in regard to trustees, a president is bound to enjoy the company of some more than others. In fear that some faculty members will strive to insinuate themselves into his good graces, as some will do, one president we talked to avoids anything that might be interpreted as intimacy with any. Another whom the faculty respect unabashedly claims the right to have some friends whose company he enjoys and does not shrink from going fishing with them. He reports that they understand that the relationship is social and not official and do not take advantage of it.

As we have seen, a president recognizes certain individuals to be power centers of influence in the faculty and realizes the importance of maintaining contacts with them. But too repeated access to the president's ear is quickly noted and apt to be resented by others. Anything interpreted as a kitchen cabinet injures his relations with others, not excluding members of the administration. "He relies on an inner circle for advice, and it is bad advice" is not an impression that generates support for his policies. At all events, he will make sure that his faculty contacts are not restricted to a group of informal admirers; nor will he overlook as mere troublemakers the gadflies who habitually oppose what he thinks should be done. Most importantly, to recall a rule of the art of administration, he will observe established channels and procedures of decision making in the faculty and administration.

In dealings with the faculty, as with all his publics, a president is in danger of speaking with two voices. "My fifth year was harder than my first," one disillusioned president is said to have remarked, "because it was then that the faculty found out I was a liar." According to William Rainey Harper, whose trumpet gave no uncertain sound, ". . . a superficial observer will find much to substantiate the accusation that college presidents are prevaricators." How often, he wrote, it has happened that in talking to one person or group the president has seemed to have a given opinion, whereas in conversation with others he expressed a different opinion on the same subject. Harper's defense against the charge of occupational prevarication was the universal tendency of people to interpret courteous consideration and a gentle "no" as approval, if only tacit, of a cherished project or an eagerly desired promotion. An honest president must try on the one hand not to be harsh and on the other not to seem a dissembler.

CHAPTER V

BUILDING
FACULTY PERSONNEL

In law and in practice the appointment and promotion of members of the faculty are by action of the board of trustees upon the recommendation of the president. Although in the great majority of the scores or hundreds of cases treated each year in a university the president perforce merely transmits as his own the judgments of others, he remains technically and morally accountable for all appointments and promotions. No longer can he, for example, emulate the small-college president who does most of his own scouting for new faculty members. Most of it will be done by others. Nevertheless, his success in building academic personnel is a prime measure of the quality of his leadership.

Unfortunately, not all presidents take this responsibility seriously enough. Some rely exclusively, or all but exclusively, on the recommendations of the appropriate dean or the academic vice-president. Neglect of adequate consideration of the critical appointments to tenured posts suggests that the president is a willing, if apologetic, captive of other concerns. By their own admission, some presidents participate energetically in personnel matters at the beginning of their terms of office, but with time they either lose interest or become increasingly so caught up in

124

other matters that in essence they delegate this all-important responsibility. Yet ideally the president's participation should be even more effective in his last years, as he develops methods of minimizing distractions and as his experience accumulates.

We do not believe that presidents of even our largest universities have a right to contract themselves out of direct—and not merely representative—involvement in the selection of tenured faculty, who, after all, may be either a source of pride or of mortification to the institution for years to come. These posts correspond to the management level in business (the nontenured ranks to middle management), and a good corporation president takes pains to become acquainted with the points of strength and weakness of members of both groups and to concern himself in decisions on appointments and advancements. True, since his routine keeps him in touch with them as they conduct their appointed tasks, the corporation head is in a better position than a university president to observe how individuals at the management, or even middle-management, level perform. A university president deals with a faculty of specialists in whose operations he is neither directly involved nor qualified to direct and from whom he is perforce relatively remote. Nevertheless, his ultimate responsibility for its quality is not so dissimilar as to justify turning it over to others.

HUMAN PRONENESS TO DETERIORATION

The tendency to deteriorate imbedded in every organization of human beings makes no exceptions in favor of the most eminent colleges and universities or of the most eminent departments or schools within them. We know that a president is duty-bound to combat apathy and to resist other forces that erode. If his institution is in stiff competition with others for improvement, he is indeed lucky. For the critical task for every president and his academic administrative staff is to assure that the college or university continually rebuilds and regenerates itself so that its performance will match changing social demands.

He will learn—perhaps the hard way—that great professors do not automatically reproduce themselves, for they can be misled in choosing younger men to succeed them. The unselfish, outgiving senior professor, so successful in stimulating others, may mistake the mere reflection of his own sparks for brilliant flashes from a junior. Others will be possessed by an urgency that their particular fields of study be perpetuated in their successors. Still others will be beguiled by imitation, an insidious means of flattery whether deliberate or unconscious.

Some assert that academia contains more built-in tendencies toward deterioration than other forms of human organization. This is debatable. Nevertheless there are certain aspects of academia that render it peculiarly subject to internal decline. The right to continuing tenure, which provides the professors a proper sense of intellectual security and a defense against maltreatment by an impetuous or weak president or uninformed trustees, also protects the mediocre in their mediocrity at the cost of a striking degree of stolid institutional inertia ("inertia" being defined as the property of matter by which it will remain at rest or in uniform motion in a straight line unless acted upon by some external force). A new president who had come to a large university from a small college reported to us that it would take ten years for his presence on the campus to be felt because of the high proportion of tenured posts in the faculty and the limited sea room he had to effect changes of direction or emphases. We predict that he overestimated the waiting period, but his appraisal of the inertia which characterizes a firmly established and proud university was not far wrong.

The entire professoriate covets membership in a department of renown, but not all are willing to pay the price. Practices that encourage deterioration are allowed, even cultivated. Bernard Berelson, referring to a senior professor's frequent preference for the appointment of one of his old Ph.D. students, has remarked that higher education is the only profession in which the makers of the product hire it back. The too frequent result of such a closed system of training and hiring is a pattern of hereditary succession through cycles of master-disciple relationships. Such a system hardly inspires young men to radical departures or rebel ideas that might distress their seniors.

There are, then, some grounds for Karl Jaspers' violent observation that freedom of a university faculty to choose its own new members theoretically favors the best but actually tends to favor the second best.[1] Whether this is too heavy an indictment or not, it is clear that, of all the many responsibilities of the president and his colleagues in academic administration, one of the most commanding is the selection of the faculty.

We by no means imply that the administration is the only influence working to combat deterioration or striving for greater excellence. Countless faculty members are just as concerned, often more concerned and more active in arousing unrest among colleagues and stirring ambitions for betterment according to severe standards. No president or dean can succeed unless the faculty is seeded with members of this sort. The president, in working with the faculty, must seek to identify them. He must then support them and see that their efforts are not nullified by opposition and indifference of their colleagues. Leadership within the faculty is indispensable, but if the administration does not supplement it, the best to be hoped for is a spotty admixture of some good departments with weak or declining ones.

In making this assertion we do not deny that colleges and universities have sustained high standards despite relatively weak

[1] *The Idea of the University,* The Beacon Press, Boston, 1959, p. 71. Jaspers writes further, with a conclusion that will annoy a goodly number in academic life, "Not only the university but all corporate bodies tend to maintain an unconscious solidarity against both the excellent and the mediocre, . . . The excellent are instinctively excluded from fear of competition, just as the inferior are rejected out of concern for the prestige and influence of the university. The 'competent,' the second-rate, are selected, people who are on the same intellectual level as oneself."

This is one more reason why appointments to vacant professorships cannot be left exclusively to the departments concerned. It should, however, be stressed that the application of administrative judgments to faculty appointments is of no value if confined to budgetary considerations and if the standards of the president and deans are not informed and rigorous.

or inept presidential leadership. Like other organizations, they
may ride for a time on acquired momentum. But if the administration is incompetent or indifferent, the germs of decay, even if
concealed, are there and will constitute a first claim on the attention of an educationally alert and energetic successor president.

Of course, a president's formal recommendations to his trustees
regarding faculty personnel are but the last step in a long
process during which the discretionary influence of the faculty,
and particularly of the department or school directly concerned,
is very great. With the exception of control over the courses of
study, in no area of university governance is their power more
formally and firmly established, as it should be.

In most colleges and universities faculty-personnel recommendations originate in the departments of instruction, except that
in those professional schools which have no departments or only
weak ones they usually come from all the full professors as a body,
or a committee thereof, under the dean. In some the departmental
recommendations rest largely in the hands of the chairman or
"head," subject to whatever the local practice may be as to the
measure of consultation with colleagues.[2] In others the recommendation at the departmental level is a thoroughly democratic determination, formalized by vote of the members of designated ranks.
In this event the chairman as a matter of law is essentially a transmitting officer, although as a matter of fact he may and should be
much more. How democratic a department is, as measured by the
members' eligibility to vote on calls and promotions, varies among
institutions and even among departments in the same college or
university. It may be restricted to full professors, or it may extend to all of tenure rank or even to assistant professors on appointments of equal or lower rank.

---

[2] We encountered departments in one university (there may be many
others) which preferred to leave selection decisions largely to the head, with
consultation as he saw fit, and believed that this gave the best results. Concentration of decision in one person left the others freer, we were told, to
go about their own work and made for a happier family because it avoided
the dissension latent in a more democratic process.

THE STRATEGIC POSITION OF THE DEPARTMENT

It is natural that the departments, or professional schools not organized on departmental lines, should be strong centers of power. Departments are composed of specialists grouped around a field of learning in which professorial colleagues in other departments usually can boast no similar competence. These specialists work closely together, so that each is in a position to appraise the work of fellow departmental colleagues on the basis of intimate acquaintance with it. Moreover, they know, or know about, their scholarly and scientific colleagues in other institutions, to whom they can turn for advice, appraisals, and recommendations. By following the literature, by correspondence, and by attending meetings of their professional associations they are prepared to identify the bright stars appearing on the horizon of their discipline. Confronted by such a concentration of specialized knowledge, the administration should be properly humble.

Nevertheless, the centrality of the department in personnel decisions carries with it some potential threats to excellence. The democratic process, focused on attaining unanimity or at least a strong consensus of the group, militates in favor of the person whom nobody is *against*, and a common-denominator solution works against the more original nonconformist. For the sake of peace and harmony, the orthodox members, apt also to be the seniors, are permitted to dominate, and not only in the less forward looking departments. Many a president, we venture to say, can report more than one case in which an eminent or promising person needed by a department was not called because of the personal objection of just one professor.

The intellectually independent, perhaps brash, young man who challenges cherished traditional views in his field, who advocates new approaches to old schools of specialization, may need protection by the administration when his reappointment or promotion comes up. Not infrequently a "young Turk" is by temperament an uneasy or inconsiderate colleague whose manners leave some-

thing to be desired, whereas the less-inspired mind, the all-round
citizen with a "better-adjusted" personality, is a more congenial
fellow.[3] Moreover, loyalties to each other and to the pervading
image each has of his department may transform it into a sort
of social club maintaining its own qualifications for admission.
As a Harvard committee observed, "A faculty made up wholly of
amiable and attractive men, or even of saints, would not as such
serve the purposes of a college or university." [4] There is some
evidence that departments in the physical sciences, where great
weight is placed these days on research productivity, are more
willing to make allowance for uncongenial colleagues whom they
recognize as creative scientists than are their confreres in the
less exact disciplines.

Although pride in one's department and jealousy for its prestige
are excellent, faculties and departments both should be diverse
enough to assure a continuing state of intellectual and professional ferment. We have observed that some professors, most
zealous in maintaining tension with the administration, have been
equally urgent in avoiding a semblance of it in their departments.
On the other hand, the desirable and necessary ferment, of course,
goes hand in hand with a reasonable degree of departmental
solidarity. The faction-ridden department is a declining one, if
not already a weak one.

[3] I well recall one case in which a likely candidate from another university,
a man of international repute, was rejected by the chairman of a department
on the basis of one paragraph in one book of several he had written. This was,
of course, an exceptionally egregious example of prejudice and probably concealed some other reasons. Nevertheless, a president may need to remind
members of the faculty on occasion that academic freedom does not run only
against trustees and presidents. More flagrant was the instance of a professor
who, until the administration intervened, became a serious embarrassment to
his departmental associates by opposing each action which involved an increase in, or call at, a salary above his own. Although salary differentials on
a merit basis naturally entail some heartburnings and resistance, it is only
fair to add that the foregoing were in my experience untypical examples.
H. W. D.

[4] *Report on Some Problems of Personnel in the Faculty of Arts and Sciences,* Harvard University Press, Cambridge, Mass., 1939, p. 77.

THE DEPARTMENT CHAIRMAN

Although a proficient chairman will solicit and receive aid from his colleagues at every step, he is usually a significant figure in building faculty strength even in the most democratically administered department. He is charged, above his fellows, with finding likely new candidates; as a rule he conducts the bulk of the correspondence with them. He solicits appraisals by colleagues in other institutions who know the candidates and their work.

If it is thorough, the search for new instructors and professors is bound to be a burdensome business. The chairman, and in turn his departmental colleagues, may easily become discouraged enough to underestimate the drawing power of the institution and to settle too quickly for second best. Here a president or a dean, as a reviewing agent, has the advantage of distance from the grind of frustrating details. This lofty position seems privileged to a chairman, yet it is salutary, since these officers, being at some remove, should be less tempted to compromise.

In not the least among his functions, the chairman is the department's planner-in-chief in maintaining a long-term personnel development program. He is the one who sees that retirements are anticipated well in advance and makes provision for replacements, who makes sure that young staff members are screened for reappointment by severe standards and that those who do not qualify are notified in reasonable time and are helped to get posts elsewhere. Whether or not there is a formal "up-or-out" regulation on the books, it is no kindness to the individual or to the institution to continue a teacher with no prospect of tenure until, to his embarrassment and everyone else's, moral rights of tenure accrue.

When a department has made up its mind in favor of a promotion or a new appointment, the chairman carries the ball with the administration and, if there is one, the faculty-review committee. He is the department's advocate for additional personnel

to strengthen or broaden its program. His colleagues look to him
to bring home the bacon.

THE DEAN AND FACULTY-PERSONNEL ADMINISTRATION

Commonly, initial recommendations go from the department
to the appropriate dean for review, thence to an academic vice-
president or a provost, if there is one, and finally to the president
himself.[5] An increasing number of institutions call for review at
some stage by a faculty committee, whose jurisdiction may extend
to the whole university or to a single unit, such as the College of
Arts and Sciences. The dean's turn for formal action on the
papers does not come until the departments file their recommendations with him. They will normally exceed budget limitations.
He must see that the available funds are equitably distributed by
judging which of the various departments—by virtue of demonstrated need, present strength, and well-conceived plans for future
improvement—deserve larger segments of the pie than others.

A wide-awake dean does not merely pass on the dossier of documents and testimonials submitted by the department; rather, he
conducts his own investigations, so as to be able to give the president an independent judgment on them. Written references from
outside authorities need to be analyzed with an expert eye. If
unfamiliar with the institution and its particular requirements,
outsiders' appraisals may not be germane to the case. Many
asked for an evaluation are unwilling to record adverse opinions
on paper; others are only too willing. Money spent on telephone
calls at this stage is well spent.

An academic dean should not hesitate to send recommendations
back for reconsideration by a department or to request that more
names be proposed. As in other matters, a weak dean throwns an
unnecessary burden of responsibility on the president. Whether

[5] As mentioned in Chap. III, the office of the academic vice-president or
dean of faculties ("dean of deans") has become a familiar feature of a
university's administrative structure. Its function, although at a higher level
of review, is so similar to that of a dean that for the sake of simplicity we
confine our discussion to the office of dean.

a president's relations with a department are at the level of big ideas and ambitious plans or are occupied with details of operation is naturally related to the complexity of the institution, but more significantly to the trust he reposes in the dean.

An alert academic dean will be conferring all through the years regarding personnel needs, plans for the future, qualifications of those on the job, and bright prospects elsewhere. He will be doing some scouting himself. The awareness of all that every recommendation is subject to critical and knowledgeable scrutiny by the administration is a powerful deterrent to slipshod methods of faculty recruitment. The dean's duties are onerous and unceasing, but they are of the highest significance. For if his standards are high, his recommendations carry great weight with his superior.

FACULTY-REVIEW BODIES

The faculties of an increasing number of institutions have established some form of self-selected body to review recommendations for appointment and advancement. Usually these committees operate in parallel column with the appropriate administrative officer or officers, and their recommendations to the administration are part of the documentation leading to final decisions. When their review does not take place until after a dean has recorded his opinion, they are less effective. Their jurisdiction may extend over the whole university, to a division, or to a single component school such as the college of liberal arts.[6]

Frequently the committees deliberate without the presence of an officer of administration; perhaps even the chairman of the department may not appear to testify unless by invitation. This seclusiveness is designed to assure free discussion unrestrained by the presence of a dean or a president. But the system contains a

[6] H. K. Newburn describes in greater detail for the universities he studied the various systems of faculty participation in personnel matters, on both a school and a university basis, with opinions pro and con. *Faculty Personnel Policies in State Universities,* multilithed for limited distribution at Montana State University, Missoula, Mont., 1959, pp. 44–54.

basic weakness: the committee and the administration do not consider cases together. Such an arm's-length relationship does not make sense in this vital area in which conference is most desirable. Both sides lose. The faculty side becomes more a watchdog than a constructive partner. In its zeal for independence, it deprives itself of light which the administration may shed on the cases under consideration. On its part, the administration is denied full access to the special knowledge of the faculty group which can best be developed face to face in an exchange of views that places individual cases in the larger matrix of university concern.

The effectiveness of such bodies varies among institutions, and faculty members disagree as to their value. The principal objections to the all-university reviewing committees are that their consideration is confined to the documents; if these are in order, their review is largely *pro forma*. It is further charged that if they do go into detailed investigations of cases, they merely retrace work already performed more efficiently by the departments and deans, contributing little but confusion to an already involved process. Balancing these criticisms are frequently cited instances of committees which have justified themselves by having compelled a department or a school to raise its standards through stricter conformity to prevailing university qualifications and whose power of review kept all departments and appointing authorities on their toes.

The most thorough and comprehensive system of all-university faculty review that we encountered was at the University of California at Berkeley. The central body is the Committee on Budget and Interdepartmental Relations of the Academic Senate, which considers all personnel recommendations relating to all ranks beginning with the assistant professor. Before taking action it refers each case for intensive study to an anonymous *ad hoc* committee, one member of which is from a nonrelated field. Approximately five hundred faculty members serve on 200 different *ad hoc* committees each year, and each assignment requires about two days' work. In its report to the chancellor, the Budget Committee may accept or reject the findings of the *ad hoc* committee. The chancellor does not become formally involved until the action of the Budget Committee is before him.

We were told that service on the Budget Committee demands about a third of a member's time for the year. Some of the faculty complain of the labor involved, but most agree to serve when asked. Although the system is undeniably cumbersome and time-consuming for those involved, those with whom we spoke were in general agreement that the whole complicated process has been influential in maintaining high standards throughout all areas and has thus contributed to the stature of the university. It is claimed that fewer mistakes are made than in the more conventional head-dean-chancellor-president route of personnel decisions. It is felt that the careful screening process enhances governance by the faculty by strengthening the force of its recommendations to the administration.

The standing committee on appointments established a few years ago in the Stanford School of Humanities and Sciences exemplifies a system operating within a single segment of the institution. It was established out of a feeling that the university-wide advisory board on personnel was superficial, that when it acted, it was essentially as a veto group passing on the written record. Being remote from the operating level it could not instigate proposals. The committee of the school consists of two representatives from each sector of the faculty (humanities, social science, and natural science) and meets weekly. The dean usually sits with it. Admittedly it consumes a great deal of time, but the reports we received united in praising it as a positive force, and its members thought it was time well spent.

The faculty of the University of Wisconsin is organized into four divisions which cut across colleges or schools. The executive committee of each division is the personnel-reviewing body of the division. While departmental proposals carry great weight, the committee may ask sharp questions and is free to go against the department. The dean of the appropriate school need not accept its advice; indeed, he may withhold from its consideration a departmental recommendation of which he does not approve, although usually he would do so only for financial reasons. But if he disregards a negative report by one of the divisional executive committees, he must make a case for his action. Divisional committees are felt to be particularly sensitive to evidence of scholarship as a qualification for promotion, as is true of the California Budget Committee also.

Ohio State University has resisted systematized procedures of review by agencies representative of the faculty as a check on departments or deans. The feeling is that essentially they serve as checks and balances that hamper bold action when needed. University officers cite cases of rapid promotion of brilliant young faculty who could not have been so readily recognized under a complex committee-screening process, which they feel would tend to hold exceptional people back by emphasizing length of service as a condition of promotion.

On the other hand, Princeton has for many years maintained with general satisfaction a standing Advisory Committee on Appointments and Advancements. It is elected by secret ballot from the slate of departmental chairmen in a manner to ensure representation of each of the three divisions of the faculty. It sits with the president, and with three deans who are entitled to talk but not to vote. The president is free to reject the advice of the committee. Departmental chairmen not only can appear on their own motion but also may be summoned to do so, and they must be prepared for what may be severe cross-examination. Indeed the faculty-committee standards are often more rigorous than those the administration of nonspecialists would feel free to apply on its own.

In making his case before the committee the departmental chairman must be prepared to speak of the department's program for the future, its personnel plans, its plans to strengthen old fields and introduce new ones. Thus, under the spur of professional colleagues—not merely of the deans and the president—the department is stimulated to develop long-range ideas.

The committee originated in a faculty demand for more

influence in appointments and promotions, and for a time it thought of itself as essentially an equalizing agency, to thwart the machinations of an administration which might be tempted by ulterior motives. It outgrew this concept as it was encouraged to develop broader interests. It has become an affirmative force in recognizing excellence out of line and so breaking the salary and promotion "lock step" tied to length of service. Thus it has exerted an influence in the promotion of brilliant younger people opposite to the fears held at Ohio State.

Experience demonstrates that the members need not be specialists in the field of the individual under review. A scholar in a tangential discipline, or even in a remote field, is often able to contribute a more impartial point of view and to ask highly pertinent questions. Naturally membership on the committee takes time from other occupations. However, election is considered an honor, and the service is cheerfully rendered. The Princeton Committee on Appointments and Advancements has become a valued partner of the administration in guarding and promoting the quality of the faculty.

Harvard's utilization of *ad hoc* committees, introduced into the Faculty of Arts and Science by former President Conant to advise the department and the president on appointments to tenure positions, has attracted wide attention.[7] The members are informed in advance of the department's choice for the vacancy and supplied with full documentation.

The chairman appears at the meeting to present the case for the candidate. If a minority of the department opposes him, one or more representatives are free to come and argue against his selection.

The president attends the meetings of the committee and finds that he learns a great deal about his own faculty as well as about those of other institutions. Ultimate decision rests with him. It is within his power to accept or reject the recommendation

---

[7] The majority of each committee are men of distinction from outside, but a minority may be of the Harvard faculty, none of whom may be members of the department concerned.

of either the committee or the department if the two disagree. Also, he may reject a joint recommendation of the two, although such instances have been few.

The evidence of outsiders who have sat on *ad hoc* committees divides, pro and con. Critics report that they exert but slight impact (the department's choice usually wins), which may suggest either that the departments do a thorough job or that they have perfected their own protective devices against external interference—probably some of both. They go on to say that there is no opportunity to see the person nominated by the department; therefore, unless a member of the committee knows him personally, his fate depends largely on the documentation supplied. Nor are the members sufficiently in touch with the departmental situation to judge how well the qualities of any candidate meet its peculiar needs. Opinions must largely be formed on the merits of publications, which are, they point out, an inadequate basis for judgment. Such critics believe that, at least for their own institutions, it is better to concentrate responsibility on the department, subject to whatever other review local procedures may prescribe.

Others who have sat on *ad hoc* committees support the official opinion at Harvard that they are beneficial. They suggest names that may not have been considered, or were insufficiently considered, by the department and often throw new light on them. Being men of distinction, the members are apt to know personally many of the promising stars in other colleges and universities as well as their publications. On its part the department is stirred to constant search for the best-qualified persons, the local candidate holding no advantage. The younger faculty, who presumably aspire to tenure, are reminded that they are in competition with scholars throughout the nation and the world, and this is good.

For one reason or another faculties of other institutions have been reluctant to adopt the system for themselves, deeming it inapplicable to their local situations. Undoubtedly the drawing power of a Harvard call aids the functioning of her *ad hoc* committees and enables her to fill her senior ranks with a much larger than average proportion of appointees from outside. A smaller proportion of the junior ranks can anticipate promotion to tenure than is usual in most American institutions, and they accept term appointments knowing this to be true.

THE PRESIDENT REQUIRES THE HELP OF OTHERS

How does a president operate effectively as a contributor to, and builder of, faculty strength? His achievement depends as much or more on what he demands of deans and department chairmen and on their ability to reflect his policies as on what he does himself. How he may participate directly we shall discuss a little later. The two categories tend to dissolve into each other, but each is essential, and the president who succeeds in carving out half his time for education will have time for both.

Obviously the first step in his program of responsibilities-discharged-through-others relates to the criteria to be employed. If he finds these criteria not as rigorous as they should be or not as clearly defined or as well understood as their more or less imponderable nature permits, he will call upon deans and faculty representatives to draft proper recommendations in conference and to present them for faculty approval. It is self-evident that no criteria or procedures which the faculty are not ready to accept will amount to anything in practice. Some say that the determination and supervision of formal criteria are all that the president of a large university can do. If this were true, it would mean the virtual abdication by the president of one of the chief historic prerogatives of his office.

But the educator-president can go further. He can, for example, insist that as a matter of policy the search for good men by others is thorough and that the best available are engaged. Many able youngsters do not automatically or quickly rise to national visibility; they must be discovered. Presidents reported to us that the simple question, addressed to a department head or a dean, "Are you sure the person you are recommending is the best obtainable for what we have to offer?" brings salutary results.

The market for quality is today highly competitive, and the smaller or more obscure institution is at a disadvantage. Yet the richer colleges and universities with greater reputation and more funds for attracting headliners by no means capture for themselves all the good minds and personalities.

While many young Ph.D.'s may prefer posts in colleges and universities with the most ample research opportunities, where they can be under the tutelage of well-known professors, the smaller, less renowned places can counter with amenities of their own. Some of these are earlier opportunities for teaching courses of one's own, a greater chance to be an important figure in the academic community, and freedom to develop even a modest research program of one's own. The simple truth is that many a teacher is happier under these circumstances than in being consigned to membership on a research team under someone else in the atmosphere of intense competition characteristic of the larger and more impersonal university.[8]

A PRESIDENT INFLUENCES CRITERIA

A president can exert a commanding influence not only in the formulation of criteria for appointments but also in the establishment of performance appraisals for measuring them. Newburn, in his study of faculty-personnel policies in eleven state universities, lists the qualifications most prominently mentioned in his interviews in the following order: teaching effectiveness, research and creative work, professional competency and activity, institutional and public service, and personality or personal factors.[9] Although the descriptions vary among institutions, these are generally employed, with the weights assigned to each differing

---

[8] When a young teacher has not qualified for continuing tenure, the separation frequently causes pain. But time and again I have observed how much more content he becomes in a new environment where he is a more significant figure and is freed from a painful and often grueling competitive struggle. H. W. D.

[9] *Op. cit.,* p. 25.

greatly among institutions as well as among segments within an institution.

One constantly encounters dissatisfaction among young faculty members on the ground that they are not told clearly what is expected of them for promotion. Their right to have the criteria and their relative weights plainly stated is unquestioned; their elucidation will not assuage the pain of the unpromoted or the unretained, although it may reduce the feeling that they have been treated unjustly. If, however, young men believe decisions are made on other than specified bases, the published standards are worse than useless. Uncertainty over probable retention, promotion, or dismissal creates a serious morale problem for junior faculty which older men are apt to have forgotten. We believe that the bases for promotion should be made as clear as possible at the start along with the possibilities of promotion.

It is much easier to draft formal criteria than to assign values to each and then apply them to cases. Indeed, faculties can fall into the liveliest discussions as to what their relative weights should be. The significance of teaching effectiveness vis-à-vis research effectiveness is an unfailing source of contention in institutions that honestly seek to apply both standards.

"RATING" TECHNIQUES

Some institutions are experimenting with "rating," or "performance appraisal," techniques similar to those employed in business and the civil service, in which formal instruments of evaluation are applied to a man's various qualities and relative weights assigned in quantitative terms. One university we visited uses a form which calls for individual judgments by each of three raters on eight qualifications in gradations of five each, initialed by each rater. Another employs a rating sheet setting forth three qualifications to be evaluated in five gradations each. Newburn describes the operation of a similar but more complicated system in one of the institutions he surveyed.[10] A committee

[10] *Ibid.*, p. 44.

rates every member on fourteen factors and ". . . allot[s] merit salary increases in terms of the difference figures in tenths of points! . . . one of the administrators judged the system to be working well because 'each year our ratings for most every person turn out to be practically the same as our subjective judgments told us they should in the beginning.' " Under these circumstances one may wonder why the rating technique is continued.

Rating forms are useful as inventory sheets to direct attention to sallient considerations and to see that none is omitted. But we question seriously whether the subsequent collating of so many individual, arithmetically expressed grades by someone in the office of the dean or president gives as sound results as nonquantified subjective evaluations molded into one group evaluation at a conference of the appropriate members of a man's department and reported in nonarithmetical terms. Giving numbers to things does not signify that the evaluations they express have been formed around a common denominator and are therefore comparable, although the presumption that they are comparable is implicit in the use of rating techniques.

The average academic mind spontaneously resists mathematically formalized systems of evaluating the competence of a teacher or scholar. It fears, with reason, that such decisions turn on statistical data at the expense of the intangibles which make a teacher great. Nor is it willing to accept the implication that relatively imponderable, highly subjective opinions take on any greater accuracy or authority by being put through a "mechanical" process.

In any case, all evaluations need to be examined for prejudice, both as to diversity of personalities and the rater's attitude toward new ideas which may disagree with his academic conceptual scheme.

Business can set its performance appraisals against a quantitative background of "goals," "targets," and "quotas"; but how does one set a similar "target" for a scientist or a teacher of literature? Do we want, it is asked, our faculties striving to show up well on uniform metrical rating sheets, to the neglect of the development of their individual, perhaps peculiar, educational potentialities? For the president or dean working to build faculty strength the answer is "no."

Nonetheless, some sort of appraisal, preferably a thorough one, is involved in any decision pertaining to the career of faculty members. Participation of the administration does not alter the fact that the center of gravity remains with academic colleagues.

EVALUATING RESEARCH

Two elements customarily control final judgment, even when a most elaborate table of qualifications is employed, viz., success and promise of growth as a research scholar and as a teacher. Research ability is a function of certain segments of the personality and can be appraised with some detachment, whereas teaching ability is more a function of the whole personality. Moreover, in assembling research evaluations it is possible to tap a larger group of informed people outside the institution who are less personally involved than are those on the ground. Their opinions, formed on the basis of publications, correspondence, exchange of ideas at scientific gatherings, and knowledge of an individual's general standing in his guild, are highly pertinent as a supplement to the judgment of departmental colleagues. Accordingly, the administration will insist on such opinions being included in the documentation as a matter of practice, maintaining its right to seek additional outside confidential judgments for itself.

Faculty members sometimes deny that the central administration—who are at best informed amateurs in most of the fields —can contribute anything of value to the appraisal of the scholarship of specialists. A self-study conducted some years ago by the faculty of the University of Wisconsin concludes:[11]

[11] Committee on University Functions and Policies, *Second Report: Internal Survey,* University of Wisconsin, Madison, Wis., July, 1951, chap. 3, p. 11.

Provided that working relations in a department are healthy, it may well be doubted if a better source of opinion with regard to a man's scholarship can be found than the judgment of his colleagues. In fact, although an administrative officer should gain as much direct information as possible concerning the members of the staff, his duty is largely collecting and weighing the judgments of those who are in a better position to form a judgment than he is, namely, the man's colleagues here and elsewhere working within the same field of knowledge as the individual under consideration.

If the import of this somewhat cloudy statement is to reduce the academic administrator to a mere canvasser of the votes of others, we cannot accept it as an adequate description of his proper role. Weighing evidence entails analyzing and evaluating it, a responsibility inseparable from a judgment regarding candidates. The president is fully within his rights when he vetoes a recommended appointment and requests faculty colleagues to make a more severe appraisal of the man on the ground or to conduct a more extensive search for a better candidate from outside.

The administration serves scholarship and research when it seeks assurance that a candidate for appointment or promotion is an imaginative and not merely a pedestrian investigator. In academia it is, alas, too frequently true that excessive rewards go to plodding, inconsequential scholarship, provided it fulfills the technical requirements of methodology. This is particularly true when the scholar has been serving as a sort of assistant to a more established senior.[12]

A president or dean can glean information about a candidate from reading specimens of his publications. One president told us that he always read at least one publication of each candidate up for promotion or appointment to a tenure post. Naturally the ma-

---

[12] We realize that universities have room for the researcher who diligently addresses himself to digging out and collating new facts and thus organizes the minutiae of knowledge with which more imaginative colleagues will weave new patterns. But they should be consequential facts, and the institution's need, as well as that of the cause of learning at large, should be assessed in each case.

terial was often too specialized for him to master, but he felt that he frequently gained an insight into the quality of the man's mind as a valuable supplement to other evidence. He added that the practice consumed a great deal of time on weekends. A candidate's bibliography may superficially appear very impressive and yet diminish in importance under analysis of its content. Uncritical stress on the "column inches" of publication, still too general in some of our universities, contributes to an unhappy publish-or-perish psychology inimical to a young scholar's development. Incidentally, at too many places the publish-or-perish threat is more than a self-induced hallucination on the part of young members of the faculty.

In considering publications as a gauge of scholarship and evidence of a lively creative mind, one must not forget that books and papers are not the only media by which the fruits of scholarship are expressed and made available to others. We have known professors with vigorous, original minds who revealed true scholarship through stimulating teaching, in criticisms and new ideas transmitted to their colleagues, but who published little or nothing during their lifetimes. The report by a committee of the faculty of Harvard College warned, "Excessive reliance on the criterion of publication may lead to a neglect of the candidate's mind as a whole, only a small portion of which is or should be represented by any published work. 'Learning' and 'cultivation' may not reveal themselves at all in print." [13]

EVALUATIONS BY ADMINISTRATIVE AGENCIES

Only slight experimentation has been undertaken to develop continuous methods for central cross-university appraisals of the quality of research carried on by individual scholars between the periods when they come up for reappointment, promotion, or salary increase. When a general university research fund is available to a cluster of departments and is allocated by a joint

[13] *Report on Some Problems of Personnel in the Faculty of Arts and Sciences,* p. 60.

committee of faculty members on a merit basis, these colleague evaluations become available to the administration. However, if the committee distributes its allowance on a "fair shares for all" basis, or if it merely follows past channels of distribution so as to disturb no one, its collective value as judges ceases to exist.

As a rule supervision of an individual's research by some overarching body, if supplied at all, is in connection with "project research" supported by government, business corporations, or foundations. A frequent procedure is that an officer of administration, perhaps a dean, certifies the scientific respectability of a proposed project, whereupon the individual is released to accept the grant or to go after funds himself, or some officer of administration is authorized to process the papers for him.

However much presidents might welcome an administrative formal court of appeal that would determine ultimately for them the quality of a man's research, second thought tells them that it would lead to the destruction of the essence of a university. Administrative agencies, which after all supply the funds and facilities for scholar-scientists, must pay due respect to the investigator's freewheeling right to roam, from which springs both the service and the glory of academic investigation. Although they may help by identifying inferior work, all systems of central review, even colleague review, of new enterprises are apt to favor the safe proposal, the one with predictable results on which everyone agrees. Actually the most brilliant discoveries have a vagrant habit of emerging from initially vague ideas, difficult if not impossible to describe specifically, with problematical possibilities of success or significance if successful. As long as universities remain universities, primary weight will continue to rest on day-by-day appraisals by colleagues expressed to one another in normal work associations, supplemented by their formalized judgments when a man comes up for promotion or is being considered for a call from outside. This is one effective aspect of the comprehensive self-cleansing process that the world of academic scholarship conducts within itself.

A recent development in the research field must be reckoned

with. Large proportions of research funds are now supplied by government and other outside organizations which assess the possibilities of success before a grant is made and frequently require reports of progress thereafter. How to reconcile the principle of organization with freedom to roam? The resultant strains are still unresolved.

Princeton is experimenting with a University Research Board. The majority of members belong to the faculty and represent broad areas of learning. It is ". . . charged with the formulation of policies for the solicitation, acceptance and administration of research grants and contracts throughout the university, and with general supervision over the implementation of such policies." The board has established orderly procedures; it requires certain conditions to be met before it grants authority to begin negotiations for a contract or apply for a grant. It inquires into the availability of facilities, prospects for employing the additional personnel needed, adequacy of the budget proposed, and the University's willingness to meet ancillary costs, all areas of decision that properly concern central authority.

The central board may demand assurance that a proposal fits within the framework of the university's teaching and research objectives, that it is soundly based and gives promise of a significant contribution. The board considers that its function is not to replace the ordinary processes of colleague appraisal but to see that all available resources for appraisal are coordinated. Here it realizes that it must tread softly, else it will invade the essential freedom and spontaneity of creative individuals. Its capacity to hew to the line between appraisal and freedom will be the measure of its success.

EVALUATION OF TEACHING

Inability to identify and assay the extremely diverse elements that comprise effective teaching and to weigh their relative importance torments everyone in the profession who takes teaching seriously. In the usual formal draft of criteria for promotion, teaching effectiveness rates at par with research. But when the chips are down, in universities it is research on which decision frequently turns. The professional vocabulary of university professors describes teaching duties in terms of "teaching loads." Although many would be the most unhappy men in the world if they were deprived of the opportunity to share knowledge with younger minds, one's status among his colleagues is apt to be measured not only by the amount and quality of scholarly publication but by the teaching he does not do.

The common charge that the stress on research above teaching in eminent institutions influences for good or ill the character of others trying to achieve eminence is substantially true.[14] There is, moreover, a widespread feeling among scientists that concentration on research promise and distinction will of itself return enough satisfactory teachers to meet the predictable needs. Departments with extrusive teaching responsibilities, as, for example, those with large undergraduate classes in English, modern languages, or mathematics, find themselves on the horns of a dilemma. If they place a heavy emphasis on effective teaching, they feel that their scholarship suffers and that their relative prestige among colleagues throughout the country suffers in proportion.

In common with the great majority of our faculties, presidents have not been enthusiastic about efforts to evaluate teaching by formal instruments of appraisal designed to introduce more objectivity. Indeed, many teachers insist that objectivity and evaluation of effective teaching are mutually exclusive terms. One thing is certain: a detached attitude free of subconscious bias is harder to achieve in evaluation of teaching than in performance appraisals of research. Educational literature contains

---

[14] Of course, such emphasis is not peculiar to the United States. On the Continent research ability is the essential criterion for appointment to a professorship. The subject has become a matter of public interest in the United Kingdom, where it is charged that the greatly expanded staffs of the civic universities are being selected primarily for proved ability in research. The University Grants Committee has sponsored a committee to study the subject of teaching in the universities.

thousands of words on the qualities of a good teacher and the need for methods of evaluating them, but most of it has been in the realm of the familiar or the abstract. It may be concluded that until new and imaginative techniques of objective evaluations are discovered, professorial reliance will continue to rest on the pooling of admittedly subjective judgments.[15]

One trouble with current appraisals of teaching performance is that the judgments are too often made at some remove. It is infra dig for both parties if a senior faculty member visits the classroom of a junior. Faculties resist direct appraisals by others —professors, deans, or presidents—which suggest a "snooper" examining how another conducts a class or delivers a lecture. Such a figure contravenes the traditional freedom of the teacher —even a beginner—from surveillance by others. Apparently, only a rare institution or a department within an institution has succeeded in creating an atmosphere in which visitations of class exercises and lectures can take place, even for the purpose of friendly criticism and to share teaching experience.[16]

At one university we were told of an abortive attempt by a former president who, from a desire to become better acquainted with professors and departments, innocently indicated his wish to visit classes and lectures if and as invited to do so. Many invitations were forthcoming, and he is on record as saying that attending a variety of lectures and teaching situations was one of the most rewarding and exciting experiences of his educational career. However, his active interest made him suspect by the

---

[15] Newburn writes, ". . . it is impossible to believe that serious efforts directed at the problem would not produce some practical results. . . . We do know too little about the effective teacher, but to continue in ignorance with the facilities at our disposal is inexcusable." *Op. cit.,* p. 36. Not all will share his optimism.

[16] Newburn believes that the traditional attitude toward visitation of classes is changing. One institution (of those he surveyed) requires deans and departmental heads to observe and report on their own reactions to the teaching of all those not on tenure. In one or two other places, indications are that senior staff members are being encouraged to visit classes and make constructive comments on the teaching of their junior colleagues. *Op. cit.,* p. 36. However, on our field trips we saw no measurable signs of change.

faculty, despite his assurance that his purpose was not to pass judgment, and he discontinued the practice. Granting the president complete honesty of purpose, the faculty had a valid basis for questioning his reassurance, since it is difficult to observe a teacher in action without forming some opinion-judgments.

We believe that this professional immunity of a young teacher from direct observation by his elders is indefensible, as is his consequent deprivation of assistance by the more experienced. It confirms the suspicion that the profession resists being judged on teaching performance, although it submits willingly to colleague appraisals of scholarship and research. Not to mention more serious deficiencies, young teachers are frequently handicapped by a nervous habit or two which they might easily cure if attention were called to them. We recall one promising instructor whose effectiveness was marred by his practice of moving his watch about on his desk, until his students began to place bets on where he would put it next.

For classroom visitations to work they must be more than occasional inspections for the obvious purpose of taking readings on a young teacher's claim to promotion. They must be a routine procedure, rooted in a desire to be helpful. They should take place over a period of time in order that they may throw light on how the class is developing, remembering that the teacher's task changes as the subject matter evolves from the simple to the more complex. The visitor and critic must be a judicious person, aware that one common characteristic of great teachers is their wide diversity of methods and mannerisms. Otherwise, consciousness that he is working under the observant eye of another who has a vote on his reappointment or promotion may impair the development of a young teacher's individuality.

One danger of occasional visitations used as performance appraisals is measurement by a table of techniques to the neglect of the fundamental factor, the quality of a teacher's mind. As Warren Weaver wrote us, "I do not think every good teacher needs to be a great research scholar, but I do most emphatically think that every really good teacher must be *intellectually alive.*"

Senior colleagues too frequently leave the young teacher to his own resources, without proffers of assistance or even expressions of interest in his development as a teacher, an example of prime professional neglect by the same men who would readily offer him criticism and help on a research project. Yet in many institutions a young Ph.D. may be more promptly and severely judged on his teaching success than on his scholarship, unless he happens to be a demonstrably poor or brilliant researcher. In our experience attempts by successful teachers to hold informal coaching sessions for young recruits evoked more enthusiasm from graduate students than from the beginners on the faculty. Support of the idea by senior colleagues, too, was disappointingly lukewarm.[17] We see no reason why the sensitivity (or laziness) of faculty seniors should continue to maintain the impropriety of direct methods of aiding and evaluating the work of young men. Young physicians, lawyers, and ministers frequently spend their first years in their professions under the supervision of men of experience and suffer no shame thereby.

STUDENT EVALUATIONS

Newburn reports that in the universities he surveyed, ". . . efforts which have been made to measure teaching effectiveness on a kind of objective basis, tend to center largely around student evaluations." [18] One dean reported to us that, in an effort to get

[17] Bernard Berelson recommends that *"All* doctoral candidates should have some actual teaching experience as part of their doctoral requirements, not less than half time for half a year, . . ."* supervised by ". . . an interested senior man . . ." deliberately assigned for the purpose. *Graduate Education in the United States,* McGraw-Hill Book Company, Inc., New York, 1960, pp. 248–249. At present, however, teaching assistantships are often overdone for the sake of meeting the financial needs of both the graduate student and the university. The consequence is that the student's progress toward his degree is impeded, and his teaching duties, performed under oppressive pressures, may develop in him a dislike for teaching which endures the rest of his life. However, service as a teaching assistant, if confined within reasonable limits as supplementary work for the postgraduate degree, can be made a rewarding internship for the beginner.

[18] *Op. cit.,* p. 36.

a line on the faculty, he used to call in the graduating Phi Beta Kappas each year and ask them who were the best and the worst professors they had had. It proved a poor arrangement for obtaining information; faculties are resentful when they discover a member of the administration "spying" to learn student opinion. The president of an excellent Eastern college each summer asks the members of the last graduating class to write back about their experience, including their views of the faculty. A few desultory attempts have been made to solicit judgments of graduates after they have been away from their alma mater for several years. We doubt if they are worth the trouble; at best they would be inconclusive, at worst deceptive. The reliability of the replies would relate to how well the inquirer is acquainted with the respondents. Does he know them to be representative samples of old grads? Does he know to what degree a nostalgia for college days or memory of single incidents has influenced judgment? Surely it would be misleading to poll only those who had achieved notable careers. Yet how can one assess the replies of failures?

When student ratings are made according to a carefully prepared bill of specifications and are conducted at the option of the instructor and the individual student, for the teacher's eyes alone and not for his superiors, with whom his fate rests, they may help him to improve his technique or to cure disturbing mannerisms. Yet several professors who had asked their students to assay the course and their professor at the end of the term told us that they had dropped the practice. One reason given was that the returns produced no fresh evidence after the first year or two, which may have meant either that the instruction was satisfactory or that the teacher was impervious to improvement.

One college testified that after many years of what it deemed to be successful operation its faculty ceased to use student evaluations as evidence in cases of promotion or advancement in salary, because it detected that they were being employed, consciously or unconsciously, as rewards for popular teachers and punishment for the unpopular. The administration reports that it misses the old system and now, after the passage of several years, a committee is pondering its restoration with modifications.

Although we believe that the students, the cash customers, have a right to express themselves regarding their teachers and that when their opinions are expressed in a responsible manner, they are not to be ignored, we do not consider that they offer substantial help to decisions on faculty promotions and advancements. At best they are as much a measure of the student as of the teacher, for a C student will apply a C level of standards and an A student an A level. How devise a mathematical formula for harnessing these and other variables derived from intensely subjective student data? One that will be an improvement upon a well-managed, nonquantitative pooling of subjective judgments of colleagues? This problem remains a challenge for the behavioral sciences.

THE INVENTORY SHEET

Pending more help from that source, methods of performance appraisals can be substantially improved, as to both research and teaching criteria, by utilizing not an arithmetical rating form but a well-conceived inventory sheet which directs the appraiser's attention to salient points and causes him to refine otherwise random opinions.

One institution we visited reported gratifying success with a form by which the department certifies that its recommendations for reappointments, promotions, and increases in salary have been made on certain specific bases. In evaluating the individual as a scholar, the department is asked to record, first, its judgment regarding his general standing as a scholar; to describe the fields of his special competence; to list his more significant publications, both books and articles, with dates, and to indicate which are primarily addressed to specialists, which to a wider audience, and which are school or college textbooks. The form calls for a report on the verdict of outside scholars on these writings, the names of the scholars, a summary of their opinions, and information as to how and where they were expressed. It further asks in what ways other than teaching and writing his scholarship has been shown and concludes with a most significant question: What promise does the individual give of further growth and productivity?

On his record as a teacher, the inventory sheet calls first for the judgment of the department regarding his general effectiveness. It then proceeds to specific evaluations of his performance as a teacher of graduate students, as teacher of upperclassmen, as teacher of lowerclassmen, as lecturer, classroom instructor, laboratory supervisor, and as supervisor of departmental students.

Each answer is developed with appropriate detail: the short-answer technique is not encouraged.

Finally the department records whether the recommendation was approved by unanimous or merely by majority vote and which ranks participated in the voting. Any member opposed to the recommendation may file a protest if he wishes. Besides directing faculty attention to the significant considerations, the inventory sheet helps to establish a common basis by which the department and the administration are better able to act in concert.

One reservation expressed about such a democratic process in departmental decisions as to who should be promoted and appointed from outside is that it runs the danger of domination by a forceful, high-ranking member. This is a hazard which the administration should be prepared to counteract. However, on the whole, we believe that the pooling of judgments ratified by vote of the department members of appropriate rank, and thus capitalizing on the "interplay of reactions and ideas" of the group, gives the best results in the long run.

The cases of junior faculty on annual or short-term appointments will naturally receive attention when the question of renewal arises. Others will be reviewed when a change in rank or salary is recommended. In fairness to all, the situation of those who have not been so recommended should be considered periodically, say, every three or five years. Accordingly, one presidential responsibility-discharged-through-others is to see that a system is established by which department heads and deans review periodically and report on those faculty members in their jurisdiction who are on continuing tenure but whose cases have not been raised by departmental action within the period. No one should be neglected, even if a call from elsewhere has not come or the individual has not been aggressive in pushing his claim to a raise in salary. Further, it is often as important for the administration to know the reasons that a man has not been recommended as the reasons that others have been.

THE PRESIDENT'S DIRECT PARTICIPATION IN CASES

We now turn to the strategic points at which the president may apply his energies in participating directly in individual faculty-personnel cases. Obviously there is a great difference here between the degree of involvement possible for a university president and that for a college president. To be effective the former has no choice but to restrict himself to important cases, which means essentially those that involve continuing tenure.

As in everything he does, the earlier the president involves himself in the faculty-personnel process, the better. There is no substitute for the habit of informal continuous discussion with deans, departmental chairmen, and faculty all through the year. There is no other way for him to get such an intimate feel of the situation, no better method for engendering enthusiasm for excellence throughout the institution. Informally, through the year, he can with grace suggest (some would say "insinuate") names of men of promise who might be called from outside and thus mitigate any opposition to them as presidential nominees. If he waits to join in the personnel process until the time for his formal decision has arrived, the president has little option but to approve or disapprove the recommendations brought before him. His usual routine is to approve them despite reservations he may have.

If he gives personal attention to tenure cases, he is in a better

position than anyone else to guard against the mistake of making
this profoundly serious commitment turn solely upon a man's
former achievements. Many a faculty has concealed within it
men chosen on the basis of their past reputations, whose future
proved to be behind them. Will the candidate continue to grow?
The faculty, or even a dean, may overlook this vital factor in
the glamor of an eminent name or thirst for quick prestige.
Incidentally, despite an occasional exception, it may generally be
assumed that a teacher who has reached normal tenure age without satisfying the usual criteria will not suddenly develop here-
tofore-concealed excellence. Kind departmental colleagues may be
optimistic about improvement, but the president must steel his
heart.

On the other hand, a department may not be ambitious enough
for greater strength or prestige to make it want to bring in new
men on terms better than those enjoyed by professors older
in the service of the institution who may themselves have coveted
the same position. Still, it has to be done on occasion. One president who carried a good faculty to even greater eminence credits
his success to insistence on departures from the normal salary
stepladder when necessary to secure the best man available. It
calls for persuasive tact and care to avoid giving the impression
that the president thinks well only of people brought from somewhere else. If such an impression gets abroad, the cleavage between the "young Turks" and the "old turkeys" will mar his best
efforts toward improvement.

A president demonstrates the art of leadership when he inspires older men to welcome imaginative new men whose philosophy
or approach to their specialties is quite different. In searching
out and calling new men to add strength to the faculty, he will
repose heavy responsibility in the faculty, where it belongs. He
will be meticulous as to procedure. He will not take advantage of
loopholes or chance the charge that he is "bootlegging" choices
of his own. If the president can involve the older faculty personally, they are far more likely to take pride in the addition of
fresh brilliance to their ranks because it is of their own doing and

are less likely to feel that the presence of new recruits reflects unfavorably on them.

Educator-presidents are fully aware that they are severely tested in their personal evaluations of the faculty. They know as well as anyone else that there is no precise gauge for predicting future intellectual achievement and that personality, as well as intellectual qualities, is involved.

Part of the president's 50 per cent of time for education can profitably be expended on interviews with candidates under consideration for calls from elsewhere. We are aware of the limitations, even the dangers, of appraisals by interviewers, especially when they cannot be conducted in depth under varying circumstances. Nevertheless, we believe that by skillful questioning a president can form some estimate of the quality of the candidate's mind, his table of values, his ambitions for himself and for his students, his sense of responsibility for the institution that he serves. The presidential interview is not an alternative to other appraisals but a supplement. On his part, the interviewee learns at first hand something of the quality of the man who heads the institution and the degree of his concern for the field of his specialization. An interview in which the president shows his interest in the man's work, elaborates the opportunity which the post offers, and outlines why the institution needs him may tip the balance in the mind of one weighing acceptance. "The president talked to me when I was here being considered for this position. It was an active conversation; he really challenged me, and I accepted." This is testimony we encountered more than once in our field studies.

The secret of a good interview, since the candidate is naturally under tension, is that the president establish a relaxed atmosphere and that he refrain from doing much talking. His questions should stimulate the interviewee to express himself freely; they should not be leading ones which suggest their own answers. He does not, like a clinical psychologist, concentrate on finding signs of morbidity, although he should be able to recognize any that appear. He seeks evidence of both strength and weakness.

THE PROBLEM OF THE WEAK DEPARTMENT

What to do about a weak department was one of the most frequent questions asked us on our field trips. To solve the puzzle, the president and dean must muster all the tact, patience, and, on occasion, firmness that they possess.

There is no sovereign remedy. Former President Henry M. Wriston confesses, "In thirty years I tried many gambits to strengthen weak departments. I was still trying when I retired." [19] A change in the chairmanship may be indicated. Or, again, it may only exacerbate the situation. The process begins with frank and friendly talks with the chairman and influential members of the department in which evidences of decline, gleaned from both intramural and extramural sources, are presented, testimony stronger than the mere personal impressions of the dean or president.

If possible, the department should be persuaded of the desirability of adding some new members of vigor and eminence, even at salaries higher than the average maxima, for the sake of the stimulus and credit they will bring and for their long-range effect on the whole salary structure. Everything said or done should be considerate of the feelings of those in the department who, while perhaps not contributing to greatness, have been bearing the heat and burden of the day.

Deterioration within a department is never easy to cope with. But when it has engulfed an entire school or college of the university, rehabilitation becomes an awesome job, and the president has no choice but to plunge in with all but undivided attention. The rejuvenation of the Stanford Medical School under the tireless, aggressive leadership of President Sterling is a notable instance. His success was achieved only through courage, hard work, and persistence in money raising, as well as tenacity in overcoming professional and other resistance.

[19] Henry M. Wriston, *Academic Procession,* Columbia University Press, New York, 1959, p. 108.

In extreme cases it may be necessary to ask an *ad hoc* advisory committee to review the department's program and personnel. Its members may be professors of tangential departments, or they may be chiefly authorities from other institutions. Naturally the committee works in consultation with the department. It is radical treatment, but the turmoil subsides after a period and may well bring about an intellectual renaissance, a happier and more co-operative department with a new self-esteem.

How can an administration or a department discover whether it is growing or declining? Although there is no absolute method of statistical analysis, some evidence is obtainable. Do the members exude pride in identifiable achievements? What do the annual reports reveal about their activities in scholarly circles? Do their publications receive critical acclaim? How do foundation officers and other qualified authorities familiar with the institution appraise them as individuals? Has the department's curriculum and research program kept pace with developments in its area of learning, or are there important gaps unfilled owing to self-satisfaction with old fields and modes of thought? Are graduate students going somewhere else after a year, for access to the newer developments or a more stimulating environment? How does the quality of faculty recruits compare with the quality of those who retire or go elsewhere? Is the faculty being recognized by calls to other places? If so, is the department able to retain its share of the quality? These and other questions are sample guidelines for self-appraisal.

There are occasional published ratings of departments in name universities, based on opinion polls taken among recognized authorities. This evidence is naturally considered seriously, but it is not readily available by similar methods to less eminent institutions. Moreover, there is generally a time lag involved, for the polls are apt to judge the departments by what they were five years before. Thus they indicate what departments were rather than what they are becoming.

REMOVING A FACULTY MEMBER ON TENURE

Removing the faculty member on tenure who has not flagrantly breached the moral code of the institution but who has proved seriously inadequate or has grievously neglected his work taxes a president sorely. "The most unpleasant thing I have had to do," reports one, and others agree, "was to arrange the separation of six men who were not good enough. I finally had to say: 'We have a moral commitment to you, but you have no future here and you should look elsewhere.' It worked."

As we mentioned earlier, the academic profession is better organized to protect a professor against dismissal than to initiate disciplinary action or accept public responsibility when dismissal or early retirement is indicated.[20] His faculty associates may desire that an individual be relieved, may urge it informally upon the president, but the onus must be borne by the administration, ultimately by the president. It is incorrect, however, to assume that faculties are indifferent to cases of physical incapacity, marked emotional instability, or major violation of the moral code. When incompetence is the sole issue, faculties are less inclined to act. They fear attacks on this score, for it has been

[20] In its report of 1958, the Committee on Professional Ethics of the American Association of University Professors concluded ". . . that the time is not ripe for a detailed code and that the most fruitful approach is to seek to develop a body of principles. . . . Any attempt to impose a uniform code of personal behavior . . . endangers the foundations of free scholarship." *American Association of University Professors Bulletin,* pp. 780, 782, Winter, 1958. In respect to the faculty taking the initiative in dismissal cases, the "Statement on Procedural Standards in Faculty Dismissal Proceedings," issued jointly by the Association of American Colleges and the American Association of University Professors, declares, "The faculty must be willing to recommend the dismissal of a colleague when necessary." "When necessary" is not spelled out, although it seems to comprehend an adequate hearing by his peers and an adverse conclusion by them. *American Association of University Professors Bulletin,* p. 271, Spring (1A), 1958.

When the time comes that faculties are prepared to adopt a code and enforce it by formal procedures, they will be less vulnerable to criticism for indifference to violations than they are today.

employed as a cloak to cover the dismissal of individuals whose ideas were unsavory to the trustees and embarrassing to the administration. Nevertheless, if the faculty's counsel is requested and proper trial procedures for disputed cases have been established, it can be anticipated that the faculty will prove understanding. If its organization includes a general advisory committee to the president, or a standing advisory committee on appointments, its cooperation will be extremely valuable. All proceedings should be kept most confidential. It is rarely necessary to invoke the trial procedures prescribed in the bylaws for dismissals; nor should they be utilized except as a last resort in extreme cases. The aim should be to secure a quiet resignation and to avoid needless cruelty to the individual.

Before concluding that forced separation or denial of future advancement as an impetus to depart is necessary, the president should see what can be done in the way of transforming the individual into a useful member of the institution. A frank discussion of his shortcomings with the individual, the department chairman, and the dean may accomplish this purpose. What he needs may be a new and different opportunity to lift him out of a dull routine, or simply overt encouragement. A change in duty assignments, a special project of his own, or freedom for some research may provide the stimulus for a fresh start. When such efforts at salvage fail, the president must face the issue squarely and persuade the faculty member to retire or go elsewhere.

Wriston[21] relates the methods he employed on such occasions. Because they were both considerate and effective, we reproduce them at length.

> In the course of thirty years I displaced no less than five men with tenure; four were full professors. It was done without a fuss with the American Association of University Professors. The method was simple in the extreme. I first checked—in confidence —with the man's colleagues, one at a time. In that way I got candid appraisals. Furthermore, no one heard anything said by a colleague that he could tell his wife, who would repeat it only

[21] *Op. cit.,* pp. 100–101.

to her best friend—until it was all over the campus. Second, I promised my advisers that they would not be brought into any unpleasantness; the full responsibility was mine and would remain undivided whatever happened. In the first two or three instances I journeyed to Washington and discussed the whole problem frankly and fully with W. W. Cook, then the executive officer of the Association.

Those steps having been taken—over a considerable period of time so that there could be no shadow of appearance of impulsiveness, I then met the professor—not in the office, or where we could be observed if the going got rough, setting tongues wagging. We met in my home in the evening. In each case I offered a year's leave at full pay, and in one case two years, in exchange for a resignation. The tone was calm, but exceedingly firm.

I had far less trouble in getting the professors to agree to resign than in getting the trustees to authorize such "extravagant" termination payments. For my part, I insisted it was a cheap price; in the long run some who had protested most vigorously came to agree with me. The college should pay some money since the error lay not alone with the professor; the responsibility rested, to some extent at least, with those who had not relieved him of his appointment before he attained "permanent" tenure.

In sum, the president's personal participation in individual cases is deeply meaningful. Advancement to tenure, reclaiming an unsatisfactory faculty member or a sick department, consultations with his deans and chairmen, or recruitment interviews—in each the standards he sets permeate the whole personnel process and either raise or lower the tone for all in building and maintaining a strong faculty.

CHAPTER VI

PLANNING, FACT FINDING, BUDGETING

One of the most common criticisms of our colleges and universities is their failure to plan. "Academic administrators," writes Corson, "generally agree that there is need for agreement about educational purpose to guide their allocation of limited resources. . . . But that they usually lack such a guiding purpose is attested to by most." [1]

ACADEMIC PLANNING IS *sui generis*

Today's rapid rate of social, technological, political, and economic change makes foresighted planning at once difficult and imperative. When well performed, the very planning process brings form to a future only vaguely glimpsed and enables a reasoned choice of attainable means for meeting its conditions.

---

[1] John J. Corson, *Governance of Colleges and Universities,* McGraw-Hill Book Company, Inc., New York, 1960, p. 122. He quotes President Griswold that the universities' ". . . sense of purpose is all but smothered; their stated purposes blurred beyond recognition."

For colleges and universities, planning presents certain considerations which do not obtain, at least in like degree, in business and which may make academic planning appear aimless when it is not. Academia cannot set production schedules, sales quotas, or the like in quantitative terms. Its aspirations being more philosophical, its measurements of success are less concrete. Moreover, in business, even with extensive consultation, planning decisions are reserved to top management, ultimately the president and the board of directors; in academia they involve the faculty as equal partners. Their divergent views must be reconciled in a more democratic manner in an atmosphere of stronger individualism. While leadership devolves upon the administration, it must conduct the process as a joint effort of faculty and trustees with reasonable concurrence by all.[2] Comprehensive planning should involve the trustees to a greater degree than is usual among the more passive directors of many business corporations.

To be meaningful, a master plan must be developed on the basis of agreed goals, and these should correspond to the contribution needed by the society and region the institution serves. That everyone should "be more like Harvard" (a frequently expressed ambition) would not be good for the nation. We respect, for example, the municipal university that defines its mission in terms of its own metropolitan area.

Corson cites with approval ". . . the success of institutions which have clearly defined and steadfastly pursued a purpose."[3] But they seem to be those which have restricted their ambitions

---

[2] We recommend that college and university administrators, particularly presidents new to their post, read chap. 1 of A. Lawrence Lowell's *What a University President Has Learned*, The Macmillan Company, New York, 1938, for a treatment of academic planning as pertinent today as it was thirty-five years ago. The author stresses that plans must not only be drafted but also be executed and admonishes presidents to retain the initiative in their own hands as far as possible.

[3] *Op. cit.*, pp. 122–123. He quotes Paul H. Davis, who "after visiting many colleges concluded that the 'best ones' . . . are usually marked by a clear, universally accepted, and relatively limited purpose." We add that, while such may exhibit a more uniform quality, the more complex universities can boast notable examples of excellence.

to relatively limited, although nonetheless essential, objectives implicit in the spirit of the place.

It is relatively easy to define a "single overriding purpose" for a Cal Tech, a Princeton, or an Oberlin, closely knit institutions compared to large multiservice universities. A true university, like most successful marriages, is a unity of diversities. Without such unity, over-all planning is more apt to be a process of dividing the spoils than a step toward attaining agreed goals. Thoughtful presidents of complex universities are troubled by insufficient intellectual unity among the parts. Without forcing all components into a single pattern, the preparation of a master plan is an opportunity to consider the interrelation of knowledge at its highest level, which a university—in contrast to a multi-versity—should stand for. The fact that a complex institution has many facets increases rather than diminishes the importance of well-defined goals, else it remains little more than a congeries of disparate parts, for which there is no educational justification and little if any economic advantage.

SOME PRACTICAL ADVANTAGES FOR THE PRESIDENT

Paraphrasing Eugene R. Black's definition of political planning, we may define academic planning as the process by which faculty, trustees, and administration are faced with an awareness of the consequences of decisions before they are made instead of afterward.[4] Even if the process results in no radical changes, a critical, periodic reexamination of traditional methods and ends is beneficial to each participant, for it tests "the faith which is by him" and its relevance to a fluid world.

A plan yields several practical advantages for the president. Physical plant development is more efficient if based on clear ideas

---

[4] *Diplomacy of Economic Development,* Harvard University Press, Cambridge, Mass., 1960, p. 32. Copyright by Fletcher School of Law and Diplomacy, Tufts University, Medford, Mass. Black goes on to remark that ". . . the concept of planning is bedeviled equally by the suffocating embraces of its idealistic champions and the cynical shafts of its detractors."

of the shape of future educational development. Is the student body to be restricted to slow growth in numbers, or are rapid increases anticipated? Will the humanities provide the core for a liberal education for all undergraduates, or will early specialization in scientific and technological subjects be the pattern? In the first instance, provisions will have to be made for appropriate reading materials and library accommodations and for an adequate staff. In the second, more shops and laboratories will be required, as well as staff.

Will the institution undertake to satisfy rising pressures for adult education programs in summer sessions and evening and correspondence courses, or will it restrict its student body to full-time residents? The first alternative creates need for new parking lots, a larger clerical staff, and a high-capacity mail room, while the second will call for more dormitories, dining halls, and recreational facilities. Will the institution admit all who apply with high school diplomas, or will it enforce rigid entrance standards? One course calls for accommodating a high percentage of freshman and sophomore students in the introductory courses, provision for remedial work in one area or another, and a larger counseling staff, while the other option requires more facilities for independent study, a greater range of advanced courses, and—in all probability—all the accompaniments of a research-oriented faculty. If plans for the future center primarily on postgraduate professional training, new faculty and buildings must be planned accordingly.

Every president is pressed by faculty for financial help to meet immediate needs. A master plan enables him to know with more assurance when to say "no" and when to say "yes"; it is a defense against imbalance in growth or makeshift and perhaps ultimately costly palliatives of faculty difficulties. Furthermore, a long-range plan guards against dilution by new, haphazard ventures urged frequently by people who have money to offer or are otherwise able to exert influence. It is against nature for trustees, as often for presidents, to refuse the proffer of a substantial donation or an initiating foundation grant. The glamor surrounding a gift tends to obscure its possible irrelevancy to institutional goals and the fact that it may entail an additional drain on the general budget. New enterprises have a way of beginning modestly and later ripening into heavy financial requirements. A comprehensive plan protects against unwittingly mortgaging future resources in the enthusiasm of the moment and makes it easier for the president to persuade his board to decline a gift out of program. It protects against corruption by mere dollar hunger. Further, more than one president has found that a well-considered plan helps him to attract gifts for essential purposes by inspiring confidence that the institution knows where it is going.

FACULTY ATTITUDES TOWARD PLANNING

Faculty attitudes toward forward planning are mixed. As we remarked earlier, the academic man's preoccupation with his own field of learning and his insistence on self-direction dims his concern for the welfare of the institution as a whole, while increasing his desire for more financial aid for his own projects. Yet a master plan should be more than a bundle of individual desires. Unfortunately, some we have seen did little more than sum up everyone's ambitions with but slight appraisal of existing weaknesses or programs that had outlived their usefulness.

Of course, no plan is realistic that does not evaluate the possibilities of adequate financing. The relative freedom of the faculty from responsibility for providing funds does not relieve them from thoughtful realization that an energetic administration, willing to live in reasonable danger, cannot be expected to provide resources to meet every desire.

Although a master plan should be courageous without rashness, it should also be more than a table of vague, worthy ideals with or without suppositive price tags attached. The president of one institution we visited was criticized by faculty members for announcing ideals but neglecting to provide defined targets.

Quick analogies with business planning are dangerous. Trustees experienced at academic planning point out that in business plans are subject to constant revision as new conditions arise and are therefore more flexible than, say, a formally adopted five-year plan for a university, which is apt to be interpreted as a promise of fulfillment by trustees and president. Disappointment that an earlier plan has not been fulfilled tends to create skepticism toward the whole concept. "What is the point of the president's urging a new set of plans when he has not carried out the earlier one?" is a comment we heard more than once.

SELF-STUDY FUNDAMENTAL TO PLANNING

The first step toward a master plan is naturally a comprehensive self-study. The impetus may come from within the faculty, but often it is in response to some external influence, such as pressure by the trustees, stimulation by an accrediting association, or a grant by a foundation.[5] The value of a self-study depends on the strictness with which it is conducted. If it is rigorous, it is bound to hurt someone. What has been termed "professorial courtesy" makes for colleague indulgence toward faculty weaknesses and deadwood in the curriculum. When a self-survey goes further than merely cataloging requirements for new buildings, more faculty personnel, lighter work loads, and the like, all of which require new money, and evaluates inefficient and obsolescent methods, failures as well as successes, decline as well as growth, its value is notably enhanced. True, "hard-nosed" appraisals of growth or decline in quality of educational programs or personnel are apt to engender bitterness and resistance to change among

[5] During the academic years 1952–1953 and 1953–1954 the Fund for the Advancement of Education made grants to thirty-eight institutions for self-studies of their four-year colleges. The results achieved and the several methods of organization and procedures employed are described by Robert S. Donaldson in *Fortifying Higher Education: A Story of College Self Studies,* published by the Fund in 1959. Some observers do not share the author's optimism regarding results obtained, believing that the subsidy bait, rather than a conviction that the study should be made, was the attraction for a number of participants.

those whose departments or divisions do not come out well, which is one reason why faculties shy away from them. But time will cure most wounds if the appraisals are so documented and presented as to inspire a sizable majority to self-improvement.

Nevertheless, the more typical survey, even if gentle toward colleagues, cannot entirely escape evaluations of weaknesses, neglect, and criticisms of inadequate and ineffectual practices.

To counter a suggestion by the regents that outside examiners be employed, the Wisconsin faculty in 1947 selected a university-wide committee which carried out an extensive survey of all aspects of university processes and policies, external and internal. The committee disavowed as presumptuous any effort to publish ratings of the quality of departments and schools, although many of its recommendations carried such judgments by implication. It worked for $2\frac{1}{2}$ years; its meetings consumed close to 5,000 man-hours, including more than 250 hours of students' time. Additional time was spent by the members in individual interviews; the gross total of man-hours approximated 10,000. The committee's chairman does not believe that so broad a study could have been done in less. While few of its recommendations relating to the over-all faculty were adopted by formal faculty action, he reports that over successive years a goodly number have been implemented by indirect action.

Although typical in other ways, the Minnesota all-university self-survey, completed in 1956, is surely one of the most all-inclusive of any we know. It was conducted by a committee of six with the help of four committees, each chaired by a member of the main committee, to which others were coöpted. Many of the findings were in the form of transmittals of the reports of the latter without appraisal by the over-all committee.[6]

No subject, however minute, seems to have been omitted. Its purview ranged from policies and procedures in the recruitment

[6] The findings were organized in fourteen separate reports bound in five volumes totaling more than one thousand multilithed pages. They are summarized and indexed in *University of Minnesota Self-Survey: A Guide to Its Contents and Recommendations*, University of Minnesota, Minneapolis, 1957.

and retention of a competent faculty and the university's role in instruction, curricular offerings, and research to better parking arrangements, a larger budget for speakers at university convocations, and improved methods for dealing with prospective benefactors and off-campus groups. Some principal recommendations were that the betterment of faculty salaries ". . . be considered a first order of University business"; that emphasis be given to closing the gap between the salaries of ". . . professional occupations and those of college and university teachers"; that at present ". . . the University had no choice but to be liberal in permitting faculty members to supplement their salaries from part-time outside employment under general control by the regents to prevent abuse"; that an all-university committee be set up to serve initially for a two-year period to examine existing curricula, to report its findings, and to propose ". . . appropriate action to improve the handling of curricular changes" in the several colleges in the future; that the office of provost, or dean of faculties, be created to assist the president in matters of instruction and perhaps with the recruitment and retention of faculty members; and that a faculty-administrative commission be established to plan new buildings and decide on space allocations.

The survey contains enough policy recommendations and proposals for further investigation to keep an army of administrators and faculty committees occupied for years. How many would cancel each other out in the process is one of the unknowns.

One cannot escape the impression that the survey would have furnished a more useful guide to the administration had the committee restricted itself to issues of primary importance and not diluted the significance of the whole by attention to a mass of relatively trivial matters.

While one may question the justification of a massive undertaking which omitted the penetrating evaluation that characterized the Pennsylvania study to be described in a moment, two obvious benefits accrued from it. One was a better acquaintance with university policies and practices gained by average members of the faculty and administration from reading the descriptive material in the reports. The other derived from participation in the very process itself, including those members of departments and schools who, in supplying statements of needs to the central committee, were stimulated to consider and evaluate their own programs and practices.

Two recent studies are worthy of attention for the exceptional sternness with which they attacked the question of progress or decline in quality. The 1959 *Report of the Subcommittee on Appointments and Promotions of The University of Chicago* is an interesting example of the sort of rigorous self-study that a university can carry out when it has the courage to view its problems realistically.[7] The investigation was part of a continuing inquiry by the Council of the Senate and its elected (steering) committee into the general academic health of the University. The subcommittee was appointed at the request of the council, and its report was received with commendable approval by both faculty and administration.

While many suggestions called for budget increases, the subcommittee confined its attention to proposals feasible through re-

---

[7] As noted earlier, this is a confidential document which we were permitted to examine and to which we have received special permission to refer. It was known locally as the *Harris Report,* after Daniel L. Harris, associate professor of physiology, who chaired the committee. The subcommittee had a broad charge and proceeded to collect a vast amount of data, which included the curriculum vitae of each faculty member employed during the preceding decade; evaluation (by his chairman) of the ability of each faculty member in respect to research, teaching, administration, and service; detailed information about procedures employed and reasons advanced for each case of promotion to tenure and each case of severance; and intensive open-ended interviews with numerous senior faculty members, as well as all departmental chairmen and academic deans, which sought opinions and recommendations regarding policy, procedures, strengths, weaknesses, etc. The subcommittee emphasizes the scrupulous care with which it preserved the anonymity of its cases and sources, even to the extent of collecting the confidential data regarding individuals by code number, so that the committee itself did not know the identity of the individuals involved. The analysis of these data was facilitated by the use of IBM machinery for the statistical portions and the discovery of methods of categorizing and quantifying the more subjective opinions.

distribution of funds currently available, a notable exception in itself. The body of the report dealt at some length with the controversial opinions regarding appointment and promotion and achieved considerable clarification of the underlying issues and problems. On any given issue, the subcommittee noted, there was a wide range of opinion, with the extremes diametrically opposed. Observing that these opinions could not all be correct, it urged the departments to useful debate. It further noted errors in appointment matters resulting from lack of emphasis on primary criteria, use of too many criteria, insufficient rigor in the application of sound criteria, and too great a reliance upon local sources for junior and senior appointments.

But, as the subcommittee proceeded, it found it necessary to go beyond a description and evaluation of methods and procedures into the field of appraisals. It concluded that while the general health of the University was good, the institution had lost strength in several important respects, owing in part but not entirely to the rise of state universities of real scholarly stature. Without naming any, it ranked the departments in several groups, beginning with those which had improved or maintained distinction and ending with those which, for various external and internal reasons, had declined, in some cases because of inadequate chairmen. Those departments that had made recovery in the face of adversity or had maintained their strength were adjudged in the vast majority of cases to have been chaired by men of rare scholarly distinction and ability or by men of unusual administrative skill.

A second rigorous self-examination was The Educational Survey of the University of Pennsylvania, begun in 1954 and completed six years later. It was directed by Dr. Joseph H. Willits, a former dean of the Wharton School, who was recalled from retirement as an officer of the Rockefeller Foundation for the purpose. The report is probably the most comprehensive self-appraisal ever undertaken by a major institution, including in its purview the board of trustees and the president's office.

The usual self-study is conducted with a minimum of help from outsiders on educational programs, although experts are called in more freely on the business side. However, the director of the Pennsylvania study stressed from the start the importance of outside consultants to supplement his faculty advisory committee, to put iron into the study by counteracting the tendency of colleagues to be too gentle to each other. As the first step, a committee of each school prepared a list of questions which it hoped the study would answer.[8] One hundred and twenty-six consultants remained for short or long terms on the campus and worked intimately with the appropriate schools, departments, and programs. Strong administrative backing was an important factor. So was a thorough system of discussion and review by committees of the faculty and schools while the study was in process. The fact that critical conclusions of the survey were made public created some problems; but in the minds of many public exposure helped to generate sentiment for improvement.[9]

As each recommendation was completed, it was first approved by the president and provost, then transmitted to the schools and agencies concerned, so that action on many began before the survey was formally completed. Despite some unhappiness, even bitterness, among those who were butts of the most severe criticism, there is wide faculty opinion that the survey made a substantial contribution to other forces which were inaugurating an

[8] The organization, methods of procedure, and principal findings of the study are summarized in a report by the president of the University, *Assaying a University,* University of Pennsylvania, Philadelphia, 1959, reissued in June, 1960, as a part of the final report, with added information and comment on the survey's continuing significance within the University.

[9] A number of special studies were published in book form, but the findings and recommendations as a whole were issued only in mimeographed form for limited circulation. The frankness and scope of the criticisms seem to have created resistance to a too wide distribution. On balance we feel that, if severe self-studies are to become common practice, their findings should be reasonably confidential documents. If they are to be published abroad indiscriminately, the candor and spirit of self-analysis which should characterize them cannot help but suffer.

era of academic revival throughout many elements of the University.[10]

ACADEMIC COST ACCOUNTING

An inescapable handicap facing self-studies generally is the same as for presidents attempting to judge the progress or decline of a department, viz., the absence of objective norms corresponding to systems of cost accounting and quality controls in industry. What a faculty does and how it does it are not subject to simple quantification in monetary terms.

The California and Western Conference Cost and Statistical Study for the Year 1954–1955 (printed at the University of California) was an exhaustive investigation of the possibilities of constructing a viable system of educational costing with full consideration of such factors as the commanding differences among institutions, diverse subjects of instruction, and variations in faculty needs for time to prepare teaching materials and to conduct research. The findings were designed for intramural guidance, and reports are that they are proving useful for this purpose. Nevertheless, if present signs hold, the time may not be far distant when many legislatures will demand that comparative cost analyses be made available to buttress requests for appropriations. Several presidents report increasing pressures from governmental agencies that unit costs be furnished to them comparable to what may be demanded of other spending units. Clearly their utility depends at best upon the wisdom and restraint with which they are employed. Failing this, they will do infinitely more harm than good.

Variations in local conditions and academic accounting systems, not to mention the difficulty of allocating overhead expenses, make the establishment of valid unit costs in even an institution's

---

[10] In addition to the two recent realistic studies described above, attention should be called to Arthur MacMahon, *The Report of the President's Committee on the Educational Future of (Columbia) University,* Trustees of Columbia University, New York, 1957, p. 282, as an example of a comprehensive investigation into the educational aspects of all components of the University and suggestions for improvement.

business operations a formidable operation, although obviously less so than in the field of education. The academic man has good reasons for distrusting the application of unit costs to teaching and research. Some presidents know from experience how deceptive their influence may be on the judgments of legislatures and governing boards in assessing programs of instruction and research and their right to financial support. Nevertheless, any college or university is well advised to record for its own use the comparative costs of its various departments and schools. Although such records of themselves form no valid basis for determining the excellence or worth to our society of a particular program of study or research, they are useful in raising questions, in calling attention to undernourished departments and schools, and in combating extravagance in others.

IMPLEMENTING A MASTER PLAN

Certain factors beyond the immediate control of the president limit the implementation of a plan and make progress toward agreed goals uneven. The personnel of some departments and schools will evince enterprise and energy; working with them will be a pleasure. Others, secure in their posts by reason of continuing tenure, will drag their feet. In spite of the most strenuous efforts, some elements will be more easily financed than others. The legislature may favor some and show little interest in others. Often gifts come through bequests or other sources for purposes either not contemplated when the plan was made or far down the line in the table of needs. Also, it takes longer for some needs to register in the minds of donors than others.

KEEPING A PLAN UP TO DATE

The preparation of a comprehensive plan which reviews and evaluates basic objectives is a major operation. It entails long hours of work by an *ad hoc* committee and protracted consultation with the faculty and administration while consensus is building up. The frequency with which it should be undertaken varies according to size, complexity, rapidity of expansion, and similar considerations. Most presidents would agree that it should not be attempted oftener than once in ten years. There are, however, real advantages in a tradition of comprehensive replanning at ten-year intervals. If it becomes accepted practice to anticipate a new look periodically, psychological forces are released which militate against institutional crystallization around the *status quo.*

Nothing would keep a faculty in turmoil and uncertainty more than to be summoned constantly to consider major changes in a master plan. Nevertheless, no plan can be viewed as ironbound. To keep it viable, it requires repeated reexamination to identify parts which have been, or are being, achieved and which are not, and to expose those which, because of changed conditions, need to be modified or even abandoned. The personal assistant to the president described in Chapter III can help him by calling such circumstances to his attention.

There is no mystique about planning that of itself fends off obsolescence or deferred educational maintenance. Primary responsibility for keeping a plan current by bringing desirable modifications before the faculty devolves upon the president and administration.[11] There is room, therefore, for a planning department within the administrative structure, not to make decisions but to supply and interpret information for others. One rapidly growing university we visited had assigned a dean to the single function of anticipating conditions five years in advance and developing proposals to meet them.

GETTING THE FACTS AS A BASIS FOR DAILY OPERATIONS

Academic presidents are well aware that "facts do not speak for themselves"; nor have methods of reporting them kept pace

[11] While a new president often begins by calling upon departments and schools for catalogues of needs and ambitions, the danger is that they may come to rest buried in his files.

with the increased complexity of the academic decision-making process. Many will agree with President Harnwell of the University of Pennsylvania that the president still "has to make many decisions out of phase with facts."

Any administrative action is based on a combination of established fact and conjecture. The circumstances leading up to a decision may be well delineated or known only in outline; its consequences may be relatively certain or almost totally obscure. Yet decisions must continually be made; the refusal to decide between alternatives constitutes a decision in itself. So the president is compelled to accept a responsibility for developments about which he can have had no sure foreknowledge. For him, as for business executives, ". . . a few facts skillfully interpreted are often more meaningful . . . than a large mass of undigested data. An executive's hunches are sometimes better than his 'reasons.' " [12]

This chronic predicament requires a degree of philosophical resignation on the part of the president, to be sure, but it also calls for effort to enlarge the scope of the known and reduce the scope of the unknown. The more facts, the better the hunches. To this end, various forms of fact-finding activity are found on every campus. Some of it is simple and routine, as the registrar's report on the number of students enrolled and the like; other portions are spasmodic, frequently highly subjective and esoteric.

The accounting systems still in vogue in many colleges and universities are one type of reporting which has not advanced *pari passu* with the president's need for information that will illuminate problems he must resolve. We heard more than one complaint that the institution's accounts were set up more for the benefit of the fiscal officers than for the guidance of management. Monthly statements of balances in the several budget authorization accounts alone reveal nothing about trends, and yet trends are one thing with which an administrator should be

[12] Edmund P. Learned, David N. Ulrich, and Donald R. Booz, *Executive Action,* Harvard University, Graduate School of Business Administration, Division of Research, Boston, 1951, p. 102.

in touch. Financial officers may object to, and deem unnecessary, the burden and expense of maintaining an accounting system that would answer every question that an administrator might ask. It is sufficient, some say, if the accounts are kept so that desired information may be dug out of them when requested. This we consider a too limited view. Surely one function of financial reporting is to suggest questions to the president and his colleagues which might otherwise escape them, not merely to answer on demand those they think to ask.

OFFICES OF INSTITUTIONAL RESEARCH

But fiscal information is only one segment of the body of knowledge needed by a president and his associates to bring their decisions into phase with institutional aims. Nor can they await the findings of periodic comprehensive self-studies, occurring at best at irregular and often prolonged intervals.

Consequently a number of the larger universities have set up offices of institutional research to supply a continuous flow of basic information. Some are offshoots of the school of education; others are part of the central administration. Occasionally, as in the case of the Bureau of Institutional Research at the University of Illinois, which is an agent of the provost's office, they make appraisals and recommendations.

The University of Minnesota was a pioneer in the field. The range of operations of its bureau, dating back to the 1920s, has been extremely broad. Operating under the supervision of a faculty committee, it has been more than a fact-finding and collating agency. Over the years its studies have touched virtually all aspects of the University's instructional activities, serving as a basis of forward planning as well as helping to guide current operations.[13] Its achievements are credited to the "involvement of

[13] Illustrations of the scope of its work over a ten-year period are presented in Ruth E. Eckert and Robert J. Keller (eds.), *A University Looks at Its Program,* University of Minnesota Press, Minneapolis, 1954. Copyright 1954 by the University of Minnesota.

the faculty as a whole" and the fact that its program has not been "dictated by deans and presidents," although, as was pointed out to us, the president's office and the deans make use of it to investigate matters of concern to them.

Universities have not usually entrusted such broad responsibilities to their offices of institutional research. The more common practice is to restrict the offices to the collection and presentation of empirical materials. Random examples are studies of the course of student enrollments subdivided into schools, departments, and programs of study; post-college career patterns of students; projections of social and economic changes relating to the number of students in the future and what their demands for instruction will be; the ratio of small to large classes with instructional costs per student, with reasons for variations; student dropouts with reasons; space utilization, with data on present and future needs for laboratory, classroom, dormitory, or other space; faculty turnover and major obstacles to faculty recruiting; salary patterns; and teaching loads and their distribution.

If the president and his colleagues find they are not getting what they need from the fact-finding operations on their campus, they may not have made their requirements clear or specified that the facts assembled be germane to pending decisions. Or, worse, they may not have ascertained and defined their problems clearly enough. In so far as the office of institutional research exists as a service agency to the university, the scholar's tendency to seize upon every iota of new knowledge as grist for his mill must be combated. Inconsequential facts conceal rather than illuminate the path of action.

Obviously the gathering of raw facts is a sterile exercise unless the implications of the facts are traced out so as to clarify the optimum distribution of resources. Prof. Lloyd S. Woodburne argues with reason that their interpretation will be accomplished more easily and more intelligently applied if the administration solicits participation by a faculty committee, selected on a rotating basis, whose sole function is to think and whose members have as few axes to grind as possible.

Here again the personal staff aide to the president, proposed in Chapter III, could be of great value. He can alert the institutional research office to the questions on which the president will most likely be needing specific information and the form in which it will be most useful. Indeed, the agency might well be an adjunct of his office. Since interpreting the research findings is just as important as gathering them, the personal aide could save his principal invaluable time by briefing and "translating" the findings of the research office's investigations as they are completed.

BUDGET MAKING

It is through the budget-making process that the hopes and dreams of educators are adjusted to the cold realities of dollars and cents. Spending proposals must be weighed against possible alternatives. Though inflated requests are common, each one is valid in itself and important to its friends. Here the president's opportunity for influencing education reaches its highest point, as he decides which projects he will cut back, which he will advance by increased allowances or new fund-raising efforts. When the document goes to the governing board for approval, it is his budget, to which his faith and credit are committed; its principal features should be a product of his most considered judgment. He cannot, of course, examine each proposal from scratch; his influence will be exercised through shaping and reviewing the work of others, in seeing that it is blended into a single joint product which will best promote the aims of the institution.[14]

[14] We shall attempt no more than a rough generalization of the various accounting and reviewing methods of the institutions we studied, by which the budget material is molded into a budget document. They vary between institutions, and there is a considerable literature written by experts on the subject. In some state institutions, governmental authority prescribes the accounting system to conform to the general practice of other agencies, in which case the university may have to prepare a parallel operational budget for its own purposes. If legislative appropriations are in the form of lump-sum grants, they are made on the basis of more detailed budget information

While broad budget-policy decisions ultimately take on the color of a presidential edict, they are with few exceptions developed in conferences with department heads, deans, academic vice-presidents, and the heads of nonacademic spending agencies, and in varying but lesser degrees with representatives of the faculty.

The process naturally begins with a careful estimate and analysis of anticipated income from all sources. The next stage is to work out and enunciate broad policies on which features are to be emphasized. For example, shall the faculty salary raises be focused on members of the lower ranks or those in tenure posts? Shall they be across the board, or shall the merit principle control? Shall new faculty posts and new faculty ventures be authorized? If so, what shall they be? Must high priority be given to a major program of plant modernization, or must it be trimmed back? What new capital developments are to be undertaken? Will anticipated income meet the additional operating expenses they entail?

At this point some administrations make tentative block allocations to component departments and schools and leave considerable discretion to the deans as to how theirs will be distributed. But the temptation to evade hard budget decisions by relying on ratios or general formulas must be firmly put aside. This practice carries an impression of fair shares for all and may be the most practicable method in case of an unexpected drop in revenue or legislative appropriations; yet it defeats the fundamental function of the budget system.

After the main points of a realistic budget basis have been hammered out in a preliminary way, the budget office calls for estimates from the individual spending units, academic and non-

---

presented for the consideration of legislators which, when approved, becomes an implied contract as to how the grants are to be spent.

In small colleges where presidential autocracy still survives, budget making is essentially in the hands of the president himself in consultation with his business officer and his chief dean. Even departmental chairmen may not be called on to submit estimates, and the faculty know little of what is going on.

academic. Along with the call it usually sends a standard form setting forth the several categories under which expenditure requests are organized and, in parallel columns, the figures for the past two or three years. With the general policy statement before them the department chairmen are ready to draft their requests.

At the other end of the budget process, final reconciliation of requests with resources in one comprehensive document for final presidential approval usually rests with a central budgetary group composed of both academic and nonacademic officers. The president may be an active member, although in big institutions he necessarily must restrict himself to policy matters, again entrusting details to his colleagues. This stage may give spending agencies a chance to appeal from earlier adverse decisions.

Naturally in the large institution the president's effectiveness depends upon the clarity and force with which he outlines major policies and how well his subordinates reflect his views. Yet if he lets the process reach its final stages before he participates, his influence, while not necessarily inconsequential, will be less than if he makes himself available for conference at the lower levels. Finally, throughout the whole process the president will naturally maintain contact with the trustees' budget committee, whose report is commonly accepted by the board *pro forma* when it comes to adopt the budget as its own.

DOES THE BUDGET MERELY PERPETUATE THE PAST?

A freshman president soon realizes that the hand of history is heavy on him; he does not write his budget on a clear slate. Basic operations must go on and be paid for against rising costs. So innocent a document as the catalogue listing of curricular offerings embodies continuing commitments, as do research programs that must be allowed to continue, even though current support has failed them, and the guarantee of tenure to large elements of the faculty. The relative immobility of the democratic organizational structure and the whole system of checks and balances characterizing academic decision making create further rigidities. "We spent this much last year; surely we have a right to count on as much or more next year" is a nearly universal attitude.

To introduce significant innovations within a year or two in the face of such inflexibility may appear all but hopeless to the president, a circumstance which helps to explain why some pass the burden of decisions to others while they engage in enterprises more personally exciting. Faculty members eager to change things or to promote their own fields complain that the very form of the budget document, with its parallel listing of expenditures of past years, holds the institution wedded to the errors or obsolescence of the past. "What this university needs to counter the weight of past figures is a wholly new scheme of priorities; we have no budget mechanism for arguing out whether a new professor of Japanese is not more essential than a new campus road." This was the complaint of one dean brought in to improve acknowledged weaknesses in the college of arts and sciences.

Of course, any attempt to build a budget that ignored the past would end in chaos. For one thing, comparisons with previous years' experience are a means, though an inadequate one in themselves, for identifying and evaluating areas of expenditure rising at an unusually rapid pace. Thus the very fact that budgets must be adopted periodically tends to raise forward-looking questions and to call the attention of administration and faculty to the danger of a laissez-faire assumption that there are no imbalances, inequities, or inefficiencies in earlier expenditure patterns, that yesterday's programs are unquestionably those most suited to society's needs tomorrow. Thus, with all its aspects of inflexibility, the budget provides the chief central instrument of control over the future.

THE FACULTY'S PART IN BUDGET MAKING

Beyond the initial formulation of departmental requests, faculty members usually have little to do with drafting the budget. Yet,

inasmuch as it is essentially a response to the faculty's voiced
needs translated into monetary terms, the budget is to a considerable degree the final assembling in one document of the day-to-day
faculty-administration decisions of the year, an adjusted re-
capitulation of the desires of the spending agencies. In one sense,
the budget-making process is without beginning or end and the
product of more consultation than formal budgetary procedures
themselves reveal.

The lack of stronger faculty representation in the adjustment
process is a subject of some complaint, although far from general,
where there is no provision for formal consultation with faculty
representatives. As Prof. John Dale Russell remarked to us, we
have no good evidence of the extent of professorial participation.
However, from our observations we judge it to be increasing, at
least in the area of more general informal consultation as the
estimates pass through their stages of revision.

Formal faculty participation begins with the formulation of
departmental requests by the chairman, possibly as his personal
judgments, but oftener as the result of conferring with departmental colleagues either individually or by formal departmental
action. His requests go to his dean for review and recommendation to the next-higher budgetary authority.

Because requests habitually exceed the funds available, the
dean is distinctly the man in the middle. He is duty bound to make
a good case for the departments. He is equally bound, as a loyal
member of the administrative hierarchy, to restrict expenditures
to income in accord with college or university policy. Several
schools in the University of Michigan have faculty executive
committees with which the dean regularly confers.

If the dean's recommendations include nonacademic costs, he
will naturally consult with the central business office before filing
them. On the other hand these needs, such as more clerical assistance and renovation of offices, may go to the chief business
officer, perhaps the vice-president for business affairs. It is this
officer's business to stress economy and efficiency. His decisions
about estimates on plant maintenance and operation and other

supporting activities are of the greatest significance. Of course, his business responsibilities cannot be divorced from academic requirements, nor should his views prevail concerning them.

At the same time the dean's superior—the "dean of deans," or the academic vice-president—may be going over the departmental requests, although he customarily awaits the report of the dean of the school. In formulating his budgetary recommendations he may confer with department chairmen as well as with deans. At Michigan the normal procedure is for him to confer with the faculty senate's advisory committee on the budget.

At Minnesota a small central administrative group compiles estimates of needs, covering the coming biennium, for presentation to the legislature. The president meets with them and, when satisfied, presents to the Administrative Committee of the faculty senate a general outline of what he intends to propose to the regents. At this stage he also confers with the faculty Consultative Committee, which usually does not recommend major modifications. He may also hold a discussion with the local chapter of the American Association of University Professors. Following action by the regents, the appropriation requests go to the legislature. When the legislature has acted, the central administrative group begins work on the university operating budget. The president, having approved it, repeats the same consultative process as outlined for legislative requests and finally takes it to the regents.

Reports agree that the discussions with the Senate Administrative Committee and the faculty Consultative Committee provide valuable exchanges of views, only rarely controversial in tenor, which give each side a better comprehension of the other's problems. One of the issues recurring most frequently is the use of money for salary increases. Three years ago, when the legislature unexpectedly cut the university's requests, the committee's views helped the administration to effect economies with least harm to faculty programs and morale.

At the University of Wisconsin it has been the practice for many years for the president's budget consultant, a member of the faculty, to discuss comprehensive budget policies with the faculty University Committee, an elected committee which habitually considers broad university problems initiated by itself or referred to it by the president. As at other places, examples of subjects on which the faculty committee is considered helpful are merit salary increases versus across-the-board raises, relative increases for full professors compared with associate and assistant professors, funds for new programs, and more money for research versus instruction. Later, when the budget has been approved by the administration and the regents, the budget consultant, who carries the chief burden of legislative relations relating to appropriations, presents an outline of it to a full faculty meeting.

The University of Oklahoma and the University of California are notable examples of formal faculty participation beyond the initial stage of departmental requests. At Oklahoma the departmental estimates, along with the recommendations of the deans thereon, go to a budget council of nine faculty members, nominated by the university senate and appointed by the president, together with three ex officio vice-presidents without power to vote. This council (also the responsible faculty agency for all academic matters, including promotions) conducts formal hearings, deliberates, and files its recommendations directly with the president, with whom final decision rests.

Faculty participation at the University of California at Berkeley, exercised through the Senate Committee on Budget and Interdepartmental Relations, is the most extensive and intensive of any university we know of. It is a partner at every stage of a complex procedure. The fact that it also reviews faculty personnel recommendations, as described in Chapter V, substantially increases its total burden of work.

Until recently, the faculty committee exercised a meticulous review of departmental requests, a most time-consuming process, inconsistent with capacity to render well-reasoned advice on larger issues. Recent reforms are designed to leave more discretion about details to the department chairmen, deans, and other staff officers within the limits of defined allocations and policies. Although the amount of work is still enormous, the faculty Budget Committee has been released to concentrate more than before on criteria and policy making. The process is a long one. It starts in the spring, fifteen months before the beginning of the fiscal year to which the budget applies. As described to us by Prof. Howel Williams, at this writing the chairman of the Berkeley faculty Budget Committee, the budgetary procedures will hereafter involve the committee at the following stages:

> The first tentative requests from the deans, based largely on projected enrollments for the year' in question, will be received by the chancellor early in the spring for the year following the next fiscal year. After thorough statistical study by his analyst and review by the Budget Committee, the requests will be discussed in June at the president's budget hearing, attended by his analysts, by the chancellor and his analyst, and by the chairman of the Budget Committee. The president will then set tentative budget targets for the campus. Early in the Fall Semester, the target requests will be revised on the basis of actual student enrollments, and, on the advice of the Budget Committee and the chancellor's analyst, tentative allocations will be made by the chancellor to the deans. The responses to these allocations will then be considered anew by the chancellor's analyst and by the Budget Committee before final allocations are made.
>
> From the foregoing, you will see that whereas much of the laborious, though essential, analytical work on the budget is now done by others, the Budget Committee, an elected body of the faculty, is given ample opportunity to express its opinions and offer its advice.

The last step is submission of the president's budget for the several campuses in the state university system to the regents. After approval by them, the appropriation requests implementing the budget go to the legislature.[15]

The universities we have described as examples of formal faculty participation in budget making are those in which the faculty's

[15] As Prof. W. H. Cowley reminds us, some states which have established centralized systems of financial control over their governmental agencies have included coordinated budgetary review of institutions of higher education. The topic of state control of financial operations is treated further in Chap. VIII.

part in decision making is well established. In the colleges and universities we visited we discovered no correlation between faculty contentment and its formal part in framing the over-all budget. The more the faculty knows about general financial situations, the better; but budget making is an extremely involved task, calling for both a broad grasp of institutional needs and a detailed knowledge of operations. How much the faculty or its representatives are willing or able to digest without regurgitating is problematical. We do not believe that a representative faculty committee is competent to pass wisely on the details of a complicated budget which is the product of months of study and analysis by deans and other administrative agencies.

We uncovered little enthusiasm in other universities for the adoption of the California system of faculty participation. Indeed, we found some opinion that a small administrative group was best able to provide equitable treatment of departments and spending agencies. In any case, the universal practice by which the ultimate decisions rest with the president and trustees, following conferences along the way, is the only serviceable system in the best interests of all.

The Harvard system of relatively independent schools and other components is reflected in its budget practice. About forty spending units submit their own budgets, on the basis of which the president makes his recommendations to the corporation. While the general pattern is one of a great deal of consultation in the formulation of several budgets, their reconciliation and authorization rests with the president and the governing board. There is no general faculty consultative committee to advise them.

TRUSTEE APPROVAL

Academic boards of trustees, or committees thereof, habitually employ the budgetary process as a contractual instrument of control more than is common among boards of directors of corporations. While in many corporations projected budgets are presented to the directors, at least to those specifically concerned with financial aspects, in others they are made by management for its own use. A director may not be called on to pass on an operating budget from one year's end to another. Usually he tends to rely on rigorous accounting controls, periodic income and expense statements, and balance sheets more than is possible for his opposite number in a university.

Several factors explain why trustees place the emphasis they do on the budgetary process. Budgets deal with figures, and trustees are more familiar with financial concepts than with abstruse educational values, which even experts disagree about. Here is one place where trustees feel at home.

Conscientious trustees feel their responsibility for guaranteeing the sanctity of fiduciary funds. They are charged by past donors and will be charged by future ones, public or private, with the duty to manage wisely and faithfully the assets entrusted to them. They have a keen sense of the importance of solvency.

Finally, trustees often mistrust, with some reason, the academic mind's ability to balance expenses against income. They should not take fright over an occasional deficit, and they should know that a college or university must live dangerously or die on the vine and that overconservative budgeting may be costly in terms of lost opportunities for strengthening the institution. But generally it makes good sense to be solvent,[16] and the president should be prepared to justify a budgeted deficit.

A president often needs intelligent checking by the trustees against his own spending inclinations and the faculty demands. When the trustees remind him that the dollar implications of a new undertaking, financed for an initial period by a foundation or private donor, extend beyond the term of original financing and ask assurance of future means to continue the project without detriment to others, they may be saving him a commitment which would rise to curse him later. Donors of buildings, for example,

[16] We do not share the opinion that each budget should show a deficit because it stimulates fund-raising efforts or that a budget must be increased each year by a specified percentage to demonstrate that the institution is still alive. Needs and opportunities should govern with due respect to funds that are available or can be made so.

usually assume that the institution should be willing to meet maintenance costs from current funds; and it is difficult, often impossible, to persuade them to include endowment for this purpose. To decline a gift may alienate the donor and discourage others, but to accept one that calls for extra income to support it may spell regret in years to come.

The budget enables trustees to trace the major trends of expenses and income and to raise questions with the administration. Another trustee service is to appraise the adequacy of reserves for meeting the contingencies they are intended to cover and to insist on proper maintenance of plant.

Reconciling dollar values with educational values is difficult, but it must be done, and it is best done when trustees keep themselves free of detail. They should trust the president and his colleagues in this respect or change them for others whom they can trust. A trustee may question the effectiveness of the student-counseling service or a special program for the more gifted and energetic students, for example; but how can he, with the time that even a most conscientious trustee can devote to the institution, express a final opinion as to whether its cost should be reduced in the interest of efficiency or be increased? But the president or a member of his administration should be able, when challenged, to validate the expenditure on the basis of experience elsewhere, the institution's own experience over previous years, and agreed goals.

Whatever hope the development of comparative costs may hold for the future, the costs are too embryonic today to serve as a reliable guide to lay trustees in approving a budget. Some presidents report increasing tendencies on the part of their boards to apply comparative monetary measurements with insufficient realization of differences in standards among institutions and the way costs vary among the several schools and departments of instruction. The president of one state university reported that it takes a great deal of his time and effort to offset the tendency of his board to make comparisons with institutions which are not comparable, to apply quantitative measurements where they are not applicable, and to equalize the costs of all educational programs without reference to inescapable variations in costs.

By its very method of compilation, the main budget document usually carries a lot of detailed information which defies interpretation except by those individuals who directly participated in its preparation, and even they will not be masters of all. Trustees, therefore, must rely largely on a condensed presentation, which regularly accompanies the main document. Its value, of course, depends upon how well it answers the sorts of questions which trustees naturally raise. As one vice-chancellor for administration stated it, "We try to see that their obvious questions are answered in advance. The real budget document that they consider is an eight-page summary."

LONG-TERM BUDGETS

Five- or ten-year budget projections, strongly urged by management consultants, are still in embryonic stages in most colleges and universities.[17] One presidential assistant remarked of his chief that he preferred to "fly by the seat of his pants." Many presidents do, among them some conspicuous for the instructional and scholarly improvements which they have brought. We submit,

[17] It is easy to overdo analogy with business long-term budgets, but the management experts are right in their criticism of the amateurish methods many college and university officers use in estimating future costs and in urging the aid which sound and inclusive accounting methods can render. Recently an instance came to our attention of one department in a university which estimated its needs for the next five years as requiring a new capital fund for laboratories and endowment of 5 million dollars, whereas a businesslike computation of all costs involved was 25 million dollars. See Sidney G. Tickton, "The Long-term Budget Projection: A New Management Tool for Colleges and Universities," in Dexter M. Keezer (ed.), *Financing Higher Education, 1960–70,* McGraw-Hill Book Company, Inc., New York, 1959, pp. 138–161. The writer describes from the accountant's standpoint the methods used by one small college in compiling a ten-year forecast and recommends a similar technique for others. However, no accounting and reporting system can correct errors in the basic assumptions or provide a formula by which a host of variables, great and small, can be distilled into guiding principles.

however, that their success would have been greater had they operated more according to plans implemented by long-term budgets. It is the latter that give reality to planning and keep administration and faculty "sensitized" to changing factors in the life of the institution and the constituency it serves.

Like long-term planning, long-term budgets are taken too seriously if they are allowed to develop into iron casts that constrict institutional enterprise. In no case should they be formulated in the detailed manner of the annual budget document. Their value is impeded, rather than advanced, by belief in the miraculous power residing in a lot of details, each one more or less supposititious at best, whose minor errors only compound the errors of the major estimates. Their utility consists in providing adaptable bench marks, against which spending proposals in operating budgets can be checked.

If intended to be stringent controls over spending, ten-year projections are tricky; they may sound more businesslike than they are, and our sympathies are with those presidents who say they're not worth the effort. Five-year budgets are more realistic. Because they can be made with a greater sense of accuracy, their preparation attracts a greater degree of serious consideration by participating departments and schools, stimulating them to examine present weaknesses as well as points of strength.

In long-term budgeting the temptation is to overestimate future income: it is easy for a president to be too optimistic about his money-raising ability. The anticipations of new funds included in long-term budgets are dangerous if they lead trustees, administration, and faculty to count on new money and relax. Less common and less serious is underestimation of windfall gifts and bequests from unexpected sources, which may come particularly to the more favored colleges and universities. The president of one of the smaller universities we observed had set a goal of fifteen new endowed chairs to be established in the near future. Early in the day four unexpected gifts to establish new chairs were received, each one acceptable but none among those he planned.

In this day of rapid change, forecasts of the course of scientific

and technological scholarship can become obsolete almost over-
night. Ten years ago many physicists anticipated that nuclear
research would all but monopolize the research interests of their
departments. But suddenly new areas, such as fluid-state and
solid-state physics, opened new vistas. New tools of research,
unavailable a few years ago, are enhancing the importance of
biochemistry for chemists and biologists alike. Indeed, chemistry
has changed so rapidly in many respects that one out of touch
with developments of the past three years reports that he is
practically an ancient in fields where he once felt at home. The new
emphasis on engineering science, something quite different from
traditional applied science, calls for radical modifications in
instruction and research; to implement them entails new costs not
generally contemplated a decade ago.

As such changes argue for flexibility, they also increase the
importance of expert and careful forward but mutable budgeting
as a guide for the future. Because scientific instruction and research involve increasingly large sums of money, an institution
should choose its fields of prominence. Otherwise it will be headed,
at worst, for bankruptcy and, at best, toward starvation of
other less dramatic but socially and culturally indispensable
branches of learning. The time has come when in the national
interest even the affluent universities must consider a more planned
division of labor among them to replace their present ambitions
to keep up with the Joneses in all branches. The same cooperation
is needed to meet mounting library costs, in which but limited
progress has been made to date.[18] Irrespective of any future
government grants, the day is approaching, if it is not already
here, when for a single institution the most practicable solution
of the problem of mounting costs of scientific research is to em-

[18] One aspect of cooperation relates to regional division of labor among
institutions within the same general area by which each develops fields in
agreement with others and makes its resources available to the others. While
there are a few commendable examples of such cooperation, the fact remains
that colleges and universities shy away from the superficial sacrifices which
cooperation entails. It is a mistake to assume that institutional rivalry is
restricted to athletics.

ploy five-year budget projections, to allot each area the maximum funds it can plan on, and to require it to decide how it will live within its means.[19]

The method which one university employs in forward budgeting may be described as follows: Some eight years ago, following a period of hand-to-mouth living and loose expenditure controls, it introduced a five-year budget, worked out with the help of a faculty committee and accepted by others as a means of implementing a reform program recognized as necessary. Provision is made for annual review and reconsideration by a consultative committee, and projections are advanced to keep the budget running five years ahead.

One of the chief purposes was to place a ceiling on requests of spending agencies by stabilizing expenditures at current levels. Departures therefrom must be justified as to need and by evidence that new sources of revenue are or will be available to cover the increases. The efficacy of the stabilization principle has yet to be tested under strain. The university has enjoyed more new gifts and new revenues from higher tuitions than were expected. A good proportion of the gifts have been for general purposes; and the problem appears to have been principally the happy one of devising principles for their allocation.

Stanford's recent experience with a ten-year financial forecast, which served as both a plan and a generalized long-term budget, is worthy of note. It was designed as a definition of broad emphases and a guide to fund raising rather than as a stringent control over expenditures. It was prepared first on the basis of minimum needs. This completed, tables of ideals reflecting more ambitious goals were constructed, and they were followed later by a middle program.

The projections were prepared initially by an administrative

[19] One provost's statement of the course of events in his university may be paraphrased as follows: In 1948 our physicists had a 12-foot linear accelerator which had cost some $50,000. Soon they needed one 220 feet long, costing about 2 million dollars. It was a great success, and now some feel that they must have one 2 miles long, costing 123 million dollars. Education has an insatiable appetite, and no institution can produce enough support to satisfy it.

group in consultation with the president. It was discovered that the way to attract and focus attention was first to put something down on paper and await the reactions of the trustees and the faculty Committee on University Policy. Following consideration and approval by each, the estimates, as amended, were adopted as a balanced forecast. It is anticipated that as the ten-year projections are updated, more specific long-term operating and capital budgets will be introduced, looking five years into the future rather than ten. Experience suggests that five years ahead is the maximum for a meaningful operating forecast.

In summary, budget forecasts are increasingly becoming recognized as essential and as helpful in revealing trends that might not otherwise be disclosed until too late, in formulating plans and setting targets, and in alerting all participants—including trustees—to problems coming over the horizon.[20]

[20] The five-year process by which British universities prepare budgets to support their applications to the University Grants Committee for their quinquennial allotments merits study by Americans considering a long-term budget for their institution. Although supplementary grants are made within the quinquennium when a case for one has been made, the significant estimates are on a five-year basis.

CHAPTER VII

THE PRESIDENT
AND SUPPORTING
ACTIVITIES

Supporting activities—business management, public relations, fund raising—offer presidents one of their best chances to buy freedom for attention to education. Although secondary in the sense of the demands they should make on a president's time, they are, of course, vital to the welfare of the institution. As indicated earlier, a reasonable mastery of the elements of administration can do much to free a president for his primary role.

NONACADEMIC PERSONNEL

Escape from entrapment in the net of supporting activities lies in finding strong subordinates to whom to delegate the widest discretion. If there is any truth in the aphorism that a lazy man makes the best chief executive, one example is the president's relation to his nonacademic administrators.

But engaging nonacademic personnel who can perform efficiently presents difficulties. Poor pay is one most frequently mentioned. Although numerable institutions have had to abandon an earlier practice of equating salaries of business officers with those of the faculty, the man from the business world whom a

196

president desires to fill a high post still faces a financial sacrifice.[1]

But the academic way of life supplies the president with potent arguments to offset smaller salary. The work is interesting, so much so that those coming from business cheerfully toil longer hours than before (contradicting the popular stereotype of academia); there is no scramble for the customer's dollar; the competitive struggle for promotion up the rungs of the prestige ladder is less intense and less searing. More than once heads of nonacademic departments reported to us that the opportunity for wider personal discretion under less bureaucratic controls brings satisfactions fully compensating for the cut in salary. One business manager who had made a substantial financial sacrifice when he came to his university said that he had never been happier in his life, partly because he found his superiors less interested in recalling past mistakes (which would have been meticulously recorded against him in his old corporation) than in his solutions of current problems. One businessman-turned-college-officer said that the need "to handle more work with a smaller staff" was an exciting challenge.

Social life in an academic community carries its own compensations for those who have become restive in a commuting suburb and are interested in ideas. The final incentive is the cause the institution serves.[2] The contagion of a president's own conviction of the importance of higher education to society can be persuasive with the type of person he is looking for.

To aid in recruiting well-qualified heads for possible future openings, some presidents keep a secret file of promising persons whom they meet as they move about. Competence in the specialized

[1] Many institutions have had to increase the compensation of nonacademic administrators over faculty ranges. After taxes, the discrepancies with business may not be overwhelming. See W. Robert Bokelman, *Higher Education Planning and Management Data, 1958–59: Salaries, Tuition and Fees, Room and Board,* Government Printing Office Circular 549, 1959, pp. 11–12.

[2] The attraction of the cause of education may extend more widely than one is apt to assume. I recall a conversation with a grounds laborer who declared, "It's a fine crowd of young men we are educating here." He wasn't polishing apples when he said it. H. W. D.

duties of the office is an obvious must, but other plus factors are required: talents and interests which will enable those officers to work in harness with the faculty, with whom they will be in daily contact and from whom they must win respect. The best work in the supporting activities comes from officers who do not merely tolerate the faculty but believe in them and take pride in their accomplishments. Accordingly, beyond technical proficiency and wisdom in worldly affairs, a more elusive qualification controls, viz., a sincere enthusiasm for the purposes of the institution in society and for the work of the faculty and students. Given this, many potential points of friction dissolve. Lacking it, nonacademic officers unconsciously exude a self-defeating condescension toward faculty, students, research, and higher education in general. The officer who, if in doubt, tells a faculty man that he will look into his request and will say "yes" if he can displays a more constructive attitude than one whose first reaction is to say "no" and then telephone him the next day to say "yes." If he must say "no," he takes pains to explain why.

However, a new man possessing all the plus factors imaginable but unfamiliar with academia will have to adjust himself and his manner to the nature of the academic man. The process can be painful and is not always successful. On his secret list, therefore, the president should note possibilities among the faculty whose teaching has related to the function of an office he has to fill; some have found excellent material there. When the chief financial officer or director of public relations has been a professor, he moves more easily back and forth across the invisible boundaries between academic and nonacademic affairs. One of the most able and respected vice-presidents for business affairs we interviewed came from the faculty of the school of business.

On the other hand, the nonacademic officer should not be the abject slave of the faculty.[3] He is, after all, the responsible

---

[3] At one place where we found the business manager universally acclaimed by the faculty for his competence and understanding, the president's wife wryly commented, "Why shouldn't he be? He gives them everything they ask for." And she proceeded to cite examples.

authority in his area. The faculty man who makes unreasonable demands on the nonacademic staff must have revealed to him the facts of life about business operations in a complex organization, including the demarcation line between collegiate authority and executive authority in business operations.

THE PROBLEM OF INTERMEDIATE ADMINISTRATIVE PERSONNEL

Without relinquishing their natural right to criticize the top officers of administration, faculties often seem more inclined, perhaps with good reason, to complain of the quality of subordinates at intermediate levels with whom they deal. Correctly or incorrectly, they are quick to attribute an appointment to the plea of a loyal alumnus who needs a job or to the influence of misguided friends who urge the appointment of a popular alumnus whom they would not consider for a moment for a position in their own organization. A president should be wary of such pitfalls prepared by friends and alumni, even trustees, who are trying to find a berth for someone who has not measured up to the demands of the business or professional world but would "fit in well" in a college.

As a protection against such pressures, as well as for other reasons, the capable head of a nonacademic department, who is most directly interested in efficient help, should be given primary responsibility for selections at the intermediate level, subject to presidential conference and approval but not interference. Above all, let the appointing officer view with a critical eye one who wants to work for an educational institution because he has not found in business or professional life the satisfactions he seeks, who is sure that his life would count more if he were working in an academic environment. He may really crave a life of semiretirement with appropriate status. Of course there are notable exceptions to this generalization, and all honor to them. What we are advocating is cautious investigation to establish that an expressed desire to switch from business to academia is honest and well grounded.

The staffing of the intermediate and lower levels of the administration is replete with problems of its own. The glamor and glory thin out as one goes down the line. The number of top policy posts is relatively small, and the line of promotion to more prominent positions is often narrowly restricted unless the institution is growing abnormally. Finally, the better pay offered by business for work of much the same nature is a more controlling incentive than for officers at the top. Colleges and universities in urban areas—and many are—are handicapped in hiring and holding secretaries and technicians who would as lief work for a business concern as an educational institution.

Unhappily, the capabilities of officials at the intermediate levels are apt to lie fallow because no one takes the trouble to keep them informed on what is going on throughout the enterprise as a whole. Such awareness would lead them to understand better how their own efforts contribute to its educational ambitions. We mentioned earlier how important it is for the chief executive to get away from his desk, to maintain contact with those responsible for particular activities under a member of the administrative council who habitually reports directly to the president. Only by doing so can he project the full impact of his personality throughout the organization.

One president we know holds a monthly meeting for all officers of administration, academic and nonacademic, of both the upper and the intermediate levels. He leads off with a report on recent significant faculty actions, after which others give news of what is happening and problems arising in their areas. As a result, all present gain an understanding of the significance of their work and an enhanced enthusiasm for it, far superior to that transmitted in meetings of the nonacademic staff alone. By taking the time to make a personal appearance, the president achieves results which no other administrative officer could accomplish.

One small university we know raised the morale of the whole staff by the simple device of a reception honoring all who had been in its employ for twenty-five years or more. Deans and professors mingled with grounds keepers on equal terms. To the surprise of some faculty members, whose lofty image of themselves at first inclined them to stay away, the occasion turned out to be enjoyable for all.

In striving for economy and efficiency, the business staff have problems exceeding, as a rule, those encountered by fund-raising or public relations officials. "Here somebody gets into a fight with the business manager every year" was the comment of one well-seasoned dean. Systems of central purchasing, inventory controls, management of automobile pools, provisions governing reimbursement of personal expenses, all necessary to avoid waste, are examples of fertile sources of friction.[4] Efficiency and economy in the management of supporting activities need not infringe on the broadest definition of academic freedom. The more efficient it is, always with due regard to the human element, the more it assists the faculty to do its work well.

Business managers are often more interested in better faculty working conditions and salaries than they get credit for. Those who take the trouble to establish a reputation for fair dealing and the time to explain why an expenditure earnestly desired by a professor cannot be allowed radically diminish their difficulties. The formula of one business officer who is generally considered successful in maintaining good faculty relations is this: "We explain why a request must be refused; we seek to convince the faculty; we try not to take the position that 'this is it.' It adds to our work, but it makes for better results in the end."

Unfortunately, not all succeed in following this rule as well as

[4] A classic misadventure of central purchasing was related to us in a tax-supported university under the control of the central state purchasing office. A biologist had devoted years to the development of a strain of fish for experimental purposes. So delicate were the young fry that the water in which they lived had to be filtered constantly through a special quality of charcoal. A functionary in the state office noted the cost of the charcoal and substituted, without consultation, a cheaper grade. Shortly thereafter, some half million young offspring were killed, and the professor's labor of almost a decade went down the drain!

they think they do. Business office personnel may need to be reminded periodically that academic problems are seldom resolved by recourse to a balance sheet. We recall the trouble into which one insensitive vice-president for business affairs got himself by calling on the academic departments for copies of all letters going out in the space of one week, as part of an investigation into the possible economies of a central stenographic pool. The faculty viewed the request as a violation of their privacy, and the reaction was prompt and decisive. As one trustee expressed it, the officer had not learned that a straight line is not always the shortest distance between two points.

A president's efforts to free himself from preoccupation with housekeeping may extend beyond attention to the fitness or unfitness of business officers to countering insistence by the trustees that he should be master of all details. Some boards which regularly approve millions for direct educational expenses may get all tangled in minor items. "How," asked one chief executive who was handicapped by such a board, "does a president develop his convictions about toilets?"

PUBLIC RELATIONS

No longer can a college or university succeed without planned attention to its public. Whatever may have been true in Emerson's time, to make a better mousetrap is of no avail today if you keep it secret. A president and his colleagues cannot afford a self-righteous rectitude or to scorn opinion of their institution. True, the term "public relations" suffers under a certain guilt by association, which doubtless led former President Hutchins to define it as ". . . a means for trying to find out what the prevailing opinion is before you act and then acting in accordance with it."

Nevertheless, a proper concern for public relations does not mean knuckling under to popular approval. An institution frequently finds itself duty-bound to a course that, far from exciting universal admiration at the moment, arouses active hostility. To sacrifice integrity or dignity for the sake of quieting dissidents destroys an institution's most honorable and formidable weapon. Yet the academic president, in so far as possible, should be aware in advance how an important action will be received by the public. Then he can take more effective measures to see that, if not approved, it is understood and respected. Thus public relations become a form of public education as an institution strives to influence its environment by promoting greater understanding of the nature of a college or university and broadening the climate of opinion favorable to freedom of teaching and investigation.[5]

As chief interpreter of his institution, and therefore the chief public relations officer, the president receives many invitations to make speeches and issue pronouncements on all sorts of issues. He should ration his speechmaking acceptances and strive to make every speech (and every public statement) count.[6] A few well-prepared speeches are more effective than dozens of entertaining afterdinner talks which leave none of his audience quite able to remember the next day whether he said anything about education or not. Being a popular banquet or convention speaker has its drawbacks. Yet a president should not spurn cultivating platform poise and power, for his publics judge him keenly on those abilities. It will comfort him to reflect that to be an effective public speaker he no longer must be an orator. We know presidents who, despite a weak voice and indifferent platform presence, hold their audiences by the cogency, clarity, and brilliance of their presentations. It is a high tribute to a president when the faculty reports

[5] Professor Merry writes us that in his experience Hutchins's definition is too narrow to fit the concept which leading businesses hold today in respect to their public relations. Instead of acting passively in accordance with prevailing opinion, they consider public relations in the active sense of an effort to change the environment. Whether or not one accepts this business view as good for society, few will deny that colleges and universities are correct in striving to create a better environment.

[6] Presidents have found it profitable to add a research assistant to their personal staff, not to write their important speeches and pronouncements, but to aid in keeping abreast of what is transpiring in areas of their interest and to dig out facts for a speech, an article, or book they are writing, or a public statement they propose to issue. Members of the faculty have them; why not a president?

that his addresses are always marked by intellectual content.

Requests for public pronouncements on educational matters or human rights cannot be ignored; thoughtful people expect him to take a stand on such things. However, our advice is to refrain from statements on political issues not immediately involved in these topics unless overruled by conscience or awareness of special competence in the field.

As remarked in Chapter I, many presidents report that they are beset by calls to serve in civic and governmental capacities. British vice-chancellors likewise seem to be drafted increasingly for various public bodies when a respected public figure, not embroiled in partisan politics, is desired. An occasional president makes it a rule simply to decline all drafts of this nature. But, quite apart from the public relations aspect, one who preaches that students and businessmen have an obligation to serve the state can hardly treat the drafts lightly himself. Of course, he must balance his acceptances against the time and energy available for his prime professional obligations. The faculty will be quick to note a president so heavily engaged in public activities that he must habitually turn over his work to others.

The public thinks of presidents as persons whose time belongs to everyone. It will not change its expectations voluntarily, for it cannot know the aggregate burden on a president's energy, time, and emotions generated by its demands. Presidents may fear that to decline to make numerous speeches or serve on public bodies will bring down criticism upon their heads, but this is not necessarily so. One courageous state university president reports with gratification how well declinations were received when he explained why his obligations to his institution precluded acceptance.

A president must make numerous *pro forma* appearances throughout the year, but he need not welcome every group coming to the campus or appear at every public occasion to which he is invited. How much he can delegate to others varies with local conditions, but we have met some who wasted a great deal of time in this way. If his predecessor has been overly generous, he may fear popular displeasure; but both he and his public will be surprised at how well others on his staff can substitute for him. By sharing the load of important speeches with his colleagues, he can develop a cadre of able spokesmen who will help to create a public perception of the university as an institution, something more than the lengthened shadow of one man. Speechmaking by popular members of the faculty may need to be controlled in their own best interest, but some members can be extremely successful in transmitting a good image of the institution's ideals.

Candor compels the admission that scholars and teachers have paid too little attention to their lines of communication with the public. Some should never attempt to communicate except to other scholars, and some of their knowledge is too esoteric to be shared with nonspecialists. But the more academic learning shares itself, the more it will gain for itself, and a faculty member able to communicate deserves more respect than colleagues are apt to pay him. A humanist, for example, who can translate humanistic truth for the public does more for the cause of the humanities than does the author of a recondite work designed for specialists.

ALUMNI RELATIONS

The old tradition was that the alumni are a hair shirt for the president. Some still are. But the early-nineteenth-century admonition of an Episcopalian bishop to the girls in his church boarding school to behave kindly to Presbyterians but not to "listen to their sinful talk" no longer applies to alumni. They are the solid rock upon which many a privately sustained college or university has built its position, and the tax-supported are increasingly enlisting their financial and moral support. If the institution pays them the compliment of assuming that they are interested in its high purposes, a gratifying and influential number will respond accordingly. Since there is no substitute for participation, opportunities should be found for them to help in ways other than financial, ways that carry the attraction of some adult education for themselves. To neglect these graduates is to open the door to the athletic fanatic who is ready to move into any vacuum open to him.

Many colleges and universities report success in cultivating and satisfying serious expectations among alumni by arranging symposia and seminars for them under faculty leadership on topics of current significance. A program for bringing back key graduates for two-day sessions to observe the growth of the institution since their graduation and to listen to deans and professors describe it is an instrument of adult education, effective in more ways than one. The same is true for conferences of nonalumni on topics of professional or citizen interest in which the faculty share. If faculty participation is wisely rationed and distributed, the experience is as good for them as for their guests.

THE DIRECTOR OF PUBLIC RELATIONS

Directors of public relations are designated by various titles, but all colleges and universities have them; their functions are similar and cover a wide range. At one end, public relations means preparing and handing out press releases, cultivating reporters, placing favorable stories and articles where they will do the most good, and striving to reduce the impact of unhappy news.[7] At the other end, it touches almost everything the institution does. Here the director becomes a high-echelon officer, advising the president and his colleagues on the public-opinion aspects of policies under consideration as well as how to prepare for and meet criticism and attacks. He is thus an officer of both offense and defense.

In his search for a head of this department, a president should look, even more than in the case of business officers, beyond practical competence gained from experience as a professional journalist or newspaperman or in the public relations department

[7] In small places these activities are part of the work of the director of public relations. In the larger they may be grouped in a division of public information under the public relations director, who should be given over-all responsibilities.

of a business corporation. If a brilliant newspaper reporter or editor is conditioned to dealing with spot news, he may not even perceive the possibilities for bringing to public notice the more intellectual activities that are the life of the institution but are hardly headline material. Thus, the president's criteria include capacity for mingling with the faculty and administration to learn what they are doing, coupled with the ability to stimulate and help them to make it known to a potentially interested audience. More than faculty members realize, the public's portrait of their institution is painted by their own hands. The most eminent institutions have enhanced their popular prestige when the writings of their professors or reports of research achievements have been presented so as to interest a lay audience.

Accordingly, the ideal public relations director makes no pretense of being a scholar, but he possesses breadth of culture and a sensitivity to scholarly life; he reads and can discuss some of the books which the faculty read. The faculty will receive such a person almost as one of their own. We know one, well qualified in the technical aspects of his work, who received the highest accolade within the power of the faculty when he was asked to help in one of its history courses. The ideal public relations officer is worthy of membership in the president's inner circle of administrators as one whose opinions are respected apart from his proficiency as an expert. The rule to follow is the same as for the selection of a psychiatrist: find one whose counsel you might solicit even if he were not a psychiatrist. He should be able to qualify as the president's coordinator of alumni programs. He should save the president from involvement in small fires of adverse publicity and be his counselor and friend in dealing with larger conflagrations.[8]

[8] We have noted how disturbed some presidents can become over minor instances of adverse publicity and how, by involving themselves in them, they can add fuel to the flames. Yet such are often signs of life and create opportunities for a proficient public relations officer to present some aspect of educational policy to an audience more attentive than usual. Patience and skillful presentation of the college or university's position will turn a goodly

An efficient public relations department can often handle complaining letters better than an official in charge of a special function, since it is in broader touch with what is going on. A president receives many letters beginning, "I am writing you because I believe in going directly to the top," when it would not occur to the writer to demand the personal attention of the president of a business corporation.

To be bowed down under the weight of correspondence is almost an occupational hallmark of academic presidents, particularly those who esteem the "personal touch." As one such remarked, "I don't own the University. It's owned by its friends. Therefore, I've got to give in a letter my reasons for saying 'no.'" One president boasted that he wrote only three or four letters a day; but we suspect his university suffered by it. Well-handled correspondence is an effective medium of understanding, but no president of a large institution can afford to think that he is the only one who can conduct it.

A proficient director will not neglect the influence of minor employees as public relations agents. Library attendants, secretaries, reception clerks, campus policemen, and janitors convey to the public impressions, good or bad, of the spirit of the place.

FUND RAISING

Colleges and universities have learned that they must organize their fund raising. The new president who strikes an agreement with his trustees that he will not be asked to engage in it (some have done so) soon discovers how naïve he was. Trustees may give

number who were hostile at first into supporters or, if not supporters, into neutrals. Of course, there will always be some irreconcilables. President Case of Colgate illustrates the situation by a story of one of his trustees when some complaining alumni were demanding that certain institutional policies be changed. The trustee likened the situation to a father who might be troubled and indignant when a young man made a pass at his daughter but would be even more concerned if no passes were made at all.

generously from their own pockets, but few are energetic canvassers of others.

Moreover, there are occasions when a trustee, even if he feels he has personal influence with a prospective donor, cannot substitute for the president. "If the matter is so important, why didn't the president come to see me?" may be an excuse for escape, but it may also close a door that would have been open to the president.

If a president believes in his cause, why should he consider money raising degrading when spending it is so honorable? But, whatever his attitude, if he is not to be submerged in it, he must have the help of what has come to be called, euphemistically, the "development office." [9] It can save him a lot of time for his educational interests by discovering potential givers, analyzing their proclivities, arranging plans of attack, and seeing that when the president is the man to make the approach, he is well briefed and, when necessary, the way is prepared for him by others. Unless the president knows the individual from past contacts, he will usually have little success with a "cold canvass."

Whether the organization chart places the head of the development office under the director of public relations or not, the requirement that the two work in harmony is obvious. We observed that not all do. The development head must keep in close touch with the faculty. Without their cooperation, his work will be fatally impeded.

Let the president remember, however, that donors—even loyal alumni—do not make substantial gifts simply for personal or sentimental reasons. Usually it is present excellence or potential for enhanced service of significance that first catches their eye. As they learn more of the possibilities for bettering these aspects,

[9] While the public are still inclined to view a professional money raiser with a somewhat jaundiced eye, his counsel regarding techniques is helpful to a college or university setting up a development office for the first time. When an institution mounts a general financial campaign, his assistance has come to be considered virtually indispensable. An *Educational Fund Raising Guide,* compiled by the American Alumni Council, surveys methods pursued in selected institutions, with some practical advice to beginners.

their interest is kindled. Here a professor can be an effective aide; often he can explain the implications of an enterprise and answer questions better than a president. "Actually the faculty are the best money raisers. We use them constantly." This was said by a vice-president of a university renowned for its scholarship. In considering grants, foundation officers appraise professors as they do the president or even more acutely.

CHAPTER VIII

THE DOMAIN OF
THE TRUSTEES

With few exceptions boards of control of non-tax-supported institutions are self-perpetuating.[1] The principal exception is the growing custom of admitting alumni representatives chosen by the alumni at large or an organization thereof. In state universities the members are of course chosen by external governmental action, as in appointment by the governor, election by the people, or election by the state legislature. Although the members of the boards of control in state universities are frequently designated "regents," we shall usually refer to them as "trustees," for that is what they are. With occasional statutory or constitutional exceptions, the legal powers of trustees over the institution are

[1] The growing practice of alumni election of a minority does not remove the center of gravity of policy making from the self-perpetuating element. In church-related colleges and universities the boards may include a proportion of ex officio church representation or require that all or a certain percentage of the membership be elected by a synod or similar body. It may occur that all members chosen by the board be subject to approval by some church body. The boards of control of Catholic colleges and universities are constituted in a variety of ways and may include representatives of the church hierarchy, the religious order which manages the institution, and sometimes the laity. The organization of Catholic institutions is worthy of study by non-Catholics, but for the sake of simplicity we have not considered them in this report.

complete. As many writers have noted, they possess, so far as the law is concerned, dictatorial power over all phases of its life. The system works, as Sir Eric Ashby has observed in respect to Anglo-Saxon political institutions, only because those in authority refrain from exercising their full powers.

In recent years, a number of writers have pointed out with misgivings certain developments which can best be summarized as "erosion" of the traditional functions and powers of the boards of state institutions.[2] In a number of states the tax-supported colleges and universities have been caught up in a general movement for consolidation of all administrative departments and agencies under the control of the central executive as a means of securing greater efficiency and economy. For typical state services this has proved a desirable reform. The trouble has arisen from a too extreme policy of assimilating the function of higher education to these other services of government.[3] It is difficult, for

[2] Malcolm Moos and Francis E. Rourke explore the impact of state administrative controls, and the politics of the legislature and of the governor's office, on the management of state colleges and universities, and point out instances where these political forces have invaded the earlier authority of their boards. *The Campus and the State,* Johns Hopkins Press, Baltimore, 1959. Lyman A. Glenny examines the several forms of state-wide coordination of public institutions, including the creation of "superboards." He provides illustrations of their effects on the principle of spreading among two or more bodies or agencies authority and responsibility once entrusted to a single lay body. *Autonomy of Public Colleges: The Challenge of Coordination,* McGraw-Hill Book Company, Inc., New York, 1959.

[3] In this era of rapid expansion of public education facilities and vigorous competition from other public welfare services, the taxpayer naturally worries about needless duplication of facilities and educational programs. Moreover, some prominent examples of waste in institutional management have given the centralizers a toe hold. Some presidents have sensibly protected their universities by bringing about greater cooperation in program and budget planning among all tax-supported institutions of higher education. Indiana is a prominent example of a state in which planning has included the privately sustained as well.

Some believe that the erosion of the rightful powers of the governing boards of state universities has not generally been as great as particular cases suggest and that the threat has spent itself. For example, the legislature of California, although refusing to give the state colleges constitutional status similar to that of the University, has acted to free them from detailed financial

example, to see why a state agency should have the power of review of salaries of new appointees above $10,000 after approval by the joint board of the four state universities and why it should feel a particular competence qualifying it to disallow such a salary for a position in a teaching hospital. Herman Donovan summarizes some of his difficulties as president of the University of Kentucky:[4]

> Only in recent years has there been a tendency to take away from governing boards their administrative authority, and to transfer to other State agencies one power after another. State agencies are chipping away the authority long exercised by the trustees of educational institutions, and the universities are slipping away from them. The issue is whether the trustees and the president administer the university, or someone else runs the university.

The "constitutional" universities in such states as California, Michigan, Wisconsin, and Minnesota have been leaders in the development of topflight programs in public institutions. Although they are subject to legislative financial control and are naturally sensitive to legislative wishes, they prize their constitutional position and attribute a share of their success to their greater freedom as a "fourth branch" of state government, relatively free of harassment by other state boards and agencies.

We noted earlier that trustees have in practice or by specific resolution delegated broad discretionary powers in educational matters to the administration and the faculty, retaining of course an ultimate but seldom-exercised legal authority. The result is a sort of bicameral system in which the upper house, the trustees, while taking many unilateral decisions in nonacademic affairs,

---

controls. Nevertheless, we agree that vigilance is indicated toward proposals to absorb the university in the administrative structure of the state government, although the threat will not be met by blind, all-out resistance to forces favoring great control. If the time comes, as Prof. Algo Henderson foresees, when state legislatures come to demand unit costs as a basis for their appropriations, the freedom of the universities and the services they render will be seriously impaired.

[4] *Keeping the University Free and Growing,* The University of Kentucky Press, Lexington, Ky., 1959, p. 79.

approve much as a matter of course the decisions taken by the lower house, the faculty, in the area of its accepted professional discretion.

Unfortunately for the efficient operation of the system, the two houses often live apart from each other in all but noncommunicating compartments, except in so far as the president is able to act as a medium of communication between them. Yet, as Harold W. Stoke correctly remarks, this ". . . apparently slight and legalistic relationship . . . is not the measure of their influence upon each other"; for "The board of trustees is a brooding force, present in spirit even when not present in body, frequently exerting influence informally more effectively than by formal resolutions." [5] Many experienced college presidents will testify that the faculty is also a "brooding force" over trustee deliberations, exerting an influence beyond what it incorporates in formal resolutions or communiqués to the board.

THE "MODERN" TRUSTEE IS MORE UNDERSTANDING

The delicate relationship between the layman, who on behalf of society exercises ultimate control, and the expert, with his special professional competence, is replete with difficulties which have not been resolved in academia any more than in government. Some tension is inevitable and desirable, for if trustees on the one hand and faculty on the other are making the contribution expected of them, their views may well diverge at least at the beginning.

Although not all is constant sweetness and light between the two, our leading colleges and universities have made notable improvements in the relationship with consequent greater unity toward a common goal. David Riesman observes that at a time when academic life in America is becoming increasingly commercial, nonacademic life is becoming more intellectual. This

[5] *The American College President,* Harper & Brothers, New York, 1959, p. 72.

"evening out" is reflected in the governing boards of our colleges and universities. The more informed trustee is beginning to set a pattern for the future, disproving Veblen's assertion of forty years ago that the life of a businessman unfits him either to understand or to respect disinterested scholarship.

In moments of discouragement college teachers may remind themselves that trustees whom they taught as undergraduates are usually more respectful of academic freedom and more informed about the propriety of faculty self-government than were their predecessors a generation or two ago. The modern trustee is working to mitigate the evils of the "natural hostility" of faculty toward trustees as mere businessmen and of trustees to faculty as temperamental theorists who have "never met a payroll." [6]

Naturally not all college and university boards are yet filled with members of this modern school of thought. One can assemble a fair assortment who, perhaps subconsciously, still view faculty members as their hired employees, predisposed to subversive tendencies, who must be watched and repressed. They are, however, no longer dominant elements in our pace-setting institutions, and we submit that their days are numbered. It bears repeating that academia is successfully erecting its own defenses against

[6] There is a growing literature on the subject of trustees. To those interested in the development of the function of lay boards, we recommend four publications: *The Role of the Trustees of Columbia University,* the Report of the Special Trustee Committee Adopted by the Trustees, Nov. 4, 1957; Morton A. Rauh, *College Trusteeship,* Institute for College and University Administrators, Boston, 1958; Donald R. Belcher, *The Board of Trustees of the University of Pennsylvania,* University of Pennsylvania Press, Philadelphia, 1960; and Beardsley Ruml and Donald H. Morrison, *Memo to a College Trustee,* McGraw-Hill Book Company, Inc., New York, 1959. Trustees are coming to examine more seriously their place in academic governance as evidenced, for example, by the Association of Governing Boards of State Universities and Allied Institutions and by the conferences for college and university trustees conducted by the Institute for College and University Administrators. The Belcher study was made at the invitation of the Pennsylvania board and represented a commendable willingness to submit itself to investigation by an outside consultant, a practice that might well be followed by others we have encountered.

them. As such trustees pass from the scene, they are increasingly being replaced by younger men with a more enlightened point of view.

THE LAY BOARD VALIDATED

Though a challenge to their right to exist crops up now and then in professorial writings, lay boards are not the major issue in academic circles that they were a generation ago. While many faculties would like to be represented on them, only occasionally does a writer argue for the professional syndicalism of Oxford or Cambridge, a system suffering attrition by virtue of growth in size, activities, and costs and expanding governmental aid and control.

America's prevailing system of nonfaculty boards of control was first formally established by specific provision in the Yale Charter of 1701. Princeton followed in its Charter of 1746. In adopting the trustee system the founders of Princeton appear to have been influenced by the example of the dissenting academies of England as well as by the Oxford and Cambridge Colleges, from which nonconformists were legally excluded. Although at first the governing structures of Harvard and of William and Mary followed the precedent of the English university colleges with a heavy element of faculty governance, after considerable contention they succumbed to what was to become our universal pattern of lay boards.

As Prof. W. H. Cowley has pointed out, however, lay trustees were not an American invention. As early as the fifteenth and sixteenth centuries, Italian universities had come under the supervision of civic boards. As James B. Conant has pointed out in respect to the early universities,[7]

Leyden, Franeker, Groningen and Utrecht, all founded before 1637, were established with boards of from three to six curators

[7] "Academic Patronage and Superintendence," *Harvard Educational Review*, p. 315, May, 1938.

or trustees who had general supervision over the university, including the power of making appointments. A similar arrangement was put into effect when Goettingen was founded in 1737, and was copied by certain German universities in the late eighteenth century. . . . This method of university organization persisted into the nineteenth century. . . .

Eventually, of course, all came under the control of the state. Nor are lay boards today peculiar to America.[8] Apart from Oxford and Cambridge, the universities of the United Kingdom, as well as those throughout the British Commonwealth generally, are governed by external boards on which laymen constitute a majority, with some university faculty representation. On the Continent the alternative to lay boards is oversight by a governmental agency representing the public's interest. Evidence abounds that government can get in the way of faculty ambitions as readily as can lay boards.

The so-called golden age of professorial freedom from external supervision at Oxford and Cambridge, which extended throughout the eighteenth century into the first half of the nineteenth, was actually one marked by somnolence ". . . more scandalous," writes Trevelyan, "than the lighter and more broken slumbers of the church." The well-entrenched dons and professors were impervious to society's demands, a blindness all the more culpable because the period was one distinguished for its vigor of intellectual inquiry by laymen with no university connection and by the faculties of the dissenting academies and the Scottish universities, who had ". . . freed themselves from the medieval scheme of studies."

It took three successive parliamentary inquiries within a span of seventy years to accomplish reform. "Though in the minds of many university people such [royal] commissions and ensuing regulations constituted undue interference . . . there is no doubt that the recommendations from lay officials proved to be the

[8] English writers sometimes share this error with American professors, overlooking in their bewitchment by Oxford and Cambridge the form of governance of their modern universities.

catalyst which stirred the universities to action." [9] All history refutes claims to exemption from social controls for academia, as for any other profession.

A common misconception concerning our system of lay boards traces its origin and present viability to the example of business organizations. Yet the founders of our early colleges could hardly have emulated today's business corporation, for the private profit concern was virtually unknown in the American colonies. Their model was rather that of the charitable trust, then the accepted form of enterprises conducted by individuals in which the community welfare was paramount.

In colonial America the right of incorporation, zealously guarded, was rarely granted except to nonprofit public welfare undertakings, such as hospitals, charity homes, academies, and colleges. Trustees were just what the name implies, guardians and governors over the use of resources, not for individual but for public gain.

COMPOSITION AND ORGANIZATION OF LAY BOARDS

Turning now to more concrete matters, one finds the widest variations among boards in size and organization. They vary from five members to fifty, sixty, or even a hundred.

Most presidents succeed in developing a *modus operandi*, whatever the number of trustees may be, and seem to think that their boards are just about the right size. Members do, too. Small boards argue that by transacting most business as a body, each trustee can maintain intimate association with all that is going on. Members of larger boards point to their broader representative character—professional, business, or geographical—and it is true that trustees who live too far away to attend more than half the stated meetings of the full board can be effective proconsuls in their several regions.

[9] George F. Kneller, *Higher Learning in Britain*, University of California Press, Berkeley, Calif., 1955, pp. 21, 22.

One danger of a large board is an inclination to meet only at long intervals, perhaps once or twice a year, in *pro forma* sessions, the real business being in the hands of an executive committee. Large boards as a rule resort to committees with wide discretion. Naturally, the structure of the committee system tends to get out of date. Another danger of large boards is that power gravitates unduly to a small proportion of the membership and others feel excluded. Thus in 1959 Wesleyan University secured an amendment to its charter reducing the trustees from the unwieldy number of fifty-seven to twenty-five. The change is said to have brought greater participation in decision making by all the membership.

Like other people, trustees prefer to serve on committees that interest them, where their business or professional equipment enables them to make their best contribution. However, if they serve only on such, they limit their comprehension of college or university operations as a whole. In some places the rule is that a portion of each committee serves on a rotating basis. This procedure develops a broader understanding of the institution and a healthier sense of participation. But members who need it most will often resist rotation, preferring to confine themselves to subjects related to their occupations.

TERMS OF OFFICE

The terms of office of trustees vary as greatly as do their numbers. In the case of short terms among the self-perpetuating boards, the privilege of reelection usually obtains. In the case of "life" trustees, the practice of compulsory retirement for age is growing, the retired members becoming honorary trustees or trustees emeriti with the right to attend meetings but not to vote. Not infrequently they continue to be useful members and natural choices for particular jobs to be done.

The introduction of compulsory retirement may entail some heartaches at the time, but on balance it is beneficial. Without necessarily losing the wisdom of the old, a retirement system makes it possible to project a schedule of anticipated vacancies and to preserve a better age distribution throughout. It also facilitates the election of an older man with a particular service to render for a time who, in the absence of a retirement system, would otherwise be automatically passed over in order to maintain a balance of younger men.

The terms of board members of state universities usually overlap and are generally shorter than among private institutions, ranging in our observation from a low of two to a high of sixteen years, although a range of four to six years is more representative. Reappointment by the governor or reelection by the legislature or the people, as the case may be, is possible. In some states there is strong precedent for reappointment or reelection, and presidents generally favor it. In others, however, a politically inclined governor or partisan political leaders may intervene on occasion to disrupt continuity to the grave embarrassment of the institution.

Cases have been reported to us by non-tax-supported institutions in which the introduction of short terms with possible reelection has improved the quality of trusteeship by providing honorable retirement for those who grow tired in service and decent exits for the disinterested who prove unwilling to work. A mixed system of "short term" and "life" or "long term," both groups being eligible for reelection, gives general satisfaction, in part because the short term affords an opportunity to try out a man's fitness for election to a long term or for "life."

A general tradition of short periods of service is undesirable. We talked with one university president whose board's senior member had served but five years. He was laboring under a serious handicap. It takes time for a trustee to learn about the university, for he has probably not encountered in his previous experience an organization so strange and complex. A trustee who begins to throw his weight about before he becomes sensitively informed can do more harm than good, as some have learned to their regret.

SELECTION OF TRUSTEES

The search for new trustees should be a constant concern, particularly for self-perpetuating boards. Nevertheless, regents of state universities are often not without influence in the process of selecting their colleagues or their successors. Neither the president nor the board should wait for a vacancy to exist before considering how to fill it. In the case of self-perpetuating boards an alert nominating committee, perhaps the executive committee, should maintain a slate of possible candidates and devote periodic consideration to it. To conduct discreetly and judiciously a thorough canvass of individuals requires time. Moreover, by holding the board's attention to the importance of a constant search for good candidates, a president can personally do much to improve the quality of an uninformed or nonworking board. Active alumni with a proved interest in the high purposes of the institution provide a pool from which to draw new members who are willing to work, but a board should not restrict itself to alumni or be beguiled into electing "good old Sam" as payment for mere activity in the alumni association.

A rough estimate of the aggregate membership of the boards of our 2,000 junior colleges, colleges, and universities gives the impressive figure of perhaps 30,000. If they were all broad-minded, knowledgeable, and hard-working men and women, who can say to what heights their institutions might attain?[10] Unhappily, too many are chosen for wrong or superficial reasons. Boards do well to follow the maxim that the only qualified candidate is the one who profoundly esteems the importance of education and wants to become wholeheartedly identified with it. If a nominee is reluctant to turn to and work, he should not be chosen, or, if chosen, he should not accept. This should be brought forcefully to his attention when he is invited to become a trustee. If it scares him off, the institution has lost nothing.

[10] The qualifications for effective service as a trustee are enumerated in *The Role of the Trustees of Columbia University*, pp. 15–18.

To choose a trustee simply because of the reflected glory his eminence will bring is as naïve as to select an uninterested wealthy man hoping that he will make substantial gifts. For one thing, such stratagems rarely succeed. They debase the office and deceive no one, least of all the individual concerned.

A governor who uses his appointive power to reward friends, to resolve political pressures, or to pack the board against a president he dislikes violates his trust. Happily, with some egregious exceptions, the state university presidents we interviewed had little complaint of political partisanship among their regents. Some did wish, however, that their boards were less timid about anticipated legislative scrutiny of the university's financial needs. A more common observation was that, until an issue had reached the state of public notice, there was a lack of interest, particularly in educational matters. A publicly sustained institution, not to mention its president, is entitled to the most diligent and far-sighted regents procurable.

Complete integrity as a qualification for a trusteeship should go without saying. However, history—not all of it ancient by any means—records cases of mortal sin by trustees who have, for example, exploited their position by directing purchases of equipment or construction contracts to certain firms or by channeling bank accounts and endowment investments to certain business concerns for personal profit. Fortunately such moral lapses are far from typical.

WHAT DO ALUMNI TRUSTEES CONTRIBUTE?

Selection of a fraction of the trustees by the alumni, an accepted practice among otherwise self-perpetuating boards, gives the alumni, who are, after all, relied on to contribute financially to the institution, some influence in its governance and provides an additional means of communication with them. Since the younger classes of alumni outnumber the older, the system, if taken seriously by the alumni, tends to return a younger group than that represented by the balance of power among life trustees, and this is good. For optimum results the election must be open to all alumni. It should not, for instance, be restricted to members or councils of a dues-paying organization, which may be heavily weighted by the storybook stereotype of the old grad, interested chiefly in athletics and fraternities.

On the whole, the quality of trustees chosen by vote of the alumni seems to give satisfaction, although in some institutions we encountered a contrary opinion. A wise president will not of course interfere with the process of alumni nomination and election. However, if the administration has tried to interest the alumni in the educational goals of the university—and they are more susceptible than some assume—a president can, by stressing excellence, exert influence which will not be regarded as inter-ference.

The contributions of alumni trustees vary with the use made of them. Because their terms of office are usually short—commonly without the privilege of reelection—they are apt to be excluded from their presumptive role in policy determination unless definite efforts are made to bring them in. When older members treat them merely as worthy freshmen, when a system of seniority assigns them only to unimportant committees and gives them no significant work to do, their value is negligible. They are likely to depart from office with a bad taste in their mouths and to spread the word among their fellows. But when accepted as full equals, they can contribute helpful points of view beyond merely reassuring the alumni of representation in high quarters. Alumni trustees feel honored by election, and they include a good proportion who are willing to work.

WIDE REPRESENTATION ON A BOARD

A well-balanced board will consist of people from various pro-fessions and occupations, not only to make different points of view available, but for the sake of specific specialized services in diverse areas of operations. A president cannot be a master of the various specialties involved in the operation of a college or university, and his knowledge in fields in which he is not expert needs supplementing. A lawyer, physician, banker, or industrialist can be extremely helpful to a president.[11]

Academic writers have criticized our trustee system as unrepresentative of our society. They say that it reflects the prevailing economic power groups in the community to the exclusion of other elements which should be represented, such as organized labor. It is true that the ranks of academic trustees contain a large proportion of professional men and businessmen. Naturally, they are influenced by their occupations (who isn't?). But it does not follow that they are thereby insensitive to social needs.

The disinterestedness that a trustee should possess is gravely diminished if he considers himself chosen to represent the demands of pressure foci. We agree wholeheartedly that "The idea that 'executives,' 'labor,' 'the professions' or other such groups should have 'spokesmen' . . ." erroneously implies that thoughtful men cannot ". . . achieve the disinterestedness that is essential to the governing of a university . . . the cure of attempting to compensate one set of prejudices with another is worse than the disease. . . . Whoever a trustee may be, he must be able to consider the university as greater than the sum of its parts." [12] Too much can be made of the duty of trustees to yield to social pressures and social trends. Often a university fulfills its commitment best by opposing a popular trend.[13] The college or university, clear as to its goals and its place in our national complex of

---

[11] Some of my most rewarding memories of trustees run to aid received from business and professional men in matters too confidential or too delicate to refer, for example, to university counsel, to the treasurer, or to the head of the health department. H. W. D.

[12] *The Role of the Trustees of Columbia University*, pp. 16–17.

[13] All credit, for example, to trustees who refuse to compromise a college's ideal of a liberal education despite donations proffered if it will transfer its center of gravity to vocational programs. All credit to those which have introduced desegregation against strong opposition. When the University of Oklahoma became the first in the South to admit Negroes to graduate school and allow them to live in dormitories, the trustees showed themselves to be more than mere mirrors of popular opinion.

higher education and wary of falling into a cult of unanimity, will still profit from a relatively like-minded board of control in contrast to one that is immobilized by enervating disagreements. Men who get things done, who are respected leaders in their several communities, are best able to act for the university in a manner to which people will respond.

PROFESSORS AS BOARD MEMBERS

Even boards that carefully include in their number members of various professions for the sake of their special contributions generally neglect the academic profession itself. This is unfortunate. An able professor from another college or university is good leavening. He can render real service to the board by interpreting faculty viewpoints. While some may object that even a trace of academia in a board's membership infringes upon the principle that trustees should be laymen, the evidence of presidents whose boards include one or more educators is overwhelmingly favorable.[14]

The effectiveness of a trustee chosen from the faculty of another institution obviously depends upon his acceptance as a full equal. This in turn runs to the personality of the individual and his capacity to interpret to laymen how the academic world operates. His value is destroyed, however, if he turns out to be a yes-man to the president or a persistent advocate of sectarian educational hobbies. At the same time he must be strong enough to uphold the president's hands, when they deserve it, in crucial academic situations. He should also be one who, however eminent in his special field (and such eminence is not to be discounted), has some familiarity with colleges and universities other than the one he is serving. Such a one can help by keeping the president and the busy lay trustees in touch with developments and new ideas else-

[14] In my experience at Princeton, alumni, when they come to vote for trustees, do not reflect the fear that an educator or two dilutes the lay character of the board unduly. The record there shows that candidates who are educators possess an advantage in alumni trustee elections. In the last forty years only one has failed of election, and he was shortly named a charter trustee. H. W. D.

where. Although a president of another institution may be of help, he may feel that "presidential courtesy" estops him from being critical. An educator-trustee who is a professor can often give more time to the institution, and more adequately reflect faculty views, than can a president.

When one comes to consider faculty members as trustees of their own institutions, the situation is altered. We have taken no opinion polls, but our impression is that a majority of the academic fraternity would favor such representation if the question were put to a vote. On the other hand, some would oppose it on the ground that a faculty member is as out of place attending and voting at board meetings as a trustee would be at faculty meetings.

Only a very small handful of American colleges and universities provide for faculty representatives on their governing boards. The data as to their value are therefore slight and somewhat contradictory, but on balance it suggests that they are not significant figures in decision making. In some instances they possess the right to debate but not to vote, in which case they are essentially only observers.[15] Prof. F. G. Marcham of Cornell, where for many years the faculty have been represented by two

---

[15] A poll of presidents would return an overwhelming vote against faculty members serving as trustees of their own institution. We have, however, encountered two exceptions. Acting President A. O. Grubb reported that in his experience at Lincoln University, Pennsylvania, the two members of the faculty elected to the board by vote of the trustees spoke freely and authoritatively on matters touching educational policies and faculty goals. So far as he has observed, their presence was not an embarrassment to free discussion by the members. However, they did not report systematically to the faculty regarding board meetings, in part because so many items on the agenda are confidential. It should be added that Lincoln is a small liberal arts college whose faculty are more like-minded than would be found in a larger and more diverse institution.

The report from Roosevelt University was equally favorable. The two mentioned can be offset, however, by equally strong unfavorable judgments. Another testified that, so far as he could see, faculty membership made no difference. Clearly faculty representation on an institution's board of control does not promise to resolve the fundamental problems of trustee-faculty relations.

members on the board of trustees, writes, "I do not think it is within the power of the faculty representatives on the board of trustees to help significantly in the management of the university. . . . The benefit occurs in the area of public relations; it has little bearing upon political action." The reason he lays largely at the door of the president. "The absence of opportunities to consult with the president has been a serious handicap to them [the faculty trustees]. They have remained ignorant of impending changes in the university until they received the agenda for meetings of the trustees." They are ex officio members of the University Policy Committee, but the administration "rarely approaches" it for advice.[16] Other evidence we received from Cornell was stronger than Professor Marcham's in asserting that the presence of faculty members on the board made no perceptible difference in policy decisions or in communicating trustee action to the faculty.

While not approving presidential neglect of trustees, whether faculty or laymen, one may ask whether Professor Marcham is not tacitly asserting a right "to work both sides of the street." Does he claim for the academic trustee the special privilege of participating in the decision-making process at the level of responsible administrative and faculty agencies and of then being able to go into a trustee meeting and there fight for or against the decision as a "free agent"? In opposing it at the faculty level, would he not be dangerously close to "interfering" in a manner forbidden to lay trustees?

In a complex university a faculty member on the governing board of his university cannot speak for the whole faculty on educational policies unless they have been formalized by a majority vote; he cannot personally be a spokesman for the diverse and often conflicting views of his colleagues, even if he sublimates his own professional predilections. Consequently, he can act as a true

---

[16] *American Association of University Professors Bulletin,* vol. 42, no. 4, pp. 617–621, Winter, 1956. Until 1956 the faculty members on the board of trustees did not have the right to vote at Cornell, but the voting privilege has reportedly not increased faculty participation in meetings.

representative only in matters of general faculty concern and consensus, and these usually relate to terms of employment, in which his private interest either will lead, or will be discounted as leading, to bias as to the interests of the university as a whole.[17]

Apart from the inevitable politics involved in elections, if the faculty considers the position really significant, many would not welcome being aggressive stand-ins for several hundred, or even a few score, of highly individualistic teachers and scholars. The two faculty members of the Cornell board are selected by the trustees from a panel of three nominees for each place. According to the bylaws, they are not considered as representing the faculty but as free agents, in order that they may be saved some of the pressures and embarrassments which arise from being "spokesmen" for others. The testimony of various individuals at Cornell that the faculty members of the board of trustees are not an effective line of communication from trustees to faculty is similar to some we received elsewhere.[18] Professor Marcham writes of the Cornell experience: "Only one has reported back to the faculty at the end of this term of office."

If professors were to become truly effective trustees in respect to faculty interests, colleague pressures would force them to be not only spokesmen but advocates. As advocates they would labor

[17] The common business practice of electing the president's subordinate officers as directors has always seemed to me not in the interests of stockholders. There are aspects of conflict of interest involved similar to those concerning faculty board members. Moreover, they are not truly independent thinkers, for their primary jobs depend upon satisfying the president. Faculty members on academic boards are under similar wraps. While subordinate officers, both academic and nonacademic, may properly attend board meetings for the light they can throw on special matters, the opportunity to go into executive session without them should always be open. H. W. D.

[18] Several vice-chancellors of British universities reported to us that while one of the functions of the academic members of the governing board was to serve as a means of communication by the board to the several faculties, they accomplished little in this respect. In Britain the degree of participation of professorial members in board discussion appears to vary among universities, in proportion to the interests of the lay members in educational matters.

under an inescapable overarching conflict of interests in the educational as well as the economic sphere.

If the board and the president are to function well together, each must be free to speak frankly and to consider, without embarrassment, the excellence or lack of it in individual faculty members, officers of administration, and component departments and schools—intensely personal matters. If frank talk is inhibited at meetings, trustees will perhaps resort to informal rump sessions to which faculty representatives are not invited or, as in the case of at least one institution, resolve the dilemma by the simple device of leaving important business to the jurisdiction of an executive committee on which faculty members do not serve.

Much of the business coming up at a meeting of trustees originates in discussions by administration or trustee committees, or in faculty action or a recommendation of one of the faculty committees. Usually it is accompanied by the president's recommendation for action, pro or con. In such circumstances a faculty-member trustee may face a difficult dilemma. Shall he follow the recommendation of the faculty or a committee thereof if he disagrees, or shall he be guided by the merits of the case as he sees them, despite faculty action? If he disagrees with the president, shall he vote against him on an issue which has passed through the mill of discussion by the faculty or the administration or both, culminating in a formal recommendation to the board? If he does, he must in a sense contradict the president and perhaps his colleagues. He would probably do so only under the most exceptional circumstances. One college board on which faculty representatives sat experienced more friction rather than less because of president-faculty differences brought along to trustee meetings. In such circumstances most boards would be inclined almost spontaneously to support the president under attack. This would not contribute to harmony.

We conclude that faculty representation on governing boards does not promote understanding between faculty and trustees commensurate with the disadvantages involved. At best it is inadequate for the purpose of presenting the faculty point of view. In a sense it is a decoy leading away from the main issue, for it is no substitute for other and more fruitful methods of communication.[19]

THE PRESIDENT AND THE CHAIRMAN OF THE BOARD

In many privately sustained institutions the president is an ex officio member of the board with full voting rights, and we think he should be. True, some who are not report that they suffer no disadvantages thereby. But if a president is the "chief spokesman" for the university, we cannot understand why he should not be a full-fledged trustee.

Although he is the chief executive officer, the president is rarely the presiding officer at board meetings. We believe that he should be, not in order to diminish the power of the trustees, but because he is the educational leader of an educational institution.[20] There are both psychological and symbolic values involved here which emphasize that education is the principal purpose for which the university and board exist. Nevertheless, nearly all boards elect a lay chairman from among themselves, which suggests less than complete confidence in the academic mind. If the president, by business standards, presides poorly, he should study to be a proficient presiding officer.

A board chairman from outside academia must possess more than ordinary powers of perception and self-control. He is the target of importuning by other trustees and the public, who think he should take critical matters into his own hands and not just

---

[19] This aspect of trustee-faculty relations is considered in the next chapter, as a special responsibility of the president.

[20] A number of presidents we interviewed did not agree that they should preside at board meetings, in part because they believed that they were freer to advocate policy if not encumbered by the duties of presiding officer. On balance, my experience did not support this position. If a president feels that the presiding role handicaps him in pressing his policies, he can turn the meeting over to the chairman of the executive committee or the senior trustee while presenting his major recommendations. H. W. D.

refer them to the president. To resist these pressures requires not only an esteem for educators but a sympathetic grasp of the values that motivate the academic mind and an ability to convey his own understanding to his fellow trustees.

The lay chairman is supposed to speak for the board; the president, for the institution. Reconciling these roles calls for a delicate harmony that is not easy to attain if both possess strong personalities. On occasion, circumstances call for the chairman, defending the institution, to speak publicly in explanation and support of a course being pursued. But he should carefully ration his public utterances. As with a new president, personal publicity can go to his head, and he too must watch for signs of inebriety.

Under all but the most crucial circumstances the president should be the only spokesman for the institution, in part because the public look to him as such. If a serious need to emphasize a united front requires that the board speak publicly as a body, usually it should do so by resolution and not through the medium of individual trustees. Public pronouncements by others undermine the president's rightful influence as the one primarily accountable for all that goes on. If he is an inadequate public spokesman, he is an inadequate president.

Some colleges and universities have labored under chairmen who are mere figureheads, especially when chosen for prestige or financial reasons. Others have suffered from domineering busybodies, "downtown presidents" who try to run the institution from their business offices. Such a one can wreck an able president. Furthermore, a board which permits itself to be dominated by its chairman, however dedicated he may be, is too permissive or will soon become so. When members are no longer free to make their collective judgment effectual, their self-respect is diminished, and so is their ardor to serve the institution.

POLICY MAKING AND ADMINISTRATION

To determine at what point policy making spills over into administrative interference is a constant problem for trustees and

presidents alike. Everyone agrees with the textbook writers that
boards should govern by policy framing, which is their business,
and not by injecting themselves into administration, which is not.
Charles A. Coolidge's oft-quoted advice to trustees is excellent:
"Don't Meddle . . . it is the president's and the faculty's job
to educate. . . . As a trustee you should see that these men are
capable . . . but you should not try to do their jobs for them.
In short you should see that the university is well run by someone
else and not try to run it yourself."[21] Advice, however, remains
only advice until it is applied to situations. No solution is possible
unless there is a fundamentally sound and cooperative relationship
between the trustees and the president.

Colleges and universities are in the public domain in a peculiar
manner, and at any time a matter of administration may explode
into a matter of policy. At precisely what point trustees cease
being trustees and become managers evades verbal definition. The
line of demarcation is more shadowy in academic institutions than
in the typical corporation. The effective trustee, for one thing,
participates more intimately in the conduct of operations than
his usual counterpart in business, who is inclined to accept, even
to prefer, management control.

SOME TRUSTEES HINDER

The trustee may accept—in theory—all the admonitions in
the book. Still there is something about the nature of a university
that tempts him to meddle. As stated earlier, trustee interference
may rarely be revealed in formal actions preserved in the minutes.
Some individuals find subtle and indirect ways in which to direct
the president about things better left to administrative discretion.
Individual members of a board may create an atmosphere of

[21] From an address to The Institute for College and University Administrators, Harvard University, Sept. 15, 1956. Published in the *Association of
American Colleges Bulletin*, vol. 42, p. 513, 1956. Mr. Coolidge has long been
a member of the Harvard Corporation.

insecurity regarding academic freedom. The resulting timidity may gravely influence the character of initial faculty appointments and promotions—all without a word in the record. Undergraduate escapades and brash student publications invite interference, for many a trustee feels in his heart that he can handle situations better than a seemingly too tolerant dean.[22]

Similarly, a trustee who exerts pressure in response to a parent's complaint that his son has been unjustly flunked or denied admission is interfering. So was the one who in his enthusiasm for a football coach undertook to negotiate the coach's salary himself. The trustee who arranged with a dean that on any question relating to the admission of students, "If I write you a letter, pay no attention to it. But if I call you on the telephone, I mean business," should have been impeached. The conscientious but overzealous board member who bypassed the president and took a room in a local hotel to interview students and faculty with a grievance over a dean was misbehaving, and so was the board chairman who invited faculty members to meet him without the presence, or even the knowledge, of the president.

Trustees should follow strictly the principle that John Dale Russell put so succinctly: "Authority resides only in the board as a whole and not in its individual members, except as the board itself may have delegated specific authority to one of its members." Broad university policies on admission requirements, academic standards, and athletics, as well as the competence of deans, professors, and officers of administration, are properly policy matters for the board, but presidents are not infrequently handicapped by boards who try to handle too much detail. Obviously, boards of control of any enterprise must, for legal reasons if no

[22] I well recall a hard-working and friendly trustee from whom I could confidently expect a phone call tomorrow morning when something to which I knew he would take exception appeared today in the undergraduate newspaper. I did not consider that his advice, which often seemed at variance with accepted university policy, was generally of help in the discharge of my over-all administrative duties. Many presidents can identify similar characters on their boards, past or present. H. W. D.

other, spend some time on *pro forma* details. Nevertheless, the reaction of one trustee, cited by Belcher, who complained that meetings were "unnecessarily long and tedious" can be matched by
others.[23] Some boards—among them some eminent ones—clog
their agenda with minutiae better left to the administration or
with the presentation of detailed committee reports which were
circulated in advance and do not need to be combed over again.
Such unwitting obstructionism automatically deprives boards of
time to consider high policy matters thoughtfully and the president of the chance to present basic and challenging educational
issues. The trustee who, when interviewing a possible president,
was impressed because the man knew more than he himself about
his university, belonged to a board that kept itself enmeshed in
details and formalities.

The excellent practice of employing a paid secretary is growing among boards. In the smaller institutions his secretarial
duties can be supplemented by others. We think the time has
come to abandon the old custom by which a member acts as
secretary, the details being carried out under his direction by a
subordinate in the administration. A board secretary can consolidate in one office duties often scattered among several people
and left to the president to coordinate. A good secretary can
arrange agenda and other material for committee meetings[24] and
help the president keep track of delegated matters. When appropriate, he can draft resolutions or statements of policy to be
recommended by committees or the president.

Attention to, and decision on, the main issues is facilitated
when members are served in advance of meetings with carefully
prepared material which concentrates on the salient factors in
any issue without irrelevant details. The secretary can make sure

[23] *Op. cit.,* p. 60.
[24] The agenda should allow ample time for the president to present his report and to raise problems on his mind. When his report is relegated to the
end of the session (in one case we encountered, to the last fifteen minutes),
when everyone is anxious to get away, the board is not playing fairly.

that this is done. Frequently the advance paper work imposed on trustees is too voluminous for busy members to master. As one victim of such a situation dryly remarked, only the lawyers accustomed to reams of written matter read it and come to raise minor issues.

The secretary of the board must work closely with the president. At the University of Michigan he serves also as the president's assistant, an arrangement said to be most satisfactory. Although he is an officer of the board, the secretary should be selected with the concurrence, if not the formal nomination, of the chief executive, as is common in business organizations. His potentials as board secretary naturally mesh with those of the new type of presidential personal aide described in Chapter III; the two can be molded into a natural functional unit.

HOW TRUSTEES HELP

Let us now turn to the valuable services to higher education that lay college and university trustees perform, frequently paying their own travel expenses to do so. They generally feel at home with business and financial operations, and their contribution in these areas is common knowledge. The experienced business executive, if he is tactful, can be of great assistance to the president with suggestions on the art of administration, particularly delegation. Lawyers and doctors make excellent trustees, but their professional experience may incline them to underestimate the weight and significance of administrative difficulties involved in even a most worthy and attractive educational policy.

Trustees can also help in a less obvious way: They can refrain from trying to make the president over into a businessman par excellence. If he is good at his primary job of educational leadership, let them be content to see his knowledge of the business world supplemented in the persons of administrative colleagues and to help generously to supplement it themselves. Management of an endowment portfolio, big or little, is a heavy responsibility, for example. A president who tries to become an expert on investments is wasting his time.[25]

Businessmen and industrialists serving on a committee on grounds and buildings can be a source of invaluable help to the business officers responsible for plant construction and operation. That is, of course, if the business officers are up to their jobs and are able to welcome criticism and suggestions based on experience in another world. Such trustees can save a president some natural and costly mistakes in building construction and the physical campus development.

In this area the president who is ambitious to improve his institution by helping the faculty do better work is particularly sensitive to pressures from the faculty with whom he lives. They, after all, do not have to provide the funds and are naturally intent on improving educational facilities, with a sense of urgency that leads them to plump for the quick cure of current deficiencies. But the quick cure is also apt to be a partial cure that neglects the institution's long-range good. Any experienced president, seeing how the short view of another day has trapped some institutions in physical development difficulties, can thank his stars if trustees of the past have rejected easy and cheap building solutions that would have alleviated deficiencies temporarily but would have militated against long-term excellence. Trustees who build for the century and not for the decade will be honored by generations to come.

Then there is obsolescence. More than one institution, particularly the privately sustained, has awakened during recent years to the cost of past neglect of their plants, costs that would have been saved under an adequate renovation program. Plant deterioration is gradual and far less visible than the need to expand libraries and laboratories. Trustees from the industrial and

[25] I have always been grateful that the investment policy at Princeton during the Roaring Twenties was determined by men of solid financial experience. We should have been in a much more serious condition when the depression hit in 1929 had the trustees yielded to the investment advice pressed upon them earlier by two or three authorities on the faculty. H. W. D.

business world are often familiar with plant-maintenance problems. They can combat the common and insidious temptation to undue economy in this area.

TRUSTEES OFTEN NEED EDUCATION
IN EDUCATIONAL RESPONSIBILITIES

When we turn to the less familiar and more imponderable problems of how trustees may serve education proper, we perceive that the question is still unresolved in many colleges and universities. A board has the power, for example, to prescribe that Greek 202 shall be open only to students who have passed Philosophy 201. Of course, even an uneducated board doesn't do anything so foolish. Naturally, like doctors, lawyers, and all experts in general, faculties want to decide for themselves what their professional relations shall be to society and to determine how they will serve it. This consideration is at the basis of George Bernard Shaw's acid remark that "all professions are a conspiracy against the laity." Cases of ignorant and prejudiced trustee interference which still occur or the memories of which still live in some professorial writings about trustees help to perpetuate a natural suspicion and some downright antagonism.

The responsibility of trustees for the educational program carries a correlative duty to educate themselves about the institution's end product. As many a seasoned board member will testify, business experience of itself is inadequate preparation for a trusteeship. Yet too rarely are any systematic steps taken to introduce a new trustee to the peculiar ethos of a college or university, its traditions, policies, and procedures. Some administrations provide briefing material for him; some—more practically —encourage him to talk with deans and other administrative officers. He will find that he is welcome.

Some presidents report that indoctrination at the hands of an old, wise trustee has proved effective and that, as a routine matter, they particularly charge a senior member with the responsibility of introducing a newcomer to the esoteric nature of academic governance. Too often trustees are left to learn by experience that to inflict a strict business kind of efficiency on the faculty as they discharge professional duties would seriously impede them as teachers and scholars. Assignment of a new member to a committee dealing with aspects of teaching, research, and student life will enable him to learn by doing much better than if his first committee contacts are restricted to the less important ones.

President Keeney of Brown University exposed the crux of the trustee problem when he complimented his board for its restraint concerning educational policies. This has, he added, "been perhaps one of its most powerful instruments" and has "created a deep feeling of partnership between the more experienced members of the faculty and the Corporation."

Yet restraint does not mean passivity. Although innovations usually originate within the faculty and administration, informed trustees have good ideas, too, and may properly approach the faculty on educational subjects through the president or conference committee relationships. Some writers on business management have asserted that the concept of corporation boards as policy makers has become but a "tired fiction." If this be true, it doesn't mean that college trustees should abdicate their function as an "organ of review, of appraisal and of appeal" in respect to educational matters.

ARE TRUSTEES INTERESTED
IN THE EDUCATIONAL PROCESS?

One hears that trustees are becoming restless because of lack of influence over educational policies. Undoubtedly the complaint is sometimes well grounded. Sometimes, however, it may spring from a trustee's misconception of his place in the educational complex and a consequent feeling of frustration at being excluded from detailed control over the curriculum and methods of instruction. Nevertheless, our interviews did not uncover any widespread discontent over being excluded.

We found more presidents, especially the good ones, complaining about the difficulty of persuading trustees to thoughtful consideration of educational policies than trustees protesting that they were being shut out. It follows that if they are unwilling to spend time and thought on it, surely trustees should not complain that they're being forced out of education. If remote from the subject matter, and thus poorly equipped to meet a crisis when it comes, trustees are in danger of rushing in without that basic understanding necessary to formulate a wise course for the university. Curbstone opinions and conditioned reflexes are no help to a president or faculty wrestling with educational policies.

The tremendous growth of specialization within the various departments and schools of an institution and the expanded autonomy of the faculty both discourage participation by lay trustees. This in turn can lead to the approval *pro forma* of even the most significant recommendations of the president. This is unfortunate. The fact that he is not a specialist in science, the humanities, or law or medicine should not rule an informed trustee out of the educational field.

A STANDING COMMITTEE ON EDUCATIONAL POLICY

It is not to be expected that each member of a board will make his most telling contribution in the educational segment. Some valuable members prefer to concentrate on finance, grounds and buildings, and the like.

We feel, therefore, that the committee structure of a board should include a strong committee on educational policy, ranking in prestige with the highest. No one unwilling to do a reasonable amount of homework belongs on such a committee. Willing members, however, will find it a welcome relief from their own business affairs and from the relative drudgery of routine university business.

Too many boards have no committee on educational policy at all, and others may make use of them only perfunctorily. Yet a well-constituted committee forms a responsible group to whom the president can look, individually or collectively, for knowledgeable counsel. It also provides a natural unit for communicating with the faculty. Since the members at best are normally generalists on the academic side, they can help administration and faculty to see the wood as well as the trees. A president or dean should be able to explain to them as laymen the significance of specialties, to define their relation to broader programs of scholarship and instruction. This committee should see that they do.

Thus, without stepping on anybody's toes, a standing committee on educational policy can exert a healthful influence simply by asking questions. It is good for educators to have to argue their case before laymen. Often a searching comment or an incisive criticism by an intelligent layman can expose some overlooked weakness in a program. The simple question, put to a president or a dean, "Is this department or that school as good as you think it is?" is always salutary. And it is even more so if the questioner knows how to appraise the answer.

Obviously, any attempt by trustees to comb through the details of proposed course changes or the scores or hundreds of faculty appointments to which they give legal approval each year and to pass an independent judgment on them would be self-defeating. However, this by no means precludes attention to significant curricular matters or to crucial faculty appointments.

We have seen in an earlier chapter how recommendations on faculty personnel originate and in due time reach the board. We have also seen that the process has become quite democratic, resting more heavily on colleague than administrative appraisal, with a corresponding built-in tendency to deterioration. Experienced trustees will naturally grant wide discretion to administration and faculty as to the scholarship and standing of nominees for promotion or appointment to tenure ranks. Presidents generally report that their trustees are interested in hearing about appointments, especially the more unusual and distinguished, but rarely review them in either a critical or a constructive manner.

We believe that a trustees' committee on educational policy has something to contribute here, without infringing upon academic freedom, for there are aspects of the whole man implicit in faculty appointments in addition to his scholarly achievements to date. In the case of significant appointments, the committee can profitably ask the president some of the same sorts of questions on which he and his deans satisfied themselves, or should have satisfied themselves, before they made their recommendations.

A most important trustee responsibility toward education is to maintain emphasis on the teaching function as well as research. If each is to enrich the other, the two must be kept in balance, and presidents will welcome trustee backing. Some vice-chancellors of British universities report that this is one of the most important uses of their lay boards of control, and their testimony can be matched by American college presidents.

TRUSTEES AS INTERPRETERS

That trustees, being laymen, are not immersed in the nuances concealed in different educational theories is an asset when they come to act as liaison between the profession and the outside world. Their very presence on the board assures that professors are not so queer and irresponsible as they may seem to the uninitiated public and that what they are doing is sound. Few outsiders appreciate the services which well-informed, respected, and courageous trustees quietly perform as public relations officers without once appearing in the public prints. Although they look to the president to be the chief spokesman, trustees perform an indispensable service as interpreters and defenders of educational policy, the faculty, and the president as opportunity affords, and the opportunities are many. As laymen they bring society's needs to bear upon the academic profession, but they also protect the institution and the faculty against hostile public opinion that would deprive them of their freedom and integrity. Even a state-supported institution, presumed to owe a particular sensitivity to the opinions of taxpayers, has rights which individuals should not invade.

There are many occasions when the defense of one vocation is best made by members of another. A president may never know how often he has been saved by the quiet good offices of trustees defending the institution and its faculty, but it happens often. The position of the latter has been strengthened, more often and more effectively than they realize, by trustees standing as a buffer between them and baneful external constraints. One may speculate that had the German universities enjoyed a tradition of strong lay boards, their resistance to Hitler would have been more effectual than that which the professoriate alone was able or disposed to muster.

We have saved to the last one aspect of trustee help not to be formalized in procedures, and certainly not implemented by prescriptions in the bylaws. A trustee who never forgets that dignity and integrity are indispensable to an institution; who, as Samuel Johnson noted about courage, recognizes that if these virtues are lost, all is lost; who fights for excellence against the cheap and the tawdry in this day of competitive publicity and struggle for attention by stunts and gimmicks—this man is beyond price.[26]

In America the position of academic trustee is one of distinct honor. That it is so derives from the service of countless individuals who not only have sustained the president, morally and materially, in his ambitions for excellence but have constantly exerted pressure on him to achieve them.

[26] There are a goodly number with whom I served over the span of a quarter of a century who are deeply etched in my memory for their unswerving insistence on excellence throughout all parts of the university. Their interest in seeing that the quality of academic departments was not only maintained but improved worked as a constant antidote to laziness and easy mediocrity, for, as remarked earlier, excellence in the democratic society of scholars does not reproduce itself automatically, nor is momentum gained and sustained without effort. H. W. D.

CHAPTER IX

THE PRESIDENT
AT WORK WITH
HIS TRUSTEES

While trustee responsibility for a sound working relationship with the president is clear, the president has a responsibility also, a principle often overlooked by one who is suffering "trustee trouble" and who fails to examine himself for the causes thereof. If he does not actually enjoy working with laymen, if he instinctively views his trustees merely as obstacles to be overcome or as troublemakers to be placated rather than consulted, he cuts himself and his institution off from the help which otherwise they would be prepared to give. The president was miscast who had to take to his bed after each meeting of his board, or the one who had to leave the room to cool off whenever the discussion was not to his liking. So was another who "clammed up" when some members took issue with him and defended his action by saying, "I won't enter into discussion with such low-grade people." However argumentative a board meeting may be, its net effect should be to leave a president with a lift in his heart; and he and the trustees have a joint responsibility to see that this comes about.

Some presidents prefer rubber-stamp boards. They may seem to ease his life, for a time at least, as for a corporation president,

243

but they do not make the contribution of which they should be capable. Some presidents particularly resist, instead of welcoming, trustee involvement in the educational process. Of course, there will be differences of opinion between the president and the board, but this should not *ipso facto* be regarded as "trustee trouble." A shrewd president does not feel that critics are automatically troublemakers. Unless the board is wholly incompetent, the president will find some stalwarts who can be developed into a source of strength and support. He soon learns that he need not lay down his body in front of the train on every debatable issue. With a little patience he will discover that often others come forward and do it for him.

THE PRESIDENT'S RESPONSIBILITY
FOR THE QUALITY OF THE BOARD

Not uncommonly a president may have to cope with an ineffectual or moribund board by bringing in new blood and letting some old blood out. The process may be rough. The president of an institution under a self-perpetuating board is in a more advantageous position for transforming its quality than the head of a state university whose regents are chosen by external governmental authority. Although practices differ from governor to governor and from state to state, where the regents are gubernatorial appointees the president is not likely to be consulted or to exert a telling influence if he is. When consulted he may be presented with a list of names whom the governor is considering, but he must be cautious and circumspect in expressing preferences. Where regents are elected, either by the people or by the legislature, the president's influence—unless he indulges in self-defeating political skirmishes and becomes identified with a particular political power group—is a passive influence if any. More than one state university head owes his enforced resignation to a taste for politics. As a citizen he may feel impelled to express his views on major public issues, particularly if they touch education, but he should avoid political partisanship.

The president of a private institution is usually an influential participant in nominations to board membership; indeed, he may be a member of the nominating committee. If the trustees ignore a president's views or exclude him from discussions of possible new members, it is time to think of resigning. For, like the chief executive of a business corporation, he has a duty to influence the board toward sustaining, and often improving, its quality. Whether he is himself a legal member of the board or not, a strong, patient man who has been diligent about educating his trustees in education frequently will find that he has succeeded in doing so. We know of more than one president who has bequeathed to his successor a more able board than he inherited. In one case that came to our attention, strong pressure by younger alumni helped to revitalize a moribund board.

Changes in membership are not the only—often not the chief— means by which an inert or seemingly incompetent board may be regenerated or, once regenerated, kept alive. The surest method is to find work for them. True, trustees who, on their own motivation or led by the president, become deeply involved in some phase of institutional operations may in their enthusiasm, as we have seen, step over the line between policy making and administration. But presidents have reported that the increased service that a hard-working trustee will deliver more than compensates for the minor incursions into their domain. By asking individuals to accept special assignments in areas of their particular competence or interests, actual or potential, many a president has uncovered unsuspected sources of help. What he had thought was a trustee's indifference may simply have been due to his own failure to find services for him to perform.

A PRESIDENT SPENDS TIME WITH HIS TRUSTEES

Naturally, if the president expects trustees to work, he must spend time working with them, collectively and individually. This is undoubtedly one of his most demanding responsibilities, for he can lose contact with the board through simple neglect.

By failure to attend important committee meetings, which some find irksome, or by relying on subordinate officers to present matters of which he himself should be master, a president may convey the impression that he is not interested in his trustees. Thereby he not only nullifies their potential for usefulness, but he weakens his defenses against a would-be dictator or opens the door to a subordinate with a power complex.

A president generally does not restrict his contacts to formal meetings of the board or its committees.[1] He engages in much informal conferring that is not revealed by discussions or actions recorded in the minutes. He will willingly spend time on the telephone; if his board is small, he may take pains to call each member on tight questions for the sake of consensus and to avoid jealousies. Most presidents find it helpful to have one influential trustee who, by virtue of his office on the board, can convey to him trustee thinking in a responsible manner and to whom he can, as a routine matter, talk frankly on any subject without risk of criticism by others who were not consulted. The board chairman should be such a one; but when there is no such office or the incumbent is inactive, the chairman of the executive committee can serve the purpose better than a "senior trustee" who has earned the title merely through long tenure. A president soon learns which trustees are the "power centers." It oils the executive machinery when chairmen of standing committees, as well as the chairman of the board or of the executive committee, are representative of such centers.

A president's social relationship with his trustees is usually of a wider significance than obtains with a business executive and his corporate directors. Opportunities for meeting his trustees soci-

---

[1] Sometimes for political reasons a state university president makes it a rule to refrain from consulting individual trustees, except the chairman, in advance of his bringing an important matter to their attention in regular sessions, in fear that he will encourage factionalism or jealousy and thereby create antagonism to his proposals before all are fully informed about them. While this may be wise in certain situations in which the regents are politically motivated, we do not recommend it as a general practice.

ally are more plentiful and more an element of his official life. Naturally, he will discover that some are more congenial off-duty companions than others, even when professional relations leave nothing to be desired. In short, some will make excellent fishing companions; others will not. Some trustees with superior judgment and a real professional friendship for the president will exhibit considerable reserve in promoting opportunities for purely social intercourse. The danger of cultivating socially congenial trustees to the neglect of others is always present, for imbalance here is quickly noted. A president should not permit intimacy with some to cut himself off from either the wisdom or the prejudices of others or lead any to feel that certain others have special access to him.

Yet no one could argue that a president must have no personal friends on the board, that he should throw a social *cordon sanitaire* between himself and the trustees. We do not suggest that an easy atmosphere of social contacts does not contribute to mutual confidence and understanding. We do argue that a too "palsy-walsy" relationship with some beclouds the objective judgment of both sides. Above all, we point out that the president who trades on personal friendships with trustees for the adoption of his policies is headed for destruction.

A president will be careful to bring important issues to the attention of the board early, while they are still under consideration. Deprived of a chance to take part in the formative stages, the trustees are faced with no alternative but formally to vote a president up or down when the matter does come before them, for Murphy has had his drink. Thus each action takes on the color of a vote of confidence or no confidence in him. Quite rightly they resent this, for it is not their function to approve all that the president recommends.

A president maintains harmony with his trustees, as with his family, only by evincing a flexibility of mind and a readiness to be convinced. This attitude does not represent passive subordination on his part; on the contrary, it strengthens his position as a capable leader. It is a weak head who tends to interpret a challenge to his wisdom or even an adverse decision as a vote of no confidence in him.

While rightfully desiring that their president possess an open mind, trustees have a right to demand that he accept full responsibility for firmly urging positions upon them, particularly positions he knows they would not take if left to themselves. As he elaborates the pros and cons of a serious matter, his obligation to express a position thereon includes the duty to propose a course of action—to show how it can be done, not merely to say it should be done. This last is often the most difficult stage. But to expect that wisdom will bubble up of itself through some quirk of group dynamics or through the innate power of truth to rise to the top is a delusion. "Why did the president let us make this mistake?" was a devastating trustee indictment of a president who was too timid or too lazy to lead in framing and executing policies.

A PRESIDENT DOES NOT WITHHOLD BAD NEWS

Above everything else a president should be honest with his board through frank disclosure of failures as well as successes. The practice of reporting that all is sweetness and light and omitting the darker aspects restricts the board's capacity to help where he may need help most. But much more serious is the damage to a president's moral position, for incomplete disclosure naturally generates distrust. According to our interviews with trustees, the qualities they respect most, without which others are worthless, are moral trustworthiness and intellectual integrity (not necessarily identical virtues). As one expressed it, "We trustees trust our president because we know that he always 'levels' with us— on the weak as well as on the strong points of his position." One of the most serious criticisms we heard of a president was that he made a habit of telling only the good news as if it were the whole truth.

True, charges of premeditated dishonesty and the sin of incomplete disclosure may be unfair in particular cases, but, even so, they emphasize the care which a president should take to establish the fact of his integrity. One who fails cannot complain that he is being interfered with or is not being allowed the sea room he requires to be a good executive. A policy of honest disclosure of failures does not demand of the president that he should eat too much crow. A too humble show of guilt generates irritation rather than confidence.

HOW AND WHAT A PRESIDENT REPORTS

Management consultants stress the causal relationship between a board's efficiency and the president's skill in communicating with it and are properly critical of the methods, or lack of them, which they often uncover. Obviously a president must make reports; equally obviously, he must be selective in what he presents. Do his reports reveal good staff work? Are his oral presentations cogent and clear? Does he spot the main issues, or does he congest the agenda with details that he should settle himself? Clearly boards should be careful not to lose themselves in minor matters, but none can function well under a president so insecure that he habitually brings up small details for its decision and thus forces it to waste time. In our interviews, trustees complained more frequently of presidents who made it a practice to shift to them decisions on items of small importance than of those who acted on major matters without previous formal endorsement by the board.

Although a wise president prepares himself well on any subject he presents, no board should expect him to be a master of every detail, and a zeal for perfection must not lead him to try to be one. It is only wisdom for him to delegate the presentation of certain educational and business matters and the elaboration of the details to subordinates, whom he should be permitted to bring to meetings with him. The practice by which certain administrative officers also regularly attend appropriate committee meetings is excellent for the help they receive as well as render. This does not, of course, relieve the president of the necessity to be master of essentials.

In his presentations the educator-president will always seek to elicit and cultivate the board's interest in education by reporting what is going on among faculty and students and by elaborating his and the faculty's ambitions for educational improvements. But he will also challenge their interest by calling attention to regional and national issues on the horizon which the institution must be prepared to meet. Throughout he will take pains to weave in his own philosophy of education, since the more his trustees know about the educational program and the rationale thereof, the more potent they become as counselors and defenders of the institution. If a president is able to devote half time to education, he will have time for attention to this phase of his work. Naturally housekeeping affairs must be attended to, and there are times when they demand broad priorities. But the president must not assume that none of his trustees has an interest in education or that one cannot be cultivated. One who wants to involve his board constructively in academic matters often will have to work at it;[2] he will get little response generated by frustration. More than one president, striving to introduce his trustees to the education milieu, labors under a sense of personal inadequacy in transmitting the sense of excitement which he himself feels in working for a university. He makes himself readily understood when a new building is being discussed but feels a gnawing sense of failure to register when a new research program or a consequential change in a program of study is under consideration. Nevertheless, we have observed institutions where presidents have been successful in the attempt, sometimes to a greater degree than they themselves seemed to realize.

[2] There are notable exceptions to this as to every generalization. For example, a member of the Harvard Corporation estimates that it devotes about half the time of its semimonthly meetings to educational concerns. No president could keep the Fellows out of such matters if he wished to.

THE DANGER OF TWO VOICES

As the chief channel of communication between faculty and trustees, and vice versa, a president remembers that he is dealing with two sorts of persons, each with its own vocational orientation. To the trustee he may seem to talk and act too much like a faculty member, while the faculty is likely to regard him as thinking and talking too much like a businessman. This complex creates a serious personal hazard—that he will barter away his identity and integrity as an educator by molding his philosophy and his presentations too readily to the predilections of the nonacademic mind. Presidents, if honest with themselves, are quite aware of the temptation to speak with two voices—one to the world of education and the other to trustees (and the lay public)—and are careful to guard against it.

The temptation is aggravated by the constant necessity to employ two vocabularies—one for communication with the world of education and the other with the world of trustees and the lay public. Translating education from professional to nonprofessional language is a demanding intellectual exercise. Yet the president who evades it is bound to acquire a reputation for prevarication as a result of repeated misunderstandings, or, equally unfortunate, for plain stupidity. At the bottom of the barrel is the president who wears two faces: he asks trustee approval of a faculty proposal on the grounds that it will help him live with the eccentric professors, and he curries favor with the faculty by depreciating the trustees.

ACADEMIC FREEDOM

The principle of academic freedom has won a widening acceptance over the past two generations. Yet it is foolhardy for a president to postpone trustee indoctrination on this difficult subject until some notable or notorious case arises to challenge it. If he should, the degree of shock suffered by the trustees when the attack comes will be reflected in their method of meeting it. How they meet it will reveal the degree of sophistication which he and his predecessors have been able to cultivate in the past. It was a farsighted president of a state university with a conservative constituency who, realizing when he took office that to many a layman academic freedom seems to contradict the behavior expected of members of a business firm or a professional partnership, warned his regents to be prepared for the day when a member of the faculty might urge, for example, the nationalization of the oil industry. He added that when that time came he would be compelled to defend the professor's right to make his position known.

The tender plant of academic freedom is extremely sensitive to its environment. Here the "brooding influence" of trustees may generate a timidity that will defeat an educator-president's dearest aspirations. Even in the most favorable environment, he will find that the necessity to sustain before his several publics the cause of free inquiry and expression is unremitting. The concept of it held by many laymen is too often derived from its manifestations in acrimonious public situations. To convince skeptical trustees that professors deserve this special kind of freedom, particularly in the less favored institution where the tradition of academic freedom is still weak, is a prime test of presidential courage and leadership.

Many presidents and trustees feel that the job would be easier and the case for freedom of inquiry and teaching stronger if the academic profession were to match its protective machinery with procedures for applying the rigorous standards of scholarship to individuals who hide a lack of integrity, incompetence, irresponsibility, shallow bias, or choler under the cloak of academic freedom.[3] It should be added, however, that a president who brings an

---

[3] The practice by which trustees, without divesting themselves of the right of ultimate decision, bring the faculty into cases involving faculty misconduct is growing. In general the procedures provide an aggrieved individual a chance to demand a hearing before a faculty committee, which reports its findings to the board or a committee thereof.

appropriate faculty body into consultation on cases of prospective separation for cause may usually anticipate judicial treatment if he is judicial himself.[4] In fairness to boards of trustees, it should be said, as others have remarked, that the cause of academic freedom is sufficiently secure in our pace-setting universities for their faculties to cease getting worked up over it and to assume a more positive role in disciplining violators.

TRUSTEE-FACULTY RELATIONS

This brings us to the question of trustee relations with the faculty and the president's role therein. As a college or university succeeds best when there are good working relations between the trustees and the president, so does it profit from good relations between trustees and faculty. Our field studies returned ample evidence that the institutions in which the trustees enjoy the confidence of the faculty are the happiest and most productive.

"Although ultimate legal responsibility for seeing that the educational policy is appropriate for the current times and is true to the traditions of learning lies with the governing board, educational policy should be developed through thorough consideration, discussion and understanding among faculty, administration, and trustees."[5] Since the president is the official channel of communications between them, this principle requires presidential implementation in such a manner as to mitigate the "built-in antagonism" between teachers and trustees. A president can do much to create a climate of cooperation by arranging opportunities for face-to-face contacts under conditions that engender mutual respect.

[4] We discussed at greater length in Chap. V the problem of removing for cause a faculty member on tenure. If conducted tactfully and with due respect for the feelings of the individual involved, the process can usually be carried on confidentially without attaining the proportions of a *cause célèbre.*

[5] From *The Responsibility of Trustees for Educational Objectives and Curriculum,* a statement adopted by a Conference for Trustees, held by the Harvard University Institute for College and University Administrators, May 30 to June 1, 1960.

Because each group speaks differently and reacts differently to similar situations, a tendency to remain aloof is as common among faculty as among trustees. Faculty attitudes derive in part from a fear that trustee interference will inevitably accompany trustee interest and in part from constraint in dealing with men of business who, they feel, rank them low in professional prestige.[6] It is as much an obligation of trustees to deserve the respect of the faculty as it is the faculty's obligation to earn the respect of the board. Although remote toleration of one for the other is better than cold war, it leaves much undone that could be accomplished if each became acquainted with the other in appropriate personal association.

Will Rogers once remarked that he was unable to dislike a person after he had become acquainted with him, and we have observed that the measure of truth in this applies to trustee-faculty relations.[7] Nevertheless, we discovered few instances of systematic programs of joint trustee-faculty conferences. If the trustee is an

---

[6] "College teachers themselves often point to the low public esteem of college professors as a deterrent in recruiting, but this is arguable. Studies of public attitudes toward various professions have always placed college teaching high on the list in terms of prestige." John W. Gardner, "Report of the President," *Fifty-third Annual Report,* Carnegie Foundation for the Advancement of Teaching, New York, 1957–58, p. 15. See also Paul F. Lazarsfeld and Wagner Thielens, Jr., *The Academic Mind,* Free Press, Glencoe, Ill., 1958, pp. 11–14. The findings of the latter indicate, however, that faculty members are more confident of their status in the eyes of college trustees than of businessmen generally. I believe that their view that they are poorly regarded by the outside community is due partly to taking too seriously some well-publicized attacks upon the academic profession to the neglect of the mass of the less articulate support which they enjoy. In their professional role of challengers of tradition and critics of the present, scholars as social irritants should expect and be prepared to absorb resistance without a sense of martyrdom. On the other hand, I have often been impressed at conferences between businessmen and teachers, on a subject of mutual interest, how each side seems to be frightened of the other at the beginning and how this feeling evaporates as the conference proceeds. H. W. D.

[7] We believe with Prof. W. H. Cowley that there has been some diminution of antibusinessman attitudes among faculty members who, as consultants, members of public bodies, and the like, have come increasingly into touch with businessmen.

old student of the college, he may know some of the faculty, but his acquaintance will be spotty and his contacts more so.

Some presidents disapprove of personal contacts between faculty and trustees. Some trustees do, too, feeling that they lead easily to a breach of the canons of orderly organizational practice. We believe this to be a shortsighted view, although many college presidents can cite experience to support it. Presidents are properly irritated by a trustee who, somewhat in the spirit of an inspector general, develops personal channels of intelligence with members of the faculty, or by a disgruntled faculty member who seeks out a trustee with a hospitable ear upon whom to unburden a grievance.[8] The way to avoid this is not to insist that the two remain apart but to provide opportunities of responsible communication between authorized representatives of each group. By this procedure the unhappy situation described by one trustee as "a continuous effort by a few faculty members to bypass the administration" is countered by the availability of a more honorable method. Moreover, the advantages derived from such a practice transcend merely the elimination of any reasonable justification for unchanneled, off-the-record contacts, cultivated by either trustees or faculty to create support for a proposal or to advance a personal or ulterior purpose.

JOINT TRUSTEE-FACULTY CONFERENCE COMMITTEE

True, some hold that there is little of benefit to be derived from organized faculty-trustee consultation. Stoke believes that faculty committees established to maintain direct relationship with trustees have not proved successful:[9]

[8] For example, the faculty handbook of Indiana University, in the section on faculty ethics, prescribes that "In no case will the teacher directly solicit any action by the Board of Trustees." Nevertheless, this does not deter the president from urging board members to visit research projects and other interesting educational programs or arranging meetings between them and faculty representatives when a subject of mutual concern is being considered.

[9] *The American College President,* Harper & Brothers, New York, 1959, p. 79.

The implications as to their mutual faith in the integrity or the efficiency of the president is a little too bald for either group to be comfortable in the presence of the other. Where such relations have been established, as, for example, at the University of Wisconsin, they usually settle down into mere social occasions.

Although their history is not one of unqualified success, our evidence does not support Stoke's appraisal of the experience of faculty-trustee conference committees in general or, as it functions today, of the Wisconsin Regent-Faculty Conference Committee in particular. In the case of Wisconsin, World War II was a period of strain and some mutual suspicion, precipitated by a dispute over a faculty appointment, and the committee became inactive or at least semiactive. Its efficacy was diminished by the faculty's inclination to view its delegation as a "fire-fighting outfit," and it was natural, therefore, that the regents did not regard the committee highly. The verdict of recent years is that it has been helpful, more so than some faculty opinion may be aware, in directing the attention of regents to policy, in dissolving lay myths about professors, and in reminding the regents of faculty rights. In 1960 the faculty side was changed from a specially chosen committee to the University Committee, the elected committee which confers with the president on any matter of faculty interest and is therefore more in the main stream of faculty thought. In 1959 the meetings of the joint committee were by law made open to the public, which places a blanket on freedom to "hash out" frankly any subject that might come up. The administration believes in the committee but also that it should not be the only faculty committee to confer with the regents, and the president is following a policy by which other committees meet with them.

We realize, of course, that it may happen that meetings of trustees and faculty amount to little more than an opportunity to air mutual complaints. When the practice is first introduced, the faculty side may view itself as a "grievance committee," but this can be overcome as immediate grievances are resolved if the president encourages frank and open consideration of educational policies as well as faculty rights and "terms of employment." Certainly if the faculty group conceives itself as only a grievance committee, perhaps exaggerating minor issues to major proportions in order to have something to talk about, it quickly becomes a bore to trustees.

Nevertheless, we would point out that business has discovered the value of a regular procedure for laying grievances out on the table in a more relaxed atmosphere than is possible in the heat of a crisis. Our evidence and experience indicate that if joint meetings of representatives of the two bodies are held on a routine schedule and not merely when dissensions make them necessary, they afford opportunities for development far beyond this limited objective.

We cannot understand why two groups, both in powerful positions in the government of the institution, should be kept apart because they find difficulty in communicating with each other. If he takes the trouble to do so, the president can raise the discussion between the two committees above trivia and minor complaints to the level of broad mutual interests. The opportunity for deans and professors to speak about significant programs in which they are engaged improves their morale and educates both sides even when the questioning is sharp. More than one teacher has expressed the satisfaction and increased respect gained for the trustees from the opportunity to discuss faculty affairs with them. On their side, trustees have found these sessions among their most interesting experiences, and as an extra dividend they gained new insights into the president's job and how to be of service to him.[10] Moreover, trustees often have limited means for finding out how a president is doing without undermining his position or chasing down rumors. In the meetings of a joint faculty-trustee

[10] My personal experience with a faculty conference committee that met on stated occasions with a corresponding trustee committee was extremely gratifying. It presented some problems at first, but none that was insurmountable. H. W. D.

conference committee they will with propriety observe him at work with an important constituency.

The natural group to meet regularly with faculty representatives is a standing committee on educational policy, discussed in the previous chapter. When the topic uppermost in the minds of the faculty group relates most appropriately to another standing committee of the board, a special meeting with it may be indicated, and the trustees should be willing to arrange it readily. The proper agent for this is, of course, the president. Such meetings, in addition to the regular schedule of the trustee-faculty committee on conference, afford distinct advantages when there is something significant to talk about.

On their part the faculty may prefer to elect a special committee on conference with the trustees, although when there is an active executive committee of the senate or a standing committee selected to consult with the president, it is a suitable agency. No formal resolutions should be adopted at the meeting, but of course there should be freedom for full discussion, and conclusions, when they are major, should be reported to each body. How free and frank the talk will be is largely dependent upon the president's attitude and the steps he takes to encourage the faculty to speak their minds. If he discourages contacts between the two groups or is afraid to allow them to expose their honest views in his presence, he may be wise to consider resigning.

A more than incidental advantage of these conferences is that the faculty are often more excellent interpreters of their work. They possess the knowledge and enthusiasm of direct participants and can often present an educational proposal more effectively than the president. In this manner a president draws strength from the faculty to aid him with his trustees.[11] In this connection, the

[11] I well recall an instance at which university policy toward a member of the faculty who might feel called upon during the McCarthy era to plead the Fifth Amendment before a congressional committee was considered in a joint meeting of the faculty conference committee and the executive committee of the board. The subsequent decision not to suspend a teacher until an offense had been judicially established but to go further and provide him

custom of faculty representatives serving as ex officio members without vote on certain trustee committees, as, for example, the committee on honorary degrees, usually results in enhanced respect for the trustees as persons as well as in valuable contributions to the decision-making process. Similar benefits accrue when appropriate academic officers of administration are ex officio members of such committees as educational policy or student life and business officers are on the committees of finance and grounds and buildings.[12]

Presidents who have organized trustee "retreats," attended by deans and other administrators and sometimes by members of the faculty, report that all participants enjoyed the occasion and profited from it. These sessions offer a favorable environment for thorough consideration of any or all phases of the university's present and future within the matrix of its educational goals. At them the nonacademic aspects of university life can be brought into more realistic focus with the main concern. Trustees have reported to us that they learned more about their institution in a two- or three-day retreat than all their previous contacts had taught them. Trustees are usually interested in what is going on at other institutions, and outside consultants may be brought in for informal talks and consultation.

Rarely do trustees engage in systematic meetings with students, at least in the larger institutions. Nevertheless, the president may do well to arrange that some representative students have a chance to talk things over with them under proper auspices. One session a year of the board's committee on educational policy may profitably be devoted to meeting a cross section of the student body and listening to their observations, their words of approval and of criticism. The committee will perceive afresh the difficulties

---

legal counsel at university expense if desired was the direct result of the spirit of frank but tolerant discussion that permeated the occasion. H. W. D.

[12] In the latter case the trustees should still be free to go into executive session without the presence of others for candid consideration of educational programs and matters of personnel.

under which age labors when it tries to communicate with youth; and it will come to a better understanding of the problems of the president and the deans.[13]

[13] Our personal experience is that trustees enjoy such meetings and profit from them, as they do sessions with faculty representatives.

CHAPTER X

SELECTION OF
A NEW PRESIDENT

By unanimous agreement trustees consider the selection of a new president their most important and critical responsibility. On the basis of national averages it is a duty they are called upon to perform once in eight to ten years.[1] However, in many institutions the normal term of office is more like fifteen to twenty years, and individual trustees may perform this vital function only once in a lifetime. Hence they have no previous experience with the problem. It is provocative to reflect that if there is any correlation between the length of a president's tenure and his success in the office, the selection of a new president has to be undertaken most frequently by those boards who have done the poorest jobs.

TRUSTEES TAKE RISKS

Informed trustees approach the task with some trepidation, even those with experience in finding new heads for their business

[1] "The average length of service of the *current* presidents in office at all types of colleges and universities is 8.1 years. . . ." William K. Selden, "How Long Is a College President?" *Liberal Education: The Bulletin of the Association of American Colleges,* vol. 46, no. 1, p. 11, March, 1960.

Contrary to popular impression, Selden believes that the average term of college presidents corresponds quite closely to that of corporate presidents.

enterprises. Members of corporation boards are accustomed to taking calculated risks, but not in calculating the risks to be run in selection of a new academic president. Attractive candidates seem to be few in number, difficult to discover; and indices of future success—let alone past success—are hard to identify and even harder to evaluate.

Unlike academia, business has its executive-development programs. It is expected of the chief executive that by his retirement he will have developed several successor possibilities for consideration by the directors. Indeed it may be considered a black mark on both his record and that of the board if it has to go outside to find a successor. In business a man seldom becomes a chief executive or even a second in command without prior qualifying experience in executive positions. Accordingly the pool of possibilities, both within and without the corporation, is more visible than in academia; the criteria are more specific, and capacity to meet them is more readily appraised on the basis of past performance. To become president is the ambition of many a businessman from the moment he qualifies as junior executive; it represents no compromise in his career or in what he has hoped to become.

Taking academia as a whole, it seems more usual to name a new president from outside than to promote from within. Nevertheless, deans or other officers of administration form a natural pool of candidates for calls elsewhere.[2] Naturally, also, the trustees' roster of possibilities always includes the names of presidents of other colleges or universities.

Whether members of the faculty other than officers of administration shy away from the college presidency as much as many assert (some observers say that the majority would like to be president but are unwilling to admit it), the truth remains that they are not career-oriented toward a presidency. Many have had

---

[2] For example, a listing of the previous careers of the presidents of the institutions composing the American Association of Universities indicates that, with few exceptions, all have had administrative experience of some sort if not in the university they are now heading.

little or no chance to display whatever executive talents they possess; the professional success of a teacher-scholar relates to capacities which have nothing to do with administration. Even deans have usually had but limited contact with the full scope of responsibilities that a president carries.

In academia trustees must seek out good candidates; there is no ready-made supply on which to draw. They need not despair, however; if they pursue their search thoroughly, intelligently, they are in a better position to name the right man than is the faculty. Provided they have been dutiful trustees, they have been in touch with the whole range of presidential functions and can estimate the diverse capacities required.

HELP FROM THE DEPARTING PRESIDENT

If the departing president enjoys the confidence of the trustees, they will naturally turn to him for counsel. He should be most cautious about giving it. The less he has to do with choosing his successor, the better. His perspective is bound to be warped by a human preference for a successor who will follow out policies which have become dear to his heart, whereas the institution may most need a radically different personality and a new set of policies.

The retiring incumbent can help by urging his board to begin looking for a new man long enough in advance to assure a smooth transition and avoid an interregnum. He can counsel it on methods for prosecuting the search; he can direct it to persons qualified to suggest nominees for consideration, although he should be extremely circumspect in passing on their merits and demerits; he can advise on methods for bringing the faculty into consultation; he should be willing to answer questions of prospective candidates but should not initiate conversations with them. Throughout the whole process he will do well to remember that the less responsibility he has for selecting a successor, even one who turns out to be an excellent choice, the happier he will probably be afterward.

TRUSTEES PREPARE TO SELECT THE RIGHT PRESIDENT

Let us now consider how boards should prepare themselves to search for a new chief executive. From interviews with trustees over a considerable span of years we are convinced that too often they neglect to clarify at the start the target they have in mind for their institution and what they should expect from their president other than money raising and speechmaking. Particularly is this true if they have not been led to interest themselves in educational policies.

Clarification embraces a clear decision on whether they as a board are willing to make massive personal efforts to raise funds to implement their hopes for the institution or whether they expect to unload this burden onto the president. Do they want to change the direction and quality of the institution's growth? Do they truly desire to move to greater excellence? Are they willing to pay for betterment in terms of criticism and opposition—often shrill —by alumni and certain elements of the public which inevitably resent change? If they want the institution to be great, are they willing to support academic freedom against hostile pressures, or do they prefer a president who will be "reasonable"? Do they really want a president who will stretch them rather than one who will make life easy for them?

Shortly after he announced his forthcoming retirement, President Herman B. Wells of Indiana University persuaded his regents to a commendable course in self-education. The board did not designate a committee of two or three but went as a group to spend a number of days at representative universities in the Middle West and in the East so as to update themselves on the directions in which higher education was moving. They familiarized themselves with teaching methods, philosophy, and research in progress, with attention to development programs. They observed presidents in action to learn of their ideas, methods, and personal characteristics. As an extra dividend they picked up some names of possible candidates and were able to take cross bearings on them on the spot.

THE LONG VERSUS THE SHORT LIST

Once trustees decide what they want their institution to become, they are ready to assemble a roster of names. Among the most common sources are officers of foundations and educational organizations who are in professional touch with educators over broad areas. Successful presidents of other institutions often are able to suggest worthwhile names, although, human nature being what it is, they cannot be expected to be eager to reveal good possibilities among their own staff.

Trustees will naturally look first to the possibilities in their own administration and faculty, and they may find there the man of their choice. If they think they have done so, they may also, because he is an insider, feel they have a fairly intimate acquaintance with him. They will still, as with outsiders, check opinions by interviews with past and present colleagues, foundation officials, officers of educational organizations who have had contact with the candidate, and, finally, when he has achieved a place on the short list, with the individual himself.

To build a long roster is easy. Suggestions, solicited and unsolicited, will come from many quarters. Checking the qualifications of even a short list is laborious and exhausting. Plainly, boiling down the long list to a short one should be an early order of business. Trustees desperate from the fatigue and frustration of prolonged examination of many names are apt to settle upon one man more or less indiscriminately and spend years regretting it. The energy required to build even a short list of impressive candidates is enormous; none of it should be drained off in wild-goose chases after second-raters. Remember that when a committee considers five men, each one against each one of the others, there are 10 pairs to be compared; but when there are ten men to be compared, each with another, 45 pairings are required; with twenty candidates the number of pairs rises to 190. Concentration on a short list may mean that a good dark horse is overlooked, but the controlling factor is the vital advantage of thoroughness in applying the chosen criteria to the select category of top candidates.

THE IMPORTANCE OF THOROUGH INVESTIGATION

Before considering qualifications for which trustees should seek, let us clear away some other aspects of the process. Avoid snap judgments, even when the pressure of time seems great. A skeptical, microscopical investigation of any individual who emerges as a serious candidate is of prime importance. Presidential failures may sometimes be attributed to trustee captivation by an agreeable social presence, by ability to make a good speech, or by the fact that a man "looks like a college president."

One example shows the danger of uncritical acceptance: A board allowed the enthusiasm of one member, who had visited the candidate at the college of which he was president, to determine their choice. Shortly after the new president took office, it became apparent that, while he was a man of ideas, brilliant, handsome, and an able speaker, he was impatient and so intolerant of opposition that he had been on the verge of dismissal at his former institution, as even slight conversation with his colleagues on the campus would have disclosed. As it developed, he was replaced within five years.

In another poor appointment, superficial investigation failed to discover that the candidate chosen was socially incompetent, a handicap compounded by marriage to a haughty wife. Obviously the stability and strength of the marriage is a potent factor. The quip that the office is one in which "two people do the work and one gets the pay" expresses the relation of a man's wife and the quality of his home life to his predictable success. Among other things, trustees are justified in examining a candidate's personal finances. Whether he meets his financial obligations responsibly is one measure of his fitness. Close examination is often required to assess a candidate's ability to meet and master crises, big and little. Similarly, only by examining his record can trustees assure themselves that he has a native passion for excellence, coloring and giving tone to all he does.

In another case a nominee was accepted without the cross checking that would have predicted poor performance largely because he was proposed by a prominent educational authority who had suggested the name of his predecessor, who had turned out to be a popular success. In still another case a closer scrutiny would have revealed that the board's choice, while president of his first university, had been losing good faculty members because he issued orders like a general. Clearly he was a poor risk in the more democratic environment of the second institution.

When a prospect achieves a strong place on the short list, the time has come to seek a personal interview. If he declines, the list will be shorter by one name, and no harm done. Rumors spring up from nowhere to embarrass individuals involved and may even cause a likely candidate to deny publicly that he would take the post if proffered. Therefore, to reduce loose talk, the interview should probably be held off campus. While it should be made clear that the early interview is not an offer of the post, there is no point in playing coy with a prospect by pretending that it is merely for the purpose of considering names of others. If he is bright enough to be president, he will know the reason for the interview.[3] How much it reveals will depend upon the manner in which it is conducted. Any candidate meriting serious consideration, whether from within or without, should be willing to submit to courteous but severe questioning. The interviewers should not eschew discussion of controversial topics. If some tensions arise, the discussion has provided at least one opportunity to put the man on his mettle and to test his reaction to stress.

---

[3] It has happened more than once, however, that an interview for the completely honest purpose of securing the individual's views regarding other candidates engendered a warm interest in the man himself.

He in turn should be encouraged to ask the most searching questions.[4] A candidate, particularly one from outside, not intimately acquainted with the institution, who does not probe into the situation should be examined for overeagerness; he is not apt to be a wise choice. The questions he asks and the conditions he imposes may reveal much about his suitability, including his general sympathy with the institution's place in the structure of higher education, or lack of it, and what he thinks should be done about it.

CRITERIA

Keep the essential criteria few and significant. Probably no college head has ever lived who succeeded in satisfying all the "essentials." Sometimes the job specifications are so detailed, so mutually exclusive, that it is folly to expect any human being to meet them. The basic principle is that, since the institution is organized for thought, competence in the field of ideas comes first, a competence more comprehensive and more rare than capacity for scholarship in a field of learning. If a president functioned in business operations alone, his role would be simpler and the job specifications clearer.[5]

Not long ago we were consulted by a trustee of a prominent university in search of a new president. In response to the question "What are you looking for?" he began to enumerate the job speci-

[4] Because some neglect to inform themselves fully before accepting, it is appropriate to stress the advisability of learning the salient features of the job in advance. What is the financial condition of the institution, the source of its funds? What do the trustees expect of him (assurance that they will not expect him to raise money should not be taken seriously)? What do the faculty expect, and is he *persona grata* to them? How well conceived are trustee and faculty ideas about future progress? Does he agree with them; can he carry them out enthusiastically? These are some of the questions he should ask. Indeed, within the limits of the situation, he should examine his prospective legacy, as recommended in Chap. II for a new president. To this end he should be released at the appropriate moment to talk to others, including administration and faculty, within the bounds of due discretion and under a seal of two-way confidence.

[5] In Chap. II, "The President and Academic Leadership," we summarized the various roles of a president.

fications as he saw them. His institution was a multiservice state university with a large and diversified staff. Therefore the new man, he believed, must first of all be a good administrator in the business sense. Next, he must be able to live on good terms with the state legislature, so that it would be liberal with appropriations. He must be able to sustain his popularity with the alumni, so that they would be generous. He should be a good speaker, reasonably religious, etc. We interrupted to ask, "Since the end product of your university is education and scholarship, did it ever occur to you that a man's educational experience and promise as an educational leader were important?"

The reply that bounced back was frank. "Gosh, I never thought of that!"

The most promising place to look for a person with the capacity for educational and intellectual leadership is within academia itself. For the time being at least, more and more trustees are coming to this viewpoint. We trust that it will become permanent. Presidents have succeeded despite the lack of an academic background, but they were men of truly intellectual interests. Nevertheless, the odds are against an outsider, as we have seen in earlier chapters. A strong and abiding conviction that in serving higher education he is ministering to a supremely great enterprise may motivate a president recruited from another occupation, but it is more likely to glow in the heart of one who has made education his lifework. For one thing, he is less likely to view his office either as a pleasant post to which to retire or as a way station or steppingstone to serve until a more attractive opening develops elsewhere.[6] We have pointed out that he has a better chance of being accepted by the faculty as an intellectual peer than one coming from an unrelated vocation. Without such acceptance he may find his efforts to lead bitterly opposed.

---

[6] Two or three times I have been asked to help find a university presidency for a man who had been defeated in an election for high public office, the idea being that it would be a better place than a financial or business post for keeping him on ice until the next election. Holding my temper on such an occasion was difficult. H. W. D.

The man from an academic background is more knowledgeable about the subtle ways in which a college or university operates. "He is one," writes a seasoned observer, "who can fight, for example, the battle of the budget with the ideals of higher education always before him." He will not suffer the frustration of one prominent public figure who thought that as a university president his work would have to do with young people but who, after a year in office, ruefully remarked that he had not yet talked to a student. A man of academic experience would not have required tutoring on how to get in touch with students.

Few errors are more self-defeating than for a new president, innocent of academic experience, to tell the faculty, "I'm not an educator, but . . ." and then confidently proceed to announce his program of action. At the other extreme is the one, also a newcomer to academia, who is so humble or solicitous of faculty favor that, for fear that he will be rebuffed, he is unwilling to venture into the academic arena at all. Sooner or later the faculty will condemn the poor fellow as intellectually bankrupt and grow restless for a more educationally dynamic head.

Sagacious trustees seek a man who, if he has not demonstrated it, possesses potential managerial ability, one element of which is a certain feeling for financial and budget matters that enables one quickly to discern the financial implications of a proposal. Presidents who feel they lack it report that they are under a handicap. Seasoned trustees desire a leader who will "pick up problems without bouncing them back on the board," but they should not, of course, rest content with these talents alone.

The head of a state institution must meet certain demands which presidents of the privately supported do not customarily encounter. Regents therefore look for a person with the temperament for meeting them in the political as well as the intellectual area. Obviously, ability to deal with a heterogeneous constituency and to "get along" with the legislature and governor eases the life of a state university president. But there is more to getting along with voters and state officials than merely a talent for fraternization. Being just a good fellow may be productive of new buildings for a while, including an athletic stadium, but in the end it lessens the support of thoughtful people who respect the office and want to respect the man who holds it.[7]

Authoritative observers of the history of state institutions can cite instances in which a governor or an organized constituency with a special interest, perhaps agriculture, or legislators with axes to grind have brought pressure on the regents to select a president to their liking. When they prevail, the chance that their choice will make an outstanding success is poor, and becoming poorer. Strong boards of strong universities resent such infringements upon their autonomy. Fortunately they seem able to resist such pressure successfully.

One criterion of interest to all boards is the matter of age, inseparable from consideration of term of office. This is the day of young men, and to a lesser degree of young women, in executive posts in both business and academia. The objection to a young man as a prospective president is that the institution will be committed to retaining him after his energy and enthusiasm have ebbed. Trustees are kindly people, and for presidents, even more than for deans who have grown gray in a deanship, there are few honorable exits. In most cases their days have been too filled with administrative duties to have allowed them to keep abreast of their old fields of learning. A return to the faculty is difficult, if not impossible, and is replete with embarrassment for one who does. Nevertheless, there are times when, in the interest of the institution, trustees must be cruel toward a president who has run down.

There is considerable theoretical sentiment favoring fixed terms for presidents, but we can trace in the lives of either successful or unsuccessful no pattern of an optimum term. Circumstances and individuals vary too widely. In an earlier chapter we observed in the lives of the seven giant academicians of the past a wide vari-

[7] How the job of the president of a state-supported institution differs from that of the head of a privately sustained one and thus calls for certain qualifications of its own was discussed in Chap. I.

ation in the terminal years of their incumbency. Some otherwise
eminent presidents faded toward the end of long terms, raising the
question "How long is too long for a president to serve?"

However, the records of successful presidents refute a fairly
popular thesis that all one can hope to accomplish must be done
in the first five years. We believe that, given average good fortune,
the competent man will find that the later years prove to be periods
of increasing influence and prestige, not ones of diminishing returns.

SELECTION TO MEET A PHASE

As institutions pass through various phases, the order of emphasis on presidential criteria in the minds of trustees will change
accordingly. If the critical problem is financial, money-raising
ability is apt to loom large, although even in this field a dedication
to education and to fitness for the long pull inspire gifts by
creating confidence in the future. The president who has been an
intimate participant in drawing up new plans for the law school
or for a new program in teaching and research in foreign relations, for example, speaks with a more convincing authority than
one who can talk only about a program worked out by others for
which it is his duty to raise money.

If the departing president has been inept in public relations or
if, in a state institution, tension exists with the legislature, the
trustees will naturally look for a successor able to function well
in extramural areas. If the institution has been riven by feuds, a
peacemaker will be sought. If rebuilding academic prestige or re-
vamping the educational program is recognized to be the chief
need, an educator will be favored. If, for example, the trustees believe that the retiring president has developed the graduate professional schools to the neglect of the undergraduate, or vice versa,
they will search for a man who can redress the balance.

But here a word of caution is in order: There is danger in
stressing the selection of a new president to meet a phase. It may
lead too easily to neglecting the criteria of educational leadership

and endurance for the long pull. A president selected to meet immediate objectives may not, as the years pass, prove competent in the other areas of his responsibilities as they reassert themselves. Or, equally unfortunately, he may lose interest in the post after he has attained the limited objectives for which he was chosen.

While new times call for new men, and the talents of the new should often be quite different from those of the old, there is apt to be an inclination to forget the predecessor's points of strength and to assess a candidate too heavily in terms of the familiar weaknesses of the old. At the other extreme is the shortsighted temptation to find a facsimile of a successful departing incumbent. Anyone who has sat on a board of directors of a corporation has observed the need to resist both these tendencies.

ASSESSING THE QUALIFICATIONS OF PROSPECTS

It is relatively easy to agree on a table of qualifications. But how to weigh them in the scale of total competence and measure the degree to which a candidate possesses them is a reasonable question that we have frequently been asked by trustee and faculty committees in search of a president. Unfortunately there is no short cut, no mystique, to obviate the methodical collection and assessment of information bearing on individuals on the short list.

Since predictions for the future are so much a projection of the curve of the past, the appraisal will naturally relate heavily to what has gone before. Yet it is difficult for presidents to make up their own minds as to which precise aspects of former experience, apart from the academic, have proved most helpful. Although those who have had administrative experience identify it as being valuable, presidents whom we interviewed felt that they had found a relevant use for all previous experience. Success as a dean is to be taken seriously, but it is no guarantee of success in a number one position, nor does it preclude the possibility of finding the right man among the faculty in a nonadministrative post.

Presidents of other colleges or universities who may be susceptible to a call provide a certain reservoir of candidates, and here some pertinent evidence is available. While growth in size these days is not an index of presidential success, growth in physical resources measured by new libraries, new classrooms, new laboratories, and increased endowment and other sources of income is. It is important to know whether growth has correctly been apportioned between the building program and growth in faculty strength, remembering, however, that adequate physical resources are essential to effective teaching and scholarship.

To appraise in concrete terms what a president has himself contributed to building a faculty during his term is difficult. Nonetheless, certain estimations are possible, and much can be learned of his success in his present institution from the opinions of informed observers. Is the morale of the faculty high? Do its members exude a conviction that they are on a winning team? Are they conscious of identifiable achievements under their present administration? Is this feeling shared by colleagues in sister institutions? The reasons that faculty members resign to go elsewhere are extremely pertinent. A president of an institution which is known to be building faculty strength naturally exposes himself to the loss of members by calls elsewhere, and this is a good sign. However, if he is unable to hold those whom the institution would like to retain and for whom lines of promotion are open, and if he has failed to attract equally good replacements, the reasons should be clearly established. If the fault lies not with him but with certain circumstances beyond his control, it should be known.

Many of the indices applicable to the appraisal of the candidacy of presidents of other institutions are relevant *mutatis mutandis* to deans and other officers of administration.

When trustees turn to members of the faculty who have not been involved in administration, appraisal is more difficult, for they do not work under the floodlight of criticism that plays on presidents and deans. Nevertheless, signs auguring success or failure are at hand, although of course none is infallible. Have a professor's colleagues entrusted increasingly important responsibilities to him in the form of crucial committee chairmanships and the like? Has he shown a sense of organization and a gift for leadership by pulling his weight in faculty governance? However, activity in faculty governance should be examined to make sure that he is not just an "old pro" who would rather attend a committee meeting than work on a lecture or a piece of research. If he has been chairman of a department, did it prosper under him? Do his peers in other colleges or universities esteem him well? Have they shown it by electing him to important offices in their professional organization or by awards of other professional honors? Is his advice sought by the administration? When the administration has delegated trouble-shooting missions to him, has he fulfilled them well? This is the day of team research and of many calls to serve as consultant to nonacademic enterprises and agencies. How has the professor succeeded in such relationships? Have they resulted in respect for him as a leader of a group as well as a scientist or scholar in his own right?

MOVEMENT FROM COLLEGE TO UNIVERSITY

How seriously is a good job as head of a college to be taken in predicting success in a university? From the relatively small proportion of university presidents chosen from the ranks of college presidents, it would seem that trustees and faculties do not consider the experience of much significance. Apparently they think that, as a group, college presidents lack the administrative capacity for the presidency of a more complex organization. Many college presidents do not aspire to be university presidents, because they have no desire to exchange their post for one in which sheer size is a burden—one which requires the ability to keep many balls in the air, which calls for delegating to others work they like to do themselves, and which spells less intimate contacts with individual students and faculty.

Nevertheless, university trustees should not cavalierly pass over the reservoir of candidates to be found in the colleges. A college presidency makes its demands on one's capacity for sustained energy and tests one's emotional toughness, reaction to pressures, and capability to surmount the crises that challenge the number one man as no other member of the organization is challenged. A seasoned college president has accumulated experience with a goodly number of situations similar to those met by his colleagues in the larger universities. He has had an opportunity to make the emotional transition from teacher to chief executive, to prove that he can live with the job. His ability to gain the confidence of others and to attain goals has been tested. One president who made a successful transition from a college to a university testifies that the experience in a simpler environment introduced him to the problem of public relations, taught him how to deal with nonacademic people, how trustees act, and how the president should behave toward them, together with experience in business operation and finance. All these matters had been a closed book to him as a professor.

At the same time, one's record as a college president must be carefully assessed. One may have been notably effective in that role and still be miscast in a university situation, where a habit of "doing it yourself" must yield to the habit of doing it through intermediaries and the ability to find satisfaction in it.

PARTICIPATION OF NONTRUSTEES
IN THE SELECTION PROCESS

While trustees, even if they want to, cannot divest themselves of legal and moral accountability for the election of a new president, other people are also concerned. Consultation with them will facilitate the new president's dealings with his several constituencies.

Alumni have a stake in the selection. Many trustees are alumni, so that their valid interests are already pretty well assured of a hearing. Nevertheless, it is natural to consult representative leaders among the alumni, and many are truly concerned about education. Yet on the whole alumni are a heterogeneous group whose specifications for a new president crystallize around their personal views. Vociferous pressure blocs may emerge, not infrequently organized around athletics, but knowledgeable trustees will know how to deal with them. With all due respect for alumni interests, it is a mistake for a board to involve the alumni association in any formal manner. One board we know announced to the alumni body that suggestions from them would be welcome. Soon the local associations picked up the ball and began to send in resolutions supporting particular candidates. The name most frequently urged was the name favored by both trustees and faculty, but this was a piece of good luck. Rarely does a candidate enjoy this degree of popular support.

More than the alumni or any other group, the faculty and non-academic officers have a personal stake in the choice of their new chief. The growing practice of trustee-faculty consultation on a new president gives better results than either side may produce alone, but it must be well conducted. Some have feared that the custom would encourage factionalism within the faculty, and on occasion it has had this effect, but, if well managed, it can have exactly the opposite effect. More than one president has reported that it would have been helpful to him if the faculty had enjoyed a voice in his selection.

As soon as a vacancy is known to be impending (the faculty will be fully aware of imminent compulsory retirement for age), it is the part of wisdom for the trustees to invite the faculty to choose a committee on conference. This approach is superior to waiting for a faculty to request that it be consulted or to demand that its committee be received to present their views, and vastly more so than relying upon the confidential sounding out of individual members. It is also better than issuing a blanket request to the faculty as individuals to submit names. In one place where this was done the board received 180 letters of recommendation. The majority urged the same man, who fortunately was the one the trustees had in mind. Had it been otherwise, the trustees might have been seriously embarrassed; as it was, they felt that their hand had been forced a bit.

The two committees should meet as full-fledged conferees. For the trustee group to ask for names but decline to meet with the faculty committee to discuss them leaves a bad taste in the mouth. The attitude of one board which came under our attention worked as a strong depressant to faculty morale. Receiving no invitation to select a committee on conference, the faculty went ahead and named one on its own motion. But the trustee committee did not consent to receive it until compelled by strong representations, and then under instructions from the chairman to listen but not to talk. To compound the damage, the faculty-committee members first learned of the new appointee in the newspapers, a development that was resented despite the fact that he met with their approval.

To a great extent the success of faculty-trustee conference committees depends on the establishment of ground rules and their observance. These should be set at the first joint meeting. Perhaps the most important rule is that the faculty committee are to act as free agents, to speak for themselves and not as mirrors reflecting colleagues' diverse opinions. Their obligation is to exercise their best individual judgment. When a faculty committee consider their function to be to canvass the faculty body for views on potential candidates and to report their findings in a sort of faculty popularity poll, trouble can be expected. Such a misconception inevitably encourages the development of factions, each with its own candidate.

The faculty side will be expected to screen possibilities and to make their own suggestions; more than one president has been uncovered by the faculty. The procedure governing correspondence about candidates will be agreed upon. Correspondence with candidates, however, will be reserved for the chairman of the trustee group or other duly appointed colleague. Throughout, the strictly confidential nature of the proceedings will be stressed.

The trustees will make it clear that the faculty committee is advisory, that its views will be influential but the power of selection remains with them.

Decision as to criteria is the next step. The faculty will naturally place academic experience at the top, while trustees, from their familiarity with the diverse roles of the president, will see the importance of other criteria. Even so, consensus will not be so difficult to achieve as one who has not been through the process might fear.

Although not insensitive to other qualifications, faculties prefer a scholar of eminence; at minimum they will urge a man from academic life, experienced in the consultative nature of academic governance, one already committed to education and sympathetic to their scholarly ambitions. They want a leader who will support academic freedom, but not a dictator. They can be rough on local prospects whose faults they know and whose points of weakness, close to, may loom large. The strong men among them have probably made some enemies. Anyone who has gained a reputation for "stirring them up" will be unacceptable to those who fear innovators. In particular, the faculty is prone to kill off the local man who seems to be eager for the job.

The experience of conferring with the faculty on a matter so crucial to them probably will give the trustees, unaccustomed to the mores of the academic world, some new insights into the workings of the academic mind. These revelations may make some demands on their tolerance, but not more than intelligent laymen will be able to meet. Out of the association may easily emerge a new mutual respect whose influence will extend beyond the circle of faculty conferees alone.

TRAINING PROGRAMS

Trustees, on the prowl for a new president and finding the field of qualified candidates limited, often ask, "Why are there no training courses in our universities for academic administrators similar to schools of business or public administration?" This is an old plaint; since the turn of the century various writers have voiced need for such programs. Schools of education may include higher education in courses designed to prepare for administrative posts in our school system, but not in the comprehensive and specialized manner of the one about to be described.

The program now being conducted at the University of Michigan, under the direction of Prof. Algo D. Henderson, is an experiment in formal education at both predoctoral and postdoctoral levels for college and university administrators who eventually may become presidents. Although recognizing that much has to be learned on the job, the program assumes that there is a body of knowledge relating to administrative behavior and organization that can be transmitted by the usual methods of graduate study and that will make the college administrator a more competent officer. Most of the available material comes from the fields of business and public administration, adapted to college and university conditions and designed for both practicing and prospective administrators. The center will arrange internships where desired. Its courses are supplemented by other offerings throughout the university as a cultural and informational foundation for more specialized work. The director, fully aware of the "almost universal prejudice toward persons who actively seek to become administrators, especially deans and presidents," reports an increasing number of requests to suggest candidates for administrative positions and a widening acceptance of the value of formal education for academic administration.

One may applaud the Michigan experiment, at the same time questioning whether academic training programs can convey more than an introduction to administrative and managerial techniques or knowledge of educational theories and problems, which a bright young man, as he works up through the ranks, will more realistically acquire on the job.[8] Furthermore, is there not danger that the prospect of heavy exposure to the managerial side, to many rather dull and, unlike the educational side, contain-

---

[8] Stoke explains why training programs have not been developed and why he believes they cannot be in these words: "The requirements of each constituency differ a little from those of every other. The processes of selection are too capricious, the chances of selection too remote. The factors which make a distinguishable college president, or congressman, are factors of individuality which are too intricate a compound of heredity, environment, personality, and experience ever to be reduced to a curriculum. There are many things a college president must learn, but they are not things which are reducible to a curriculum—and who could teach them?" *The American College President,* Harper & Brothers, New York, 1959, p. 14.

ing none of the richest rewards of the office, may deter vigorous and intellectually alert young men from entering the lists?

"Short courses" for practicing presidents and deans, on the other hand, have brought noteworthy results. The Michigan center conducts an annual Institute on College and University Administration. Each day's discussion centers upon some major theme. The local staff is supplemented by outsiders of experience and distinction in the various fields of administration.

The program of The Institute for College and University Administrators, located at the Harvard Graduate School of Business Administration under its own board of trustees, provides another productive short course. Under the direction of Prof. Robert W. Merry, it conducts separate annual conferences for academic deans (of one to five years' experience), presidents (of not more than three years in office), and trustees. Some members of the Harvard faculty participate, with a larger number of speakers drawn from outside. Employing the case method, the institute devotes a considerable amount of time to questions and to exchanges of experience from the floor. We interviewed several who had attended one of these short courses, and the general conclusion was that it was a valuable educational experience.

For a good many years the Carnegie Corporation has conducted an activity by which it invites selected junior administrators to accept grants enabling them to visit several institutions during a period of approximately three months. The reports that they have written indicate a widening of their horizons—they have observed problems on a national scale. An incidental result has been a higher visibility for those who enjoy this opportunity, which helps to promote their careers.

On the other side of the coin is the fact that active distrust of formal academic curricula for training college and university presidents lies deeply imbedded in the minds of many presidents and faculties alike. "I can think of nothing worse than a formal training program for academic administrators, including deans and presidents," writes the head of a leading law school. "My own notion is," he continues, "that any institution which picked such deans and presidents would be well on its way towards ceasing to be an educational institution. I would myself prefer not to be connected with it."

How can the imponderables of educational leadership, the really exciting elements of a president's life, the quality of intellectual and emotional sensitivity which successful presidents possess[9] be revealed and transmitted in a curriculum? Moreover, as Stoke asks, where will teachers of the elusive art of leadership be found? As with political leaders, its most successful practitioners are not as a group blessed with the capacity to elucidate its subtleties for others. Scholars may ultimately succeed in disclosing them, but laying bare the mystery is not tantamount to success in the office. When the last word is said about the art or science of heading a college or university, educational leadership remains an exceptionally intuitive gift, and "intuition is a name for the inexplicable." We confess to a large degree of sympathy with this viewpoint.

On the other hand, despite the skepticism which many entertain, it would be foolish to conclude that no academic training can ever be developed which can transmit something of the indispensable intangibles. As in any other art, practice has its intellectual aspects. Indeed, this book is in part an attempt to describe them. In any case, however, the analogy with the graduate training programs in public administration must be accepted with some reservation. These have succeeded more in turning out competent civil servants than in developing notable political leaders.

It is a commentary on the schizoid personality of a college or university that an avowed desire from a young man to become a dean or a president is viewed in academic circles as a disqualification. The faculty suspects, rightly or wrongly, that the motivation derives more from the glamor and ego satisfaction attached to the office than from ideals of service. As long as prevailing faculty attitudes persist (and they seem unlikely to change for a

[9] As defined by an old faculty colleague, "sensitivity" is "an inclination on the part of a college president to do what you want him to do." It is more than this, although the professor's definition expresses one aspect of it.

long time), announced intention to be a president will count against a man. By and large, successful presidents rise through the academic ranks of teacher and scholar, and we trust it will always be so. The president is already separated from the body of the faculty by the nature of his job. If he has had training or experience in administration, but none in the world of scholars, the estrangement will be disastrous.

THE APPRENTICESHIP APPROACH

However one may question academic training programs of any or all sorts, the formidable question remains: How long will academic presidents and deans of wisdom, courage, imagination, and skill continue to emerge through existing vagrant processes of selection in numbers sufficient to the mounting demands?

We cannot wait for training courses to be perfected and universally accepted by the academic profession. We must take active steps to equip young men to become competent administrators for our colleges and universities. Presidents especially have an obligation to draw likely junior faculty into the administration to try them out and to give them experience. Some presidents have made it a practice to do so, but far too few.

Under an in-service development program, the young faculty members serve on a rotating basis, either full or part time, and then return to their full-time faculty posts. These "apprentices" acquire experience while helping to lighten the load of the administrative cadre and increasing the depth of the administrative reserve corps.

Rotation of the faculty in administrative posts brings with it another benefit, in that the incumbents are able to reflect, for the benefit of administrative officers, current faculty opinion relatively unadulterated by the "administrative point of view." Also, having learned about phases of the university operation generally unknown to the faculty, the returnee is able to contribute a broader perspective to the faculty decision-making process. This rather informal method of cultivating latent administrative talent falls far short of full-fledged "apprenticeship," not to mention an executive-development program, but it is as far as academia is yet prepared to go. Indeed, whether it ever should go further will be debated for years to come.

Two objections are leveled against even such a denatured apprenticeship system. One is that since so many presidents and deans are poor administrators themselves and so incapable of training assistants, it would promote confusion rather than order. To this we reply that some exposure to confusion can be quite educational to a bright young man: it gives him the advantage of learning how not to do something. The other objection is that deans and heads of administrative departments are too busy, or think they are too busy, to take time for coaching. The fact is that one fresh from the faculty can be of real help to a more seasoned superior, and this may be the chief argument in persuading a promising young person to accept the assignment. It does indeed require some time and energy from the senior to familiarize an assistant on rotation with his job, but if the choice has been sound, it will not be formidable and will be worth the effort.

A BRIEF RECAPITULATION

We shall not undertake to add further to the volume of words already written on the subject of leaders. If trustees correctly dissect their expectations of a new president, the essential qualifications for the leadership that they seek will emerge almost of themselves. We realize that our prescription for the ideal college president set forth in the preceding chapters seems to call for a superman. However, if he succeeds in arranging his work so as to devote half time to education, a less than "super" man can fill it.

A very great deal of advice has gone into these chapters, much of it distilled from trial-and-error experience, much from observation and firsthand examination of places and people. Certainly no one, even if it were physically possible, is going to follow all the admonitions herein. Just as his institution differs markedly from the usual business and industrial organization, so the college or university president needs to possess and develop abilities not called for in the average career. So, also, we have seen that the dominant qualifications required may vary between college and university, as well as among categories of colleges and universities themselves.

Nevertheless, there are constants to be sought for in all college and university presidents. Because the president is expected to be the chief interpreter of the institution, the trustees or regents should satisfy themselves of his ability to represent it with dignity and in a manner to generate confidence. No chief executive succeeds who so needs to be loved that he avoids stirring things up, but a dash of the homely virtue of getting along with people is indispensable. The president who cannot suffer tolerantly, if not gladly, others who disagree or who goes off "half-cocked" when others cannot think as rapidly as he will not inspire confidence. On later evidence such a one may have to beat an embarrassing retreat from positions held stubbornly or taken too hastily. A sense of humor protects against being bruised too easily and helps relax tension both within himself and within others. That physical and nervous health and a high level of energy are desirable in any president goes without saying. Sagacity is a prime requirement, of course, but there is no substitute for ability to attend, if need be, more dinners than there are days in the week. As one adviser of many presidents once remarked, with pardonable hyperbole, "It is desirable that he have the wisdom of Solomon and the heart of a lion, but it is indispensable that he have the digestion of a goat."

Above everything, trustees and regents should avoid becoming enamored of prominent names, eminent public figures who may welcome a try at being a college president, only to become disillusioned and bored in the job. This is no place for a retired governor or general per se or a minister whose congregation or bishop wants to kick him upstairs. An equal chance is taken in the selection of a famous scholar merely for the sake of the prestige he will bring. The man to be desired is one whose fame will be made by how well he performs in the office. If he possesses the capacity for growth, if he is not an uncompromising educational sectarian unable to integrate sharply differing views, the job will make the man.

INDEX

DATE DUE

JY 8 74			
GAYLORD			PRINTED IN U.S.A.